THE NEW
Classics
Cookbook

THE NEW Classics Cookbook

Family Favorites Made Healthy for Today's Lifestyle

By Anne Egan

Managing Editor, *Prevention* Cookbooks;
former Food Editor, *First for Women* magazine

Rodale Press, Inc.
Emmaus, Pennsylvania

Interior and Cover Designer: Christina Gaugler
Front Cover Photographer: Angelo Caggiano
Back Cover and Flap Photographer: Kurt Wilson/Rodale Images
Interior Photographers: Kurt Wilson/Rodale Images and Angelo Caggiano
    (pages 283 and 286)
Illustrator: Sandra Bruce
Food Stylist: Diane Simone Vezza
Prop Stylist: Debrah Donahue

Library of Congress Cataloging-in-Publication Data

Egan, Anne.
    The new classics cookbook : family favorites made healthy for today's
lifestyle / by Anne Egan.
        p.   cm.
    Includes index.
    ISBN 0–87596–503–2 hardcover
    1. Cookery.   2. Low-fat diet—Recipes.   3. Low-calorie diet—Recipes.   I. Title.
TX714.E335   1999
641.5'638—dc21   99–30421

Distributed to the book trade by St. Martin's Press
2   4   6   8   10   9   7   5   3   1   hardcover

Visit us on the Web at www.rodalecookbooks.com, or call us toll-free at (800) 848-4735.

───── OUR PURPOSE ─────

*We inspire and enable people to improve
their lives and the world around them.*

This book is dedicated in fond remembrance to
Bernadette Sauerwine

*In all Rodale Press cookbooks, our mission is to provide
delicious and nutritious low-fat recipes. Our recipes also
meet the standards of the Rodale Test Kitchen for
dependability, ease, practicality, and, most of all, great
taste. To give us your comments, call 1-800-848-4735.*

Contents

Acknowledgments

Many thanks to all who contributed their time and talents in creating *The New Classics Cookbook.*

Thomas P. Aczel

Keith Biery

JoAnn Brader

Debrah Donahue

Kathy D. Everleth

Christina Gaugler

Michelle Gavin, C.C.P.

Chavanne B. Hanson, M.P.H., R.D., L.D.

Suzanne Lynch Holderman

David Joachim

Marge Perry

Sharon Sanders

Darlene Schneck

Anita C. Small

Shannon Stovsky, R.D., L.D.

Diane Simone Vezza

Teresa A. Yeykal

And Other Truths about Healthy Eating

Everybody loves food. Whether your relationship is true love, love-hate, a weekend fling, or a lifelong companionship (that you may sometimes ignore), it's still love. Why? Because you want it. You crave it. You need food to survive. And like most basic necessities of life, such as clothing and shelter, food brings with it great pleasures to both body and soul.

You might assume that this pleasure, this love of food, goes out the window when you eat "healthy," as if eating healthfully is something that you're supposed to do stoically, like taking medicine. Nothing could be farther from the truth. In fact, according to research, you may find yourself loving food more than ever before.

"We've found that food with less fat allows people to more fully enjoy the experience of eating," says John La Puma, M.D., director of the CHEF (Cooking Healthy Eating Fitness) pilot study at Alexian Brothers Medical Center in Elk Grove, Illinois. "It's almost as if fats form a layer over your palate, preventing an appreciation of food's other flavors and textures." After 10 weeks of lower-fat food, subjects in this study reported an increase in their range of flavor appreciation. "There is a shift from appreciating mainly the full, rich, heavy, round flavors in fat to appreciating the bright, clean, citrusy, fresh flavors of foods with less fat. Eating less fat may actually broaden your palate and your enjoyment of food," says Dr. La Puma.

The fact is, the simple act of choosing to eat better deepens your relationship with food. It causes you to look at food more closely than you ever did before. When reaching for a snack, you may find your-self thinking more about the food itself, its nutritional content, what you really want to eat, and what your body is really hungry for. When cooking, you will discover more about how food works, like what makes some foods crisp and crunchy and other foods rich and creamy. Best of all, you'll find out how to achieve these textures and flavors in your favorite foods without piling on the fat or calories. To read some of these cooking tips right now, turn to the next chapter.

Still skeptical? Still think that "eating healthy" and "true love" don't belong in the same sentence? Go ahead and try any one of the more than 200 recipes in this book. They all prove the point. Or, read on. Let's de-bunk the most popular myths of healthy eating, right here, right now.

MYTH #1: I'll always be hungry.

Not a chance. Just the opposite is true. When you eat foods that are lower in fat and calories, you can actually eat a *greater* amount of food. Sounds impossible, right? It's really simple. Fats are a dense source of calories. When you eat less of them, you have calories to spare. That means that every mouthful of healthy food you eat has fewer calories. So you can eat more! To see which foods to eat more of, turn to page 11.

MYTH #2: I'll have to give up my favorite foods.

This entire book dispels that old myth. I've taken more than 200 beloved classics and made them healthier. What tops your list? Potato salad? Macaroni and cheese? How about pork chops, meat loaf, and lasagna? Flip through the recipes or the index to find your favorites. You'll also find ways to update your favorite recipes for today's lifestyle. The next chapter contains dozens of simple tricks to boost flavor, cut fat, and save time when you cook. You'll know how to spot excess fat and calories in every recipe you read. When you see an appealing dish in a magazine or newspaper, you'll know just what changes to make.

MYTH #3: I'll have to learn to cook weird new foods.

What's strange about Beef Stroganoff, Turkey Tetrazzini, Molasses Baked Beans, and Spaghetti with Meatballs? Healthy food doesn't have to be exotic to be good. All the ingredients for the recipes in this book are readily available, and most are already familiar to you. To keep your tastebuds awake, I also threw in a variety of newer classic dishes, like Barley Risotto with Mushrooms and South Pacific Crisp. Now there are two perfectly good reasons to eat healthfully.

MYTH #4: I'll have to eat foods that I don't like.

Food is about pleasure. If you don't like a food, there's a simple remedy: Don't eat it. Why suffer when there are hundreds of wonderful, healthful foods out there to enjoy? You can get all the nutrients you need from foods that you love, even if you're a finicky eater.

MYTH #5: I can eat all the fat-free food I want.

Not so fast. Some fat-free foods are just as high in calories as their full-fat counterparts. This is particularly true of snack-food products. When manufacturers remove the fat, they often dump in loads of extra sugar. And that means more calories, sometimes just as many as the original product. If a fat-free cookie satisfies your craving just as much as a regular one, by all means have one. Less fat is still a good idea, even if the calories are the same. But there are other options. For a quick look at these, see "Snacks for Health" on page 71.

MYTH #6: I can't ever eat another egg.

Never say never. The key is moderation. And, in the case of eggs, that may mean more eggs than you think. The American Heart Association (AHA), which recommends that healthy adults limit cholesterol intake to less than 300 milligrams a day, says that it's okay to eat up to four egg yolks per week. That's an increase from earlier recommendations because laboratory evidence shows that dietary cholesterol in a large egg is 213 milligrams, not 274 milligrams as previously thought. Plus, the AHA has no restrictions on egg whites. The whites are a low-calorie source of protein that contain no cholesterol or fat. So don't rule out omelets, quiche, or baked goods that use whole eggs. And the whites have important binding and leavening properties that make them an invaluable cooking ingredient.

MYTH #7: I'll have to eat fish so often that my house will smell like low tide.

Fresh fish, stored properly and cooked right, won't make your house smell bad. When buying fish, do the nose check. Truly fresh fish should smell clean and almost sweet, but not fishy. Do the finger check, too. The flesh should be moist and firm. To store, wrap fillets in plastic and place them in an ice-filled colander. Set the colander in a bowl and refrigerate. Try to use within a day. When you realize that fish contains healthy omega-3 fatty acids—a kind of fat that's good for you—you'll want to work more seafood into your meals anyway. Try Teriyaki Tuna with Pineapple on page 303 or Pasta with Beans and Cajun Salmon on page 143.

MYTH #8: I won't be able to eat at restaurants.

Almost every restaurant offers healthy choices. For the top picks, see "Menu Minder" on page 16. The real key to dining out is understanding that restaurant portions—particularly, portions of meat, fish, and poultry—are sometimes enormous. Take a peek at the guidelines beginning on page 7 to see what normal portions should look like. When your meal is served, use these mental images to divvy up your plate and push the extra to one side. Then, ask to have the extra wrapped to take home. That way, you'll get two healthy meals for the price of one.

MYTH #9: I can't eat at friends' homes anymore.

Sure you can. And you should. Half the fun of eating food is sharing it with family and friends. Nonetheless, you may want to plan ahead for social situations where you don't control the menu. Try having a small healthful snack before you go out, to take the edge off your appetite. That way, you'll be less tempted to nibble on high-fat appetizers. When the main meal is served, remember that you don't have to eat everything on your plate, especially if you are leaving room for a bit of dessert. And if the food is laden with cream and butter sauces, focus mainly on the meat, chicken, or fish and leave the sauce on the plate. When dessert comes, start with just a forkful or two and savor every bite. After a few bites, you may find that you're completely satisfied and don't want the entire portion. Planning ahead makes these occasional indulgences taste even better.

MYTH #10: My family won't like what I serve.

What's not to like about Baked Potato Skins, Grilled Cheese Sandwiches, and Oven-Fried Chicken? This is normal food. And these days, just about everybody thinks that it's a good idea to eat a little more healthfully. With dishes like these, your family and friends will be paying you compliments left and right. They'll say, "This is delicious. Is it really low-fat?" and "You're such a good cook" or "Can I have the recipe?" Never fear bland food again. With my simple tips on cooking methods and vibrant seasonings, your dishes will taste better than ever.

MYTH #11: Healthy foods are more expensive.

Actually, the reverse is true. Graham Kerr, television's former Galloping Gourmet, found that when he cut meat from his grocery list, he also cut his expenses by 50 percent. Meat is usually the most expensive item in your shopping cart. When you buy less meat and more beans, grains, fruits, and vegetables, you'll save money. Now there's a hidden benefit of healthy eating that you'll see right away—right in your checkbook.

MYTH #12: Healthy foods take longer to cook.

If recipes take too much time and effort, you aren't going to make them. Nobody has hours to spend in the kitchen. So I offer dishes that can be prepared as easily as some of the old standbys that you've been making for years. I've included recipes for easy-to-prepare weeknight suppers as well as make-ahead dinners for entertaining that will fit right into your lifestyle. All recipes include the hands-on time and total time so that you can tell at a glance if a recipe fits into your schedule for that day.

MYTH #13: I'll have to become a nutrition expert to eat healthfully.

You don't have to take a course in nutrition to learn how to cook and eat for good health. This book has all the basics that you'll need to know, like which foods you should eat more of and which you should eat less of.

MYTH #14: I'll have to use those substitute food products so my food will taste almost like it's supposed to.

Please don't! You don't need "fake" food to prepare healthful fare. Fresh and minimally processed ingredients are the keys to great flavor. Plus, highly processed ingredients are often sky-high in added fat, sodium, and sugar. In the next chapter, you'll discover how to use the best and most versatile fat-free ingredients, such as milk and plain yogurt, how to include small amounts of higher-fat flavorful foods, such as nuts and avocado, and even how to use minimally processed convenience products, such as seasoned diced tomatoes.

MYTH #15: I'll have to shop at specialty markets to get the ingredients I need.

No one wants to make a career out of grocery shopping. All of the recipes in this book use ingredients from a standard supermarket. There's no reason not to explore the ethnic foods section as well as the produce department of your local store. Many supermarkets now stock bulk grains, dried beans, whole-grain breads, and high-flavor foods like chili-garlic sauce. You may just find a new ingredient that you'll grow to love.

MYTH #16: I can never eat red meat again.

Not true. In fact, there are cuts of pork and beef that have nutritional profiles comparable to that of a skinless chicken breast. And red meat contains important nutrients such as iron, thiamin, and zinc. I'll show you the best lean cuts to choose, such as beef flank steak and pork tenderloin. Then I'll show you how to use these cuts in classic dishes like pot roast and meat loaf as well as newer dishes like Roast Pork with Cherry Sauce and Southwest Round Steak.

MYTH #17: I can never eat dessert again.

Say it isn't so! No one should go through life without dessert. If you've tried to deny yourself this universal pleasure, you know how hard it is. Moderation is essential, but so are our knock-your-socks-off desserts like Apple-Cheese Strudel, Fudgy Chocolate Brownies, and Peach Tart. The American Dietetic Association agrees that you can average your fat intake over several days to allow yourself flexibility in food choices such as dessert. With the healthy treats in this book, you can fully enjoy occasional indulgences and not worry about falling off the wagon.

MYTH #18: Eating and cooking won't be as much fun anymore.

This last misconception is true: Eating and cooking won't be as much fun anymore. They will be *more* fun than ever before. With the practical tips and easy recipes in this cookbook, you'll be eating and feeling better than ever.

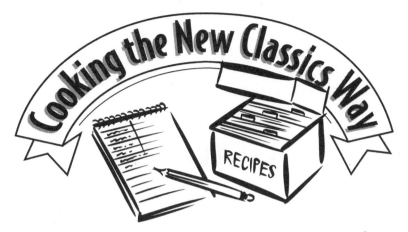

I t's an exciting time for food. Supermarket shelves are brimming with great-tasting healthy products. Most restaurants now offer a few healthy options. And thousands of home cooks have discovered countless ways to prepare good-for-you food that's absolutely delicious. Really. If you want proof, try any one of the recipes in this book.

Eating healthfully is more than just a good idea. First, it costs less. Second, it makes you feel better and more energetic. And third, it keeps you fit as a fiddle well into your golden years, which can also save you loads on medical bills. Exactly how to go about cooking and eating healthfully is the real question now—how to do it on a daily basis with familiar foods that are readily available, that taste good, and that don't take lots of your valuable time.

Lucky for you, I scoured the country to find the best healthy cooking and eating tips available. Some are from nutritionists. Some are from folks just like you. All of them are perfect for today's lifestyle. Here's a complete guide to updating your eating and cooking habits.

Visualize Portion Size

The first rule of healthy eating is watching how much you eat. This may not come naturally. Many of us grew up thinking that a proper portion size was whatever was put on our plates. You can learn to judge portion sizes fairly easily. Just pull out nature's built-in measuring device: your hand.

- The palm of your hand is about the size of a 3- to 4-ounce serving of meat, fish, or chicken. Just the right size. Another good mental image is a deck of cards.
- When munching on snacks, it's easy to get carried away and eat the whole package. Instead, focus on eating one small handful. That's

Why Eat This Way?

Good-for-you food has more benefits than you may realize. Most of the benefits stem from reducing the fat in your diet, particularly saturated fat. Here are some the biggest payoffs you can expect.

You can eat more. Hallelujah! When you cut back on fat, you can actually eat a greater amount of food. That's because fatty foods are a denser source of calories than healthier, carbo-hydrate-rich and protein-rich foods. One gram of fat contains 9 calories, but 1 gram of carbohydrate or protein contains only 4 calories. Eat fewer fatty foods, and you'll have calories left over. That means you can pile your plate with more eats.

You'll save money. Premium meats and processed foods usually cost more than healthy foods like chicken, vegetables, fruits, and grains. When you buy fewer high-fat items, you automatically lower food costs, according to thrift whiz Amy Dacyczyn, author of *The Tightwad Gazette* books. Plus, as you continue to eat more healthful foods, you save on the potential hidden costs of health care. It's no secret that eating too high on the hog increases your risk of weight gain, heart disease, diabetes, and other potentially expensive illnesses, says Dacyczyn.

You'll lose weight. Want to lose a few pounds? Experts agree that one of the best ways to do it is with a better diet. Study after study shows that eating fewer calories (which comes naturally from eating less fat) can help you lose weight. Not only will you look and feel better, but losing weight also cuts your risk for just about every major illness out there, including heart disease, high blood pressure, diabetes, stroke, and certain cancers. All this just from eating more healthy foods like fruits, vegetables, beans, and grains—even lean meats and dairy products.

You'll cut heart attack risk. I thought this was so important that I had to include it. It's clear that eating healthfully can help prevent disease. But it can also help reverse it. Eating naturally low fat foods like grains, vegetables, fruits, and lean proteins can actually help reverse the buildup of deposits (plaque) in the blood vessels and reduce your risk of heart attack. That's pretty powerful. If you think a lifetime of overindulgence can't be helped, think again. It's never too late.

about 1 ounce, the recommended serving size for most snacks (and usually enough to satisfy those cravings). For larger snack foods, like pretzels or low-fat chips, two handfuls equals 1 ounce.

- Are you a cheese-lover? Instead of eating a whole wedge, think of the top joint of your thumb. That handy digit is the perfect serving size: 1 ounce.
- Follow your thumb when it comes to butter, peanut butter, and mayonnaise, too. The top joint of your thumb is equal to about 1 teaspoon of these foods. For 1 tablespoon, count three thumb joints.
- Close your fist. That's the size of a serving of cereal, pasta, vegetables, or fruit—about 1 cup. Or, think of a tennis ball. Of course, you'll want to eat more than a fistful of these foods because they're so good for you.

Shop Smart for New Classic Ingredients

When you prepare food at home, you have the opportunity to eat exactly what you want, in precisely the amount you want, in exactly the way you want it cooked. In other words, you can make and eat food that positively thrills you. In what other area of your life can you exert such complete control?

A pantry, refrigerator, and freezer that are well-stocked with a variety of foods make it easy to cook wonderful dishes. And these days, everything you need to cook healthy meals is right in your local supermarket.

When shopping, stick to the perimeter of the store. That's where the freshest and most healthful foods are located because they generally need to be kept refrigerated. Shop the walls to find produce, dairy products, fish, meat, and poultry. You'll want to make wise selections within each category.

Good-for-you foods can also be found in the aisles, but you need to be careful about products that contain added fat, sugar, and salt. In general, look for foods with few or no added ingredients, such as canned beans, canned pureed pumpkin, canned tomatoes, canned fruits packed in juice, whole grains and flours, dried pasta and rice, and plain frozen fruits and vegetables. Here's how to shop in every aisle of the store.

This Fat, That Fat

Not all fats are created equal. Some fats, like monounsaturated fats, are actually good for you. "Fat is an extremely important nutrient that provides calories, supplies energy, and assists many vital bodily functions," says licensed dietitian Chavanne B. Hanson, R.D., of the University Hospitals of Cleveland Synergy Program in Ohio. The key is understanding which fats to eat more of and which to eat less of. Here's the scoop.

Eat More of These

Monounsaturated fats. This type of fat is liquid at room temperature and becomes partly firm if chilled. Monounsaturated fats are healthy because they may help lower your total blood cholesterol levels. It is best to get up to 15 percent of your daily diet in the form of monounsaturated fat. That means swapping solid fats like butter and margarine for liquid oils like olive, canola, and peanut.

Polyunsaturated fats. Also found in liquid oils, polyunsaturated fats are abundant in corn, safflower, sunflower, and soybean oils. Like the "monos," the "polys" are liquid at room temperature, but the polys stay liquid in the fridge. These fats tend to lower blood cholesterol levels when they replace saturated fats like butter in your diet. Getting up to 10 percent of your daily diet as polyunsaturated fat is recommended.

Another healthful type of poly fat is called omega-3 fatty acids. These are found mostly in fish. Studies show that omega-3's may help reduce the risk of heart attacks by up to 50 percent. So start eating fishes such as salmon, Atlantic mackerel, bluefish, trout, sablefish, and tuna (fresh and canned).

Eat Less of These

Saturated fats. These fats come mostly from animal sources, such as red meat, butter, and egg yolks. But there are some plant sources, too, like coconut oil and other tropical oils. Eat these fats sparingly because they tend to raise blood cholesterol levels, increasing your risk of heart disease.

Trans fatty acids. Also called trans fats, these are found in partially hydrogenated oils—the kind used to make most processed snack foods like chips, crackers, and cookies. Many margarines and shortenings are also high in trans fats. These fats tend to act like saturated fats because they can raise blood cholesterol levels. To eat fewer trans fats, go easy on processed foods containing hydrogenated oils and try to use less margarine and shortening.

Cholesterol. This fatlike substance is found only in animal-based foods such as meat, poultry, dairy products, and seafood. Although dietary cholesterol is not a saturated fat, it can contribute to increased blood cholesterol levels. Keep your cholesterol intake to no more than 300 milligrams per day.

Produce. If you shop once a week, pick fresh vegetables and fruits that keep for several days, such as onions, carrots, bananas, and oranges. Also choose some that must be used within two to three days, such as asparagus, broccoli, and strawberries. Let color be your guide. Do you have light and dark green, orange, red, and yellow in your cart? A wide range of rich colors will ensure the best nutrition. Choose at least one vegetable for every night of the week that you'll be home and plenty of fruits for snacks and desserts. If you don't use them up by the end of the week, you can use any that are left to make a stir-fry, a casserole, or a pot of soup. Store these in the freezer for quick weeknight meals.

Buy plenty of salad fixings. Many types of lettuce and vegetables are now sold ready-to-use. Or, wash and chop salad vegetables early in the week. Keep them wrapped in a paper towel in an open plastic bag so that they don't go limp. Another option is to buy pre-cut produce and salad fixings at your supermarket's salad bar. Having the ingredients ready to use makes you much more likely to eat more vegetables, especially on busy nights.

Don't forget frozen and canned vegetables and fruits. These are ultra-convenient and often have vitamin and mineral profiles comparable to those of fresh. Frozen corn, peas, peaches, and blueberries and canned tomatoes and beans will be used often. What's more, they keep for months.

Dairy. Don't assume that you have to choose fat-free dairy products every time. Sometimes reduced-fat or even full-fat dairy in smaller amounts is a better choice because even just a bit of fat coating the palate makes the flavor linger, so it's more satisfying. A few highly flavored higher-fat products, such as blue cheese, feta, and goat cheese, can do wonders for the taste of your dishes.

Of course, fat-free ingredients work beautifully in recipes, too, especially when you want to extend another flavor or texture; that is, when there's another ingredient that gives the dish most of it's "oomph." You get a lot more bang for your fat buck when you combine high-fat blue cheese with fat-free sour cream.

Meat. Go for select grade, and if the package lists trim size, choose ¼" trim or less. Choose red meats with the words *round* or *loin* in the name, as in eye of round, top round, sirloin, and tenderloin. These are the lowest in fat. Buy cuts of pork with *loin* in the name, such as pork tenderloin.

(continued on page 14)

Color Me Healthy

Tonight, when you sit down to dinner, take a good look at your plate. Ask yourself this question: "Are there a variety of colors on my plate? Do the colors come from minimally processed foods?" Color is a simple indicator of vitamins and minerals. A mix of green, orange, yellow, and red on your plate indicates the presence of many different nutrients. And many flavors, too. "Foods that deliver a lot of nutrients can also deliver a lot of taste. We sometimes forget that those go together," says Roberta Duyff, R.D., author of *The American Dietetic Association's Complete Food and Nutrition Guide*. Here's a full spectrum of colorful foods, the nutrients they are high in, and why they're good for you.

Apricots. Vitamin A, potassium

Artichokes. Iron, magnesium, potassium

Asparagus. Riboflavin, folate

Avocado. Vitamin B_6, vitamin E, potassium

Bananas. Potassium, vitamin B_6

Beans. Folate, pantothenic acid, thiamin, calcium, iron, magnesium, potassium, zinc

Beet greens. Potassium, vitamin A, vitamin C, riboflavin

Bok choy. Vitamin A, vitamin C, calcium, potassium

Broccoli. Folate, vitamin A, vitamin C, calcium, riboflavin, vitamin B_6

Brussels sprouts. Vitamin A, vitamin C, vitamin K, folate, potassium

Cantaloupe. Vitamin A, potassium

Cauliflower. Vitamin C, folate

Cheese. Calcium, vitamin B_{12}, riboflavin

Curly endive. Vitamin A, folate, vitamin K

Eggs. Vitamin A, vitamin B_6, vitamin B_{12}, biotin, riboflavin, vitamin K

Fish. Vitamin B_6, vitamin B_{12}, niacin, pantothenic acid, iron, zinc, potassium

Kale. Vitamin A, vitamin C, calcium

Lentils. Folate, iron, magnesium, zinc

Mango. Vitamin A, vitamin C

Meat. Vitamin B_{12}, niacin, pantothenic acid, iron, potassium, zinc

Milk. Vitamin A, vitamin B_{12}, riboflavin, vitamin D, vitamin K, calcium, potassium, zinc

Mustard greens. Vitamin A, vitamin C, folate, calcium

Oranges. Vitamin C, folate, potassium

Oysters. Vitamin D, zinc

Peaches. Vitamin A

Peanut butter. Vitamin E, magnesium

Peanuts. Vitamin B_6, folate, niacin, vitamin E, magnesium

Peas. Folate, riboflavin, thiamin, calcium, iron, magnesium

Peppers. Vitamin C

Pork. Vitamin B_6, vitamin B_{12}, niacin, pantothenic acid, thiamin, zinc

Potatoes. Vitamin B_6, niacin, riboflavin, thiamin, vitamin C, iron, magnesium, potassium

Poultry. Niacin, vitamin B_6, vitamin B_{12}, pantothenic acid, iron, zinc

Pumpkin seeds. Iron, magnesium, potassium, zinc

Rice. Vitamin B_6, riboflavin, thiamin, iron

Romaine lettuce. Vitamin A, vitamin C

Salmon. Vitamin B_6, vitamin D, vitamin E

Soybeans. Vitamin B_6, folate, riboflavin, iron, magnesium, potassium, zinc

Spinach. Vitamin A, vitamin C, vitamin B_6, vitamin B_{12}, folate, riboflavin, magnesium, potassium

Sunflower seeds. Vitamin E, folate, thiamin, iron, magnesium, zinc

Strawberries. Vitamin C

Sweet potatoes. Vitamin A, vitamin B_6, vitamin C, vitamin E, potassium

Tofu. Calcium, iron, magnesium

Tomatoes. Vitamin C, potassium

Tuna. Vitamin B_6, vitamin D, niacin, iron

Watermelon. Vitamin B_6 thiamin, vitamin C, magnesium, potassium

NUTRIENT	WHAT IT DOES
Vitamin A	Essential for vision; enhances immunity; builds and maintains bone
Thiamin (B_1)	Helps turn food into energy; essential for nerve impulses
Riboflavin (B_2)	Helps turn food into energy; regulates hormones and red blood cells
Niacin (B_3)	Helps turn food into energy
Pantothenic Acid (B_5)	Helps metabolize foods; helps produce red blood cells and neurotransmitters
Vitamin B_6	Helps metabolize proteins and fats; helps make red blood cells
Vitamin B_{12}	Helps make new cells; protects and maintains sheath around nerve fibers
Biotin	Necessary for energy metabolism; makes fatty acids; breaks down amino acids
Folic acid	Helps form DNA in new cells
Vitamin C	An antioxidant; strengthens resistance to infections; helps in absorption of iron
Vitamin D	Promotes bone mineralization by raising calcium and phosphorous levels in blood
Vitamin E	An antioxidant; helps protect cells from damage
Calcium	Essential in bone formation and maintenance
Iron	Helps carry oxygen in the bloodstream
Magnesium	Helps metabolize food and transmit messages between cells
Potassium	Helps transmit nerve impulses, contract muscles, and maintain normal blood pressure
Zinc	Necessary for growth, immune function, wound healing and sperm production

Poultry. Choose boneless, skinless chicken for stir-fries and grilling. Buy breasts left on the bone for baking. To keep bone-in breasts moist, bake with the skin on and remove the skin just before serving. Turkey cutlets make a great alternative to chicken breasts, and ground turkey breast is a versatile ingredient for burgers, meat loaf, and casseroles. But don't be misled by packaging that says "lean ground turkey." Some ground turkey and ground chicken contain all parts of the bird and sometimes the skin, which can be quite high in fat. Look for 100 percent ground skinless turkey or chicken breast, which contains the lowest amount of fat.

Seafood. Think of fish and shellfish as falling into two categories: either very low in fat or full of health-promoting omega-3 fatty acids. Either way, you come out a winner.

Be sure to choose and store seafood properly because it is highly perishable. Find out when your market gets fish delivered and try to buy and cook it that day (even if you have to refrigerate the cooked fish and eat it later). Also, consider keeping frozen fish on hand. Generally displayed near the fresh seafood case, you'll find a variety of frozen products such as shrimp and fish fillets. Experiment to discover which ones you'll use and enjoy. Lean canned seafood, such as tuna packed in water or canned clams, is also excellent to have on hand in the pantry.

Deli foods. Most deli cases stock a variety of reduced-sodium and reduced-fat lunchmeats. Many contain nitrites, which have been shown to cause cancer, so you'll want to use them sparingly. By all means, buy roasted turkey breast, which is minimally processed and makes an ideal lunch. While it is a little more expensive than the processed versions, the difference in nutritional benefits and flavor makes it well worth it.

Baked goods. The bakery is filled with healthful choices. Sourdough bread, Italian semolina bread, French bread, bagels, English muffins, and pitas tend to be low in fat. Whole-wheat bread is more nutritious and higher in fiber than these. Be sure to buy true whole-wheat bread. If the label says "wheat," "cracked wheat," or "sprouted wheat," the bread may be made mostly from white flour. The first ingredient in whole-wheat bread should be "whole-wheat flour."

Cereals. Select cereals that you enjoy with as little sugar and as much fiber as possible (aim for 3 grams per serving). If you're new to healthful cereals, eat them with sliced fruit, raisins, or even a sprinkling of sugar. Adding a teaspoon of sugar to cereal often increases the sugar content less than buying a sweetened cereal. Cereals also have myriad nonbreakfast uses. Whole-grain cereals make a sweet, crunchy topping for frozen yogurt. Toasting cereal with garlic powder and Worcestershire sauce makes a tasty low-fat snack.

Pastas and grains. You can't go wrong filling your shopping cart with pastas and grains. Experiment with the wide variety of rices available: white, brown, Jasmine, basmati. For time-pressed evenings, stock quick-cooking grains such as couscous and bulgur. Barley is also available in a quick-cook version. Choose plain grains and season them yourself with herbs and spices instead of high-sodium seasoning packets. Try new pasta shapes, too.

Spices and baking goods. Go crazy in the herb and spice section of your supermarket. You may discover exciting new ways to add flavor and zest to your foods.

When buying flour, bear in mind that many low-fat baked goods turn out better when you use cake flour instead of all-purpose flour. Buy cocoa instead of solid baking chocolate. To boost chocolate flavor, keep some instant coffee granules on hand. Seek out flavor extracts such as vanilla and almond. And don't forget the cornstarch; it thickens sauces and adds body to foods without fat.

Cookies, crackers, and other snack foods. Try healthier choices such as vanilla wafers, graham crackers, fig bars, and animal crackers. But read labels and eat minimal quantities of products made with partially hydrogenated vegetable oils, which can raise blood cholesterol levels.

Pretzels, air-popped popcorn, and rice cakes are all decent choices for snacking. Again, be sure to read nutrition labels. Some popcorn is amazingly high in fat, even though it says "air-popped" on the label. Nuts make a healthy snack in moderate amounts. Almost all candy is empty sugar calories. But to satisfy a sweet tooth once in a while, choose licorice, gumdrops, or jelly beans, which all have a negligible amount of fat. Small, individually wrapped candies offer built-in portion control.

Low-fat and fat-free frozen yogurt also make good treats, but don't assume that all frozen yogurt is low in fat and calories. As with anything else, read the nutrition label.

(continued on page 18)

Menu Minder

In today's fast-paced world, you can't always eat home-cooked meals. Besides, eating out is one of modern life's greatest pleasures. Just be sure you know what you're getting. Strike up a conversation with the wait staff to find out how the restaurant's food is made. Ask simple questions like, "How is the fish prepared?" and "Is there a lot of cream or butter in the sauce?" If the preparation seems a little too heavy for you, ask them to bake or broil the fish instead of frying it. Or ask them to go easy on the cream or butter in the sauce. It's actually a lot of fun customizing your meals this way. And why not? You're shelling out the bucks for the meal; you should get what you want. Most restaurants realize this fact and are very accommodating.

Even if you'd rather not get chummy with the wait staff, you can still order smart from restaurant menus. Here are some terms to watch for and a complete guide to the best choices in today's most popular eateries.

- "Coated," "breaded," and "battered" usually describe dishes that are fried. Ask to have yours baked with a quick brush of oil instead.
- "Sautéed," "pan-fried," "pan-seared," and "fried" are all cooking methods that require additional fat. Ask them to use just a touch of oil in your dish.
- "Rich" or "enriched" often refers to sauces or other dishes that have added butter, oil, or cream. Ask that a light hand be used with these ingredients.
- "Light" can be a very misleading term. A light cream sauce can be laden with fat, and "lightly fried" is at least partially immersed in oil. Ask to find out what you're getting.
- "Au gratin," "alfredo," "in cheese sauce," and "parmigiana" are typically high-fat dishes.
- "Fresh," "baked," "roasted," "broiled," "grilled," "seared," "braised," "poached," and "steamed" indicate the healthiest choices.

Chinese

The first thing to remember about Chinese restaurants is that the portions tend to be huge. That's what makes Chinese such a great value. You only have to order one entrée for every two people. Get plenty of steamed rice, too. To play it safe and cut back on sodium, request that everything be made without monosodium glutamate, or MSG.

Healthy choices: Szechuan shrimp, lo mein chicken and/or vegetables, chicken chop suey, steamed and stir-fried vegetables, Hunan tofu, soft noodle dishes, steamed rice

Think twice about these: Egg rolls, Kung Pao chicken, fried wontons, spareribs, sesame chicken, crispy noodle dishes (called bird's nest), sweet-and-sour pork or chicken

French/Continental

Contrary to popular belief, not all French food is riddled with fat. Many classic dishes are naturally lean and satisfying, like *pot-au-feu* (literally, "pot of fire," or slow-cooked beef and vegetables). Just skip the high-fat butter and cream sauces.

Healthy choices: Bouillabaisse, grilled shrimp, grilled asparagus with lemon sauce, petit filet mignon, blackened tuna, coulis sauce

Think twice about these: Beef Wellington, veal Oscar, chicken cordon bleu, any dish made with aïoli, béchamel, hollandaise, Mornay, or velouté sauce

Italian

Italian restaurants are a mecca of healthful choices. Two caveats here: olive oil and cheese. Try not to go overboard on either one.

Healthy choices: Spaghetti with tomato sauce, spaghetti with meatballs, linguine with red or white clam sauce, pasta e fagioli, pasta primavera, baked whole fish

Think twice about these: "À la Parmigiana" dishes, fettucine Alfredo, lasagna, ravioli, stuffed shells, Caesar salad

Mexican

Some Mexican restaurant dishes tend to be high in sodium and fat, but plenty of flavorful healthy choices are available. Just keep an eye on the side dishes and condiments, like guacamole and sour cream. That's where most of the fat and calories add up. Salsa is the one exception. Eat as much as you want of this healthy sidekick.

Healthy choices: Chicken, shrimp, or vegetable fajitas; chicken, shrimp, or vegetable burritos; chicken, shrimp, or vegetable soft tacos; black bean soup

Think twice about these: Guacamole, cheese quesadillas with sour cream, cheese nachos, enchiladas, chimichangas, salads in fried taco shells, fried taco chips

Seafood

Good seafood is a godsend. Prepared right, it's simple, healthy, and tasty. The key is freshness. Always ask the wait staff what is the freshest seafood on the menu.

Healthy choices: Steamed lobster, crab, or shrimp, fish or shellfish broiled or grilled without added fat, blackened fish, seafood gumbo, cioppino, bouillabaisse, seafood paella, fish or shellfish on pasta in marinara or tomato sauce, any teriyaki dish, kabobs

Think twice about these: Fish and chips, fried seafood, baked stuffed shrimp, any "Newburg" dish, any "Thermidor" dish, any "au gratin" dish, *zuppa di pesce*

Beverages. Choose low-calorie, caffeine-free beverages like bottled water, herbal iced tea, or reduced-sodium tomato juice to meet your minimum need for 8 cups of fluid daily. Go easy on carbonated beverages, which give a false sense of fullness by filling your stomach with air.

How to Update Your Favorite Recipes

With the more than 200 fantastic recipes in this book, you're off to a sound start in cooking the new classics. But what if you crave one of your old favorite high-fat dishes or long to try a recipe that you see in a magazine? Here's what you can do to make over a recipe. First, identify the high-fat ingredients. From there, it's a matter of substituting low-fat ingredients for high-fat ones, boosting flavor where necessary, and troubleshooting to get the textures just right. Apply the following standards to any main-dish recipe for four.

- *Meat, poultry, and fish portions* should be 4 to 6 ounces per person. If a recipe calls for more than that, you have two choices. First, you can make the dish and refrigerate or freeze the leftovers for another meal. This option saves you time because you get two main dishes from cooking only once. The second solution is to scale down the amount of meat, poultry, or fish to the number of servings that you need. Keep the vegetables and grains the same as stated in the recipe.
- *Meat, poultry, and fish recipes* should have no more than 1 tablespoon of added oil. If the recipe calls for more, ask yourself why it's there. Is the oil used to fry? You can brown foods in a nonstick skillet with nonstick spray instead. Is the oil part of a sauce or dressing? If so, consider replacing it with broth, vegetable juice, fat-free or reduced-fat sour cream, or fat-free evaporated milk, depending on what style of sauce it is.
- *Meatless main dishes* should limit oil to 2 tablespoons. With plant foods generally containing far less fat than animal foods, you can afford a little more oil, particularly if it's a healthful monounsaturate like canola or olive oil.
- *Full-fat cheese* should be limited to no more than ½ cup per recipe. For recipes using low-fat cheese, allow up to 1 cup. Or, for larger casseroles that serve 8, allow up to 2 cups.

- *Olives, nuts, seeds, and other high-fat additions* should be kept to less than 2 tablespoons. These foods are all nutritious but are high in calories because they're dense sources of fat. If a recipe calls for ¼ cup of olives, reduce the amount to 2 tablespoons and chop them to disperse the flavor throughout the dish. For nuts, ½ cup can be reduced to ¼ cup when you toast the nuts to boost their flavor and chop them finely to distribute the flavor throughout.

Adapt Your Cooking Style

Nonstick cooking pans are the gold standard in today's kitchens. With just a whisper of cooking spray, you can brown foods with virtually no fat. Look for flavored sprays, such as garlic or Cajun, to expand flavors. Or, make your own sprays by pouring flavorful oils, such as olive or toasted sesame, into clean plastic spray bottles.

Another useful technique that you can use to bring out the flavor of garlic, onion, and other aromatics is to simmer them in a bit of chicken or vegetable broth in a nonstick skillet. Here are some other little substitution tips and techniques that can add up to big fat savings.

- *Pump up flavor* by increasing herbs, spices, and other seasoning ingredients. Experiment with shallots, scallions, fresh ginger, dried mushrooms, grated citrus peel, sun-dried tomatoes, and balsamic vinegar. All add depth of flavor and no fat. If these ingredients are new to you, try to incorporate one new seasoning a month into your pantry.
- *Prevent pasta from sticking* without adding oil to the water. Simply save a few tablespoons of the cooking water before draining the pasta. Toss the pasta with the reserved water before adding the sauce, and it won't clump.
- *Poultry will stay moister* if it's cooked with the skin on. Remove and discard the skin before serving.
- *Moisten poultry stuffing* with fat-free broth and bake it in a pan separately from the chicken or turkey so that it won't absorb any of the fat from the bird.

(continued on page 24)

Simple Substitutions

Whittling away fat and calories is a matter of making small substitutions in your cooking. Use this list when you're doing a recipe makeover. Included are troubleshooting tips for times when things need tweaking to make them just perfect.

Baked Goods

Butter
Replace with: Nonstick spray, for coating pans
  OR less butter plus drained applesauce, pureed prunes, or pureed silken tofu
  OR less butter plus oil and buttermilk or fat-free evaporated milk
  OR less butter plus reduced-fat cream cheese
Troubleshooting tips: If rubbery or tough, add a small amount of grated apple to the batter for moistness
  OR increase the ratio of butter to pureed fruit or tofu
  OR increase the ratio of butter to oil and buttermilk or fat-free evaporated milk
  OR add chopped dried fruit or nuts to the batter to add a different texture
  OR if too wet, decrease baking temperature and increase baking time
  OR if too wet, add whole-wheat flour, wheat germ, or oat bran to batter to absorb moisture

Chocolate
Replace with: Cocoa powder plus oil, pureed prunes, drained applesauce
Troubleshooting tips: For more chocolate flavor, add a small amount of grated solid chocolate
  OR add a teaspoon of instant espresso or regular coffee granules
  OR replace some of the liquid with strong brewed coffee
  OR add or increase vanilla extract

Chocolate chips
Replace with: Fewer mini chocolate chips

Troubleshooting tip: For more flavor, add chopped nuts

Coconut, shredded
Replace with: Less coconut, finely shredded for better distribution
  OR a small amount of coconut extract

Cream
Replace with: Fat-free evaporated milk
  OR buttermilk
  OR a small amount of half-and-half
Troubleshooting tips: If not enough body, add a small amount of grated apple to the batter for moistness
  OR if not enough structure, add beaten egg white before baking

Cream cheese
Replace with: Reduced-fat or fat-free cream cheese, or Neufchâtel cheese
Troubleshooting tips: If not enough body, add beaten egg white to the batter
  OR use reduced-fat instead of fat-free cream cheese

Eggs
Replace with: Egg whites (2 for each whole egg)
Troubleshooting tips: If too gummy, add beaten egg white to provide structure
  OR if too wet, decrease baking temperature and increase baking time
  OR if too wet, add flour, wheat germ, or oat bran to batter to absorb moisture

Flour
Replace with: Whole-wheat pastry flour

Milk
Replace with: Fat-free evaporated milk
  OR buttermilk

Nuts
Replace with: Fewer nuts, toasted and finely chopped to better distribute flavor

Rum
Replace with: Less rum
OR a small amount of rum extract

Sour cream
Replace with: Reduced-fat or fat-free sour cream
OR reduced-fat or fat-free yogurt
OR buttermilk
OR Fat-free evaporated milk plus lemon juice (1 tablespoon for each cup)
Troubleshooting tips: If not enough body, add beaten egg white to the batter
OR if too wet, add flour, wheat germ, or oat bran to the batter to absorb moisture

Sugar
Replace with: Less sugar
OR less sugar plus pureed fruit such as apple, banana, or apricot

Casseroles

Butter or margarine
Replace with: Less butter or margarine
OR reduced-calorie margarine
OR oil
Troubleshooting tips: If too thin, add beaten egg white before baking to provide structure

Cheddar cheese
Replace with: Reduced-fat or fat-free Cheddar cheese
Troubleshooting tip: If a tough crust forms on top, finely shred the cheese so that it melts evenly
OR use reduced-fat cheese instead of fat-free cheese
OR cover the casserole during baking

Cream
Replace with: Fat-free evaporated milk
OR buttermilk
OR a small amount of half-and-half

Troubleshooting tips: If too thin, add a smaller amount of fat-free evaporated milk or buttermilk OR stir in a teaspoon of arrowroot or cornstarch, bring to a gentle boil, and cook and stir for 1 minute

Cream cheese
Replace with: Reduced-fat or fat-free cream cheese, or Neufchâtel cheese
Troubleshooting tips: If too thin, add beaten egg white before baking to provide structure
OR use reduced-fat instead of fat-free cream cheese

Cream soup
Replace with: Reduced-fat cream soup
Troubleshooting tip: For more flavor, add seasonings

Feta cheese
Replace with: Mixture of feta cheese and reduced-fat cottage cheese
Troubleshooting tip: For more flavor, add a small amount of lemon juice or vinegar

Ground beef
Replace with: Extra-lean ground beef
OR ground skinless turkey breast
Troubleshooting tip: If the taste of ground turkey is too unfamiliar, use a mixture of ground beef and ground turkey breast

Mayonnaise
Replace with: Reduced-fat or cholesterol-free mayonnaise

Milk
Replace with: Fat-free evaporated milk
OR buttermilk

Oil-packed tuna
Replace with: Water-packed tuna

Pork bacon
Replace with: Turkey bacon
OR Canadian bacon

(continued)

Simple Substitutions —Continued

Ricotta cheese
Replace with: Reduced-fat ricotta cheese

Sausage
Replace with: Turkey, chicken, or tofu sausage
Troubleshooting tip: For more flavor, add
  crushed fennel and sage

Sour cream
Replace with: Reduced-fat or fat-free sour
  cream
  OR reduced-fat or fat-free yogurt
  OR buttermilk
  OR fat-free evaporated milk plus lemon juice
  (1 tablespoon for each cup)
Troubleshooting tip: If too thin, stir in at the very
  end and cook just until heated through

Icings and Frostings

Butter or margarine
Replace with: Less butter or margarine plus
  marshmallow creme
  OR less butter and reduced-fat cream
  cheese
  OR a dusting of confectioners' sugar and/or
  cocoa powder

Pie Crust

Butter or shortening
Replace with: Less butter or shortening plus re-
  duced-fat cream cheese
  OR less butter or shortening plus oil
  OR replace pie crust with phyllo dough crust
Troubleshooting tips: If too stiff, add more oil or
  ice water
  OR if too crumbly, use less butter or shortening
  and more ice water; also avoid overmixing dough
  OR if too tough, add more butter or shortening;
  also avoid overmixing dough
  OR if difficult to work with, use very cold ingre-

dients and roll out between sheets of plastic or
waxed paper; carefully transfer to pan
OR if soggy, increase the oven temperature or
increase the baking time

Sauces, Dips, Dressings, and Gravies

Butter or margarine
Replace with: Less butter or margarine
  OR reduced-calorie margarine
  OR oil
  OR other liquids such as stock, sherry, wine,
  vegetable juice, or pureed cooked
  vegetables
Troubleshooting tip: For more flavor, add sea-
  sonings

Cream
Replace with: Fat-free evaporated milk
  OR buttermilk
  OR a small amount of half-and-half
Troubleshooting tips: If too thin, add a smaller
  amount of fat-free evaporated milk or
  buttermilk
  OR stir in a teaspoon of arrowroot or corn-
  starch, bring to a gentle boil, and cook and stir
  for 1 minute

Cream cheese
Replace with: Reduced-fat or fat-free cream
  cheese, or Neufchâtel cheese

Milk
Replace with: Fat-free evaporated milk
  OR buttermilk

Oil
Replace with: Reduced amount of oil
  OR chicken or vegetable stock
  OR vegetable juice
  OR fruit juice

Troubleshooting tip: If too thin, stir in a teaspoon of arrowroot or cornstarch, bring to a gentle boil, and cook and stir for 1 minute

Pan drippings
Replace with: Defatted pan drippings plus chicken, beef, or vegetable broth
Troubleshooting tip: If too thin, stir in a teaspoon of arrowroot or cornstarch, bring to a gentle boil, and cook and stir for 1 minute
OR if too thin, add fat-free evaporated milk mixed with flour
OR for more flavor, add sautéed mushrooms and seasonings

Sour cream
Replace with: Reduced-fat or fat-free sour cream
OR reduced-fat or fat-free yogurt
OR buttermilk
OR fat-free evaporated milk plus lemon juice (1 tablespoon for each cup)
Troubleshooting tip: If too thin, for cooked sauces, stir in at the very end and cook just until heated through; for uncooked sauces and dips, gently stir in; avoid overstirring

Yogurt
Replace with: Reduced-fat or fat-free yogurt
OR reduced-fat or fat-free sour cream
OR buttermilk
Troubleshooting tip: If too thin, for cooked sauces, stir the yogurt or sour cream in at the very end and cook just until heated through; for uncooked sauces and dips, gently stir in the yogurt or sour cream to avoid overstirring

Soups, Stews, and Chowders

Butter or margarine
Replace with: Less butter or margarine
OR reduced-calorie margarine
OR oil

Cheddar cheese
Replace with: Reduced-fat or fat-free Cheddar cheese
Troubleshooting tip: If cheese is stringy, finely shred the cheese so it melts evenly; cook over low heat, stirring constantly, just until melted OR use reduced-fat cheese instead of fat-free cheese

Cream
Replace with: Fat-free evaporated milk
OR buttermilk
Troubleshooting tips: If too thin, add a smaller amount of fat-free evaporated milk
OR if too thin, stir in a teaspoon of arrowroot or cornstarch, bring to a gentle boil, and cook and stir for 1 minute

Cream soup
Replace with: Reduced-fat cream soup
Troubleshooting tip: For more flavor, add seasonings

Milk
Replace with: Fat-free evaporated milk
OR buttermilk

Pork bacon
Replace with: Turkey bacon
OR Canadian bacon

Sausage
Replace with: Turkey, chicken, or tofu sausage
Troubleshooting tip: For more flavor, add crushed fennel and sage

Sour cream
Replace with: Reduced-fat or fat-free sour cream
OR reduced-fat or fat-free plain yogurt
OR buttermilk
OR fat-free evaporated milk plus lemon juice (1 tablespoon for each cup)
Troubleshooting tip: If too thin, stir in at the very end and cook just until heated through

- *Use fat-free salad dressings* to marinate chicken, turkey, meat, and fish before broiling or grilling.
- *Puree cooked vegetables as a base* for silken soups and sauces. Enrich with a bit of fat-free evaporated milk.
- *Keep fat-free condiments on hand*, like mustards and salsas. If you crave mayonnaise, mix the low-fat version with flavor enhancers, such as chopped fresh herbs, hot-pepper sauce, chopped pickles, or capers.
- *Spread bagels and toast* with fruit jams, fruit butters, or yogurt-cheese spreads mixed with fresh fruit or chopped herbs instead of butter, margarine, or full-fat cream cheese.
- *For fat-free salad dressings*, use canned fat-free broths, vegetable juices, and fruit juices as a base.
- *Rub dry spice seasonings* into lean meats, chicken, or fish before broiling or grilling.
- *Instead of frying fish*, bake or grill fillets in foil packages along with fresh herbs and thinly sliced vegetables of your choice.
- *Use lean Canadian bacon* instead of regular bacon. For smoky flavor with no fat, try chipotle chile peppers (smoked jalapeño chile peppers). These will also add fiery heat. For smoky flavor with no heat, try a drop or two of liquid smoke seasoning (available in the spice or condiment aisle of most supermarkets).
- *Create a crisp crust* on fish or fowl cutlets without frying. Dredge the cutlets alternately in flour, beaten egg white, and seasoned bread crumbs. Coat both sides with nonstick spray and bake in a preheated pan.

Adapt Your Baking Style

Breads, muffins, and other baked goods can be an important source of complex carbohydrates. To get the flavors and textures just right, use the following tips.

- *Substitute cake flour or whole-wheat pastry flour* (sold in some supermarkets and natural foods stores) for all-purpose flour in fat-reduced baked goods to produce a more tender result.
- *To reduce butter*, try substituting half the amount called for with prune puree, drained applesauce, mashed banana, pureed silken tofu, fat-free cream cheese, or drained fat-free yogurt. This substi-

tution is particularly effective for muffins, quick breads, and denser snack cakes.

- *To reduce saturated fat*, experiment with replacing some of the butter with canola, safflower, or other heart-healthy vegetable oil.
- *Cut down on eggs* by replacing each large egg with either 2 egg whites or ¼ cup fat-free liquid egg substitute. For 2 large eggs, use 1 whole egg and 1 egg white. Too many egg whites can dry baked goods, so be sure to include at least 1 egg yolk in your recipe.
- *Replace sour cream and yogurt* with their fat-free counterparts.
- *Get great chocolate flavor* but reduce the amount of saturated fat by using cocoa instead of solid chocolate. For 1 ounce of unsweetened chocolate, use 3 tablespoons of cocoa plus 1 tablespoon of canola oil. You can use the same substitution for semisweet chocolate, but you may want to increase the sugar in the recipe by about 4 tablespoons to keep the sweetness in balance. And try adding a teaspoon of instant coffee granules to bolster chocolate flavor.
- *Cut chocolate chips* by using half the amount of miniature chips. The smaller chips disperse the flavor throughout the baked good.
- *Cut each cup of nuts* to ¼ cup. Toast nuts in a skillet over medium heat for about 5 minutes, or until fragrant, to heighten the flavor. You can also chop the nuts finely to disperse them more thoroughly throughout the baked good.

All about Breakfast

Breakfast has long been touted as the most important meal of the day. But for many of us trying to lose weight or save time, breakfast is often the first meal that we ignore. Yet there's compelling evidence that breakfast is not only the most important meal of the day, but breakfast also may positively impact our health, our attitudes, and our work.

"Breakfast gives your body the ability to refuel after an evening of rest. Individuals who eat breakfast tend to have more strength and endurance as well as better concentration and problem-solving skills," says Jill Stovsky, R.D., licensed dietitian with the Preventive Cardiology Program of the Cleveland Clinic Foundation in Ohio.

"We encourage patients to stick with breakfast," Stovsky says. "We find that they maintain their ideal weight more easily when they evenly spread their caloric intake throughout the day. Studies have shown that individuals who eat only one or two large meals a day accumulate more fat than those who eat smaller meals more frequently. In fact, breakfast is the meal most often skipped by overweight people."

Good Morning Foods

Start your day off right with whole-grain breads, whole-grain cold cereals and instant hot cereals, fruit juices, ready-cut fresh fruits, dried fruits, or low-fat yogurt. These healthful convenience products provide the fiber, vitamins, minerals, and energy that you'll need to keep you going strong throughout the day.

If you typically have several rushed mornings a week, prepare portable items that you can grab and go. Pack small plastic bags each with a serving of bite-size shredded wheat and a tablespoon or two of raisins or dried cranberries. Keep ripe bananas in your pantry and individual serving cartons of fat-free milk in the refrigerator.

On weekend and weekday mornings when you have a bit more time, turn to the satisfying breakfast dishes in this chapter. Many can be made in 30 minutes or less. Some can even be prepared the night before. As you savor each bite, remind yourself that today is the first day of the best breakfasts of your life.

Recipes

Breakfast Wrap

Hands-on time: 10 minutes
Total time: 15 minutes

2   eggs

6   egg whites

1/4   teaspoon salt

4   ounces mushrooms, sliced

4   plum tomatoes, chopped

1   small zucchini, chopped

1   small onion, chopped

1/2   teaspoon dried basil

4   whole-wheat tortillas (8" diameter)

1/2   cup (2 ounces) shredded low-fat mllozzarella cheese

In a medium bowl, whisk together the eggs, egg whites, salt, and 2 tablespoons water.

Coat a large nonstick skillet with nonstick spray. Set over medium-high heat. Add the mushrooms, tomatoes, zucchini, onion, and basil. Cook, stirring occasionally, for 4 to 5 minutes, or until the vegetables are soft.

Add the egg mixture. Cook, stirring often, for 3 minutes, or until the eggs are cooked. Remove from the heat.

Meanwhile, wrap the tortillas in a paper towel and place in the microwave oven. Cook on high power for 30 seconds to heat. Place the tortillas on a cutting board. Spoon some of the egg mixture down the center of each tortilla. Sprinkle with the mozzarella. Roll into cylinders and cut in half diagonally.

Makes 4 servings

Per serving

Calories 214	*Sodium 547 mg.*
Total fat 6 g.	*Dietary fiber 4 g.*
Saturated fat 3 g.	*Protein 18 g.*
Cholesterol 114 mg.	*Carbohydrates 19 g.*

WRAP UP NUTRIENTS

Play it Again!

Breakfast wraps are the perfect vehicle for using vegetable side dishes left over from the previous night's dinner. Figure on needing 2 cups of cooked vegetables for 4 wraps. Try adding some drained and rinsed canned beans for extra fiber and great taste.

Florentine Omelette

Photograph on page 56
Hands-on time: 10 minutes
Total time: 25 minutes

2 cups liquid egg substitute

1 teaspoon Italian seasoning

1/4 teaspoon salt

8 ounces mushrooms, sliced

1 onion, chopped

1 red bell pepper, chopped

1 clove garlic, minced

2 ounces (1 packed cup) spinach leaves, chopped

3/4 cup (3 ounces) shredded low-fat mozzarella cheese

In a medium bowl, whisk together the egg substitute, Italian seasoning, salt, and 3 tablespoons water.

Coat a large nonstick skillet with nonstick spray. Set over medium-high heat. Add the mushrooms, onion, bell pepper, and garlic. Cook, stirring often, for 4 to 5 minutes, or until the bell pepper starts to soften. Add the spinach. Cook for 1 minute, or until the spinach wilts. Transfer to a small bowl and cover.

Wipe the skillet with a paper towel. Coat with nonstick spray. Set over medium heat. Pour in half of the egg-substitute mixture. Cook for 2 minutes, or until the bottom begins to set. Using a spatula, lift the edges to allow the uncooked mixture to flow to the bottom of the pan. Cook for 2 minutes, or until set. Sprinkle with half of the reserved vegetable mixture and half of the mozzarella. Cover and cook for 2 minutes, or until the cheese melts. Using a

spatula, fold the egg mixture in half. Invert onto a serving plate.

Coat the skillet with nonstick spray. Repeat with the remaining egg-substitute mixture, vegetable mixture, and mozzarella to cook another omelette. To serve, cut each omelette in half.

Makes 4 servings

Per serving
Calories 155	*Sodium 505 mg.*
Total fat 4 g.	*Dietary fiber 2 g.*
Saturated fat 2 g.	*Protein 20 g.*
Cholesterol 12 mg.	*Carbohydrates 10 g.*

STICK WITH NONSTICK

Nonstick cookware and nonstick spray are true heroes of healthy cooking, allowing you to effortlessly slash fat and calories. For example, if using nonstick spray affords a savings of 1 tablespoon of cooking fat per person per day (probably a conservative estimate), that works out to a reduction of 4,964 grams of fat and 43,882 calories a year!

All about Eggs

Eggs are inexpensive, nutritious, versatile, and easy to cook. But they also contain a relatively high amount of cholesterol—about 213 milligrams each, which approaches the daily maximum of 300 milligrams recommended by the American Heart Association (AHA).

Many people who are trying to eat more healthfully mistakenly think that they can never again enjoy their favorite omelets, scrambles, and frittatas. This simply isn't true.

Keep in mind that saturated fat has a greater impact than dietary cholesterol on raising the level of cholesterol in the body. One large egg yolk contains just under 2 grams of saturated fat. So moderation is the key to enjoying eggs. The AHA recommends up to four yolks a week and unlimited amounts of egg whites, which contain no cholesterol or fat.

And most liquid egg substitutes, which are made from pasteurized egg whites, contain no cholesterol or fat. Egg substitutes are a fine replacement for those who want to further reduce cholesterol and fat in their diets. They can be used in place of whole eggs in most recipes calling for beaten eggs.

Here are some tips for getting the most from eggs.

- Eggs remain freshest when stored in their cartons. Push to the back of the shelf where it is coldest, and never put them in the door, as this is the warmest spot in the refrigerator.
- Scramble or poach eggs instead of frying them to cut back on the amount of fat used in preparation.
- You can always substitute two egg whites for each egg in any recipe in order to further reduce the fat and cholesterol. When baking, however, keep at least one yolk in the recipe to prevent the recipe from drying out.
- Salmonella is the bacteria most commonly associated with eggs. Proper handling and storage and thorough cooking can minimize the risk of this food-borne illness. Remember, because liquid egg substitutes are pasteurized, the threat of salmonella is removed.

South-of-the-Border Frittata

Hands-on time: 5 minutes
Total time: 20 minutes

1 egg

5 egg whites

1 can (15 ounces) black beans, rinsed and drained

1 cup corn kernels

$^2/_3$ cup ($2^1/_2$ ounces) shredded low-fat Monterey Jack cheese

$^3/_4$ teaspoon chili powder

1 bunch scallions, sliced

$^1/_4$ cup (2 ounces) fat-free sour cream

$^1/_4$ cup salsa

In a medium bowl, whisk together the egg, egg whites, beans, corn, Monterey Jack, and chili powder.

Coat a large nonstick skillet with nonstick spray. Add the scallions. Coat lightly with nonstick spray. Cook, stirring, over medium heat for 1 to 2 minutes, or until wilted.

Add the reserved egg mixture to the skillet. Cook, stirring occasionally, for 7 to 8 minutes, or until the eggs are set on the bottom. Reduce the heat to low. Cover and cook for 4 to 5 minutes, or until the eggs are set on the top.

To serve, cut into wedges and top with the sour cream and salsa.

Makes 4 servings

Per serving
Calories 229	*Sodium 751 mg.*
Total fat 6 g.	*Dietary fiber 7 g.*
Saturated fat 3 g.	*Protein 20 g.*
Cholesterol 67 mg.	*Carbohydrates 27 g.*

Try it — EGGS FOR DINNER

For Jane Biggar, a mother of four, two of whom are vegetarians, South-of-the-Border Frittata provided a welcome addition to her meatless meals repertoire. "We had the frittata for dinner with a fruit salad and grilled chicken. It was a great main dish for the vegetarians. It was quite filling and delicious with the sour cream and salsa."

Great Western Quiche

Hands-on time: 15 minutes
Total time: 55 minutes

1 bunch scallions, sliced

1 small green bell pepper, chopped

2 ounces Canadian bacon, chopped

$^1/_2$ cup (2 ounces) shredded low-fat Cheddar cheese

1 cup fat-free evaporated milk

$^3/_4$ cup liquid egg substitute

2 teaspoons Dijon mustard

$^1/_4$ teaspoon ground nutmeg

1 tablespoon ($^1/_4$ ounce) grated Parmesan cheese

Preheat the oven to 350°F. Coat a pie pan with nonstick spray.

Coat a medium nonstick skillet with nonstick spray. Set over medium-high heat. Add the scallions, bell pepper, and bacon. Cook for 3 to 4 minutes, or until the bell pepper has softened. Spoon into the prepared pie pan. Sprinkle with the Cheddar.

Meanwhile, in a large bowl, combine the milk, egg substitute, mustard, and nutmeg. Pour into the pan over the Cheddar. Sprinkle with the Parmesan.

Bake for 35 to 40 minutes, or until golden and a knife inserted in the center comes out clean.

Makes 6 servings

Per serving
Calories 98   Sodium 367 mg.
Total fat 2 g.   Dietary fiber 0.7 g.
Saturated fat 1 g.   Protein 12 g.
Cholesterol 10 mg.   Carbohydrates 8 g.

Cooking Note

Bake quiches, pies, and tarts in the lower third of the oven. The bottom crust will get crisp and the top won't get overly brown.

BETTER BACON

All breakfast meats are not created equally lean. One ounce of turkey bacon has 69 calories, 6 grams of fat, and 2 grams of saturated fat. It's clearly a better nutritional choice than regular pork bacon, which provides us with 163 calories, 14 grams of fat, and 5 grams of saturated fat per ounce. However, the best choice of all is lean and flavorful Canadian bacon, which contains only 52 calories, 2 grams of fat, and 1 gram of saturated fat per ounce. It pays to read the nutrition label.

Smoked Turkey Hash

Photograph on page 56
Hands-on time: 15 minutes
Total time: 35 minutes

2 teaspoons vegetable oil

1 large onion, coarsely chopped

1 small green bell pepper, coarsely chopped

1 pound cooked red potatoes, cubed

1 smoked turkey drumstick (1 pound), skinned, boned, and cubed

1 egg white, lightly beaten

2 tablespoons chopped parsley

$^1/_2$ teaspoon dried thyme

$^1/_8$ teaspoon salt

3 tablespoons fat-free milk

Warm the oil in a large nonstick skillet set over medium-high heat. Add the onion and bell pepper. Cook for 3 minutes, or until the bell pepper starts to soften.

In a large bowl, toss together the potatoes, turkey, egg white, parsley, thyme, and salt. Add to the skillet. Cook, stirring occasionally, for 10 to 12 minutes, or until lightly browned. Pour the milk around the edges. Cook, stirring, for 3 minutes, or until the milk is absorbed.

Makes 4 servings

Per serving
Calories 220	*Sodium 620 mg.*
Total fat 5 g.	*Dietary fiber 3 g.*
Saturated fat 1 g.	*Protein 20 g.*
Cholesterol 68 mg.	*Carbohydrates 24 g.*

Good for You

FORTIFY FOR FITNESS

Get the maximum benefit from your workout by consuming a 200- to 300-calorie snack 30 to 45 minutes before you begin. Choose complex carbohydrates or protein snacks such as high-fiber cereal with fat-free milk, a whole-grain bagel with low-fat cheese or peanut butter, or fat-free yogurt sprinkled with low-fat granola to provide the extra energy that you need.

Sunrise Casserole

Hands-on time: 15 minutes
Total time: 55 minutes

1 large onion, chopped

1 green or red bell pepper, chopped

6 ounces low-fat turkey sausage, cut into bite-size pieces

1/4 teaspoon ground sage

2 1/2 cups 1% milk

3/4 cup liquid egg substitute

1/2 cup (2 ounces) cubed low-fat Cheddar cheese

1/4 teaspoon salt

4 cups bread cubes, crusts removed

Preheat the oven to 350°F. Coat an 8" × 8" baking dish with nonstick spray.

Coat a large nonstick skillet with nonstick spray. Set over medium-high heat. Add the onion and bell pepper. Cook for 3 to 4 minutes, or until almost soft. Add the sausage and sage. Cook, stirring often, for 5 minutes, or until the sausage is no longer pink.

Meanwhile, in a large bowl, combine the milk, egg substitute, Cheddar, and salt. Add the bread cubes and the sausage mixture. Stir to mix, making sure that the bread cubes are moistened. Pour into the prepared baking dish. Press with the back of a spoon to pack the mixture.

Bake for 35 to 40 minutes, or until browned and slightly puffed.

Makes 6 servings

Per serving

Calories 228	Sodium 562 mg.
Total fat 6 g.	Dietary fiber 3 g.
Saturated fat 2 g.	Protein 17 g.
Cholesterol 28 mg.	Carbohydrates 26 g.

Good for You

ORDER RIGHT

When dining out for breakfast, look for the healthiest menu items. Many restaurants offer whole-grain breads and cereals, low-fat muffins, hot oatmeal, mixed fruit, and egg-white omelets and scrambled eggs. Keep in mind when you order to ask your server to have your dish prepared with minimal oil. Ordering a healthful breakfast will set you on the right nutritional course for the day.

Apple Skillet Cake

Photograph on page 55
Hands-on time: 15 minutes
Total time: 1 hour and 15 minutes

1   tablespoon butter or margarine

3   apples, peeled and sliced

2   tablespoons packed light brown sugar

$^1/_2$ teaspoon ground cinnamon

$^1/_2$ cup raisins

$^3/_4$ cup unbleached or all-purpose flour

$^1/_3$ cup sugar

$^1/_8$ teaspoon salt

$1^1/_2$ cups 1% milk

2   eggs

1   egg white

2   teaspoons vanilla extract

Preheat the oven to 375°F.

Melt the butter or margarine in a 10" ovenproof skillet over medium-high heat. Add the apples. Cook for 2 minutes, or until slightly softened. Add the brown sugar, cinnamon, and raisins. Cook for 5 minutes, turning occasionally, or until the apples are tender when pierced with a knife.

Meanwhile, in a large bowl, combine the flour, sugar, and salt.

In a medium bowl, whisk together the milk, eggs, egg white, and vanilla extract. Add to the flour mixture. Whisk just until smooth. Pour into the skillet with the apple mixture.

Bake for 40 to 45 minutes, or until golden brown and puffed. Remove to a rack to cool for 5 minutes.

To serve, cut into wedges. With a pancake turner, lift each wedge and turn, apple side up, onto a plate.

Makes 6 servings

Per serving
Calories 270	Sodium 114 mg.
Total fat 5 g.	Dietary fiber 2 g.
Saturated fat 2 g.	Protein 7 g.
Cholesterol 78 mg.	Carbohydrates 51 g.

PICK APPLES

Apples are a readily available and portable fruit, which makes them an appealing choice to meet your minimum quota of five fruits and/or vegetables a day. One medium unpeeled apple contributes 13 percent of our daily vitamin C and 15 percent of our daily fiber requirement.

Autumn Oatmeal Muffins

Hands-on time: 10 minutes
Total time: 40 minutes

2 cups unbleached or all-purpose flour

1 cup oats

$^1/2$ cup packed light brown sugar

2 teaspoons baking powder

$^1/2$ teaspoon baking soda

1 teaspoon ground cinnamon

$^1/2$ teaspoon salt

$^3/4$ cup buttermilk

$^1/2$ cup apple butter

$3^1/2$ tablespoons vegetable oil

1 egg

1 apple, chopped

3 tablespoons chopped toasted walnuts

Preheat the oven to 375°F. Coat 12 muffin cups with nonstick spray.

In a large bowl, combine the flour, oats, brown sugar, baking powder, baking soda, cinnamon, and salt.

In a medium bowl, combine the buttermilk, apple butter, oil, and egg. Add to the flour mixture. Stir just until blended. Stir in the apple and walnuts. Spoon into the prepared muffin cups.

Bake for 30 minutes, or until a wooden pick inserted in the center of 1 muffin comes out clean. Cool in the pan on a rack for 5 minutes. Remove to the rack to cool completely.

Makes 12

Per muffin

Calories 224	*Sodium 256 mg.*
Total fat 6 g.	*Dietary fiber 2 g.*
Saturated fat 1 g.	*Protein 4 g.*
Cholesterol 18 mg.	*Carbohydrates 39 g.*

Cooking Note

These muffins can be frozen for up to three months double-wrapped in plastic wrap. Thaw at room temperature or in the microwave oven.

SNACK SEAL OF APPROVAL

For Julie Avery, a clinical dietitian, these muffins are a perfect combination. Professionally, she appreciates the nutritional profile. One muffin supplies 8 percent of the daily requirement for fiber as well as providing lean protein and ideal amounts of favorable unsaturated fat (monounsaturated from the vegetable oil that she used and polyunsaturated from the walnuts). On a personal level, Avery loves the great flavor and the quick prep time using ingredients that she had on hand.

Cranberry-Orange Coffee Cake

Photograph on page 57
Hands-on time: 15 minutes
Total time: 55 minutes

STREUSEL

3/4 cup unbleached or all-purpose flour

2/3 cup packed light brown sugar

1 teaspoon ground cinnamon

1 tablespoon butter or margarine, cut into small pieces

2 tablespoons frozen orange juice concentrate

1/4 cup chopped toasted almonds

CAKE

2 1/4 cups unbleached or all-purpose flour

1 cup sugar

1 teaspoon baking powder

1 teaspoon baking soda

1/2 teaspoon salt

1/4 cup butter or margarine, softened

1 egg

1 egg white

2 teaspoons vanilla extract

1 cup (8 ounces) fat-free sour cream

2 cups (8 ounces) cranberries

To make the streusel: In a small bowl, combine the flour, brown sugar, and cinnamon. Stir with a fork until no lumps remain. Add the butter or margarine. Press with the fork to work into the dry ingredients. Add the orange juice concentrate and almonds. Toss until coarse crumbs form. Set aside.

To make the cake: Preheat the oven to 350°F. Coat a 9" round cake pan with nonstick spray. Line the bottom with a round of waxed paper. Coat lightly with nonstick spray.

In a medium bowl, combine the flour, 1/2 cup of the sugar, baking powder, baking soda, and salt.

In another medium bowl, combine the butter or margarine and the remaining 1/2 cup sugar. With an electric mixer on medium speed, beat until creamy. Add the egg, egg white, and vanilla extract. Beat until smooth. Add the flour mixture and the sour cream alternately to the batter, beating on low speed just until blended.

Spread half of the batter into the prepared cake pan. Sprinkle evenly with one-third of the streusel. Spread evenly with the remaining batter. Sprinkle with the cranberries and the remaining streusel.

Bake for 40 minutes, or until a toothpick inserted in the center comes out clean. Cool in the pan on a rack for 5 minutes. Run a knife around the sides of the pan. Turn onto the rack. Remove and discard the waxed paper. Place a plate on the cake and turn it right side up.

Makes 12 servings

Per serving
Calories 336   *Sodium 252 mg.*
Total fat 7 g.   *Dietary fiber 2 g.*
Saturated fat 1 g.   *Protein 6 g.*
Cholesterol 18 mg.   *Carbohydrates 63 g.*

FRUITFUL IDEAS

If you don't have cranberries or it's not cranberry season, you can still make this delightful breakfast cake. Replace the cranberries with blueberries, golden raisins, or chopped pitted dates.

Cornmeal Flapjacks

Photograph on page 58
Hands-on time: 25 minutes
Total time: 25 minutes

1 cup cornmeal

3/4 cup unbleached or all-purpose flour

1 teaspoon baking soda

1/2 teaspoon salt

1 1/4 cups buttermilk

1 egg

2 tablespoons maple syrup

1 tablespoon vegetable oil

Preheat the oven to 200°F. Coat a baking sheet with nonstick spray.

In a large bowl, combine the cornmeal, flour, baking soda, and salt.

In a medium bowl, combine the buttermilk, egg, maple syrup, and oil. Beat with a fork or whisk until blended. Add to the flour mixture. Stir until a smooth batter forms.

Coat a large nonstick skillet with nonstick spray. Warm over medium heat. Pour the batter by 1/4 cupfuls into the skillet. Cook for 2 minutes, or until tiny bubbles appear on the surface and the edges begin to look dry. Flip the pancakes. Cook for 1 to 2 minutes, or until golden on the bottom. Transfer the pancakes to the prepared baking sheet. Place in the oven to keep warm.

Coat the skillet with nonstick spray. Repeat with the remaining batter to make a total of 15 pancakes.

Makes 5 servings

Per serving
Calories 248	*Sodium 557 mg.*
Total fat 4 g.	*Dietary fiber 3 g.*
Saturated fat 1 g.	*Protein 8 g.*
Cholesterol 44 mg.	*Carbohydrates 45 g.*

A New Twist

CORNMEAL CRÊPES

To make cornmeal crêpes, omit the baking soda and maple syrup. Decrease the cornmeal to 1/4 cup, add 1 more egg, 1 egg white, and 1 teaspoon of sugar. Let the batter sit for 30 minutes. Stir in 1 tablespoon finely chopped fresh herbs. Coat a small nonstick skillet with nonstick spray. Set over medium-high heat until hot. Whisk the batter. Ladle about 3 tablespoons batter into the pan. Quickly tilt the pan so that the batter spreads evenly. Cook for 30 seconds, or until the bottom is lightly browned. Loosen the crêpe and flip. Cook for 20 seconds, or until the bottom is set. Transfer to a plate. Continue with the remaining batter to make a total of 12 crêpes.

Breakfast under the Big Top

Try these toppings to make your pancakes a little bit more exciting. But don't stop there. These toppings are terrific on fat-free ice cream, too.

Apple Harvest. Coat a large nonstick skillet with butter-flavored nonstick spray. Place over medium-high heat. Add 3 peeled and thinly sliced Granny Smith apples, ¼ cup apple juice, 2 tablespoons sugar, 1 tablespoon lemon juice, ½ teaspoon ground cinnamon, and ¼ teaspoon ground nutmeg. Cook, stirring occasionally, for 7 to 8 minutes, or until the apples are tender. Serve warm or at room temperature. Makes 2 cups.

Berry Berry Sauce. In a medium saucepan, combine ¾ cup water, ¼ cup sugar, and 2 teaspoons cornstarch. Cook, whisking constantly, over medium heat until the mixture boils and thickens. Add 1½ cups berries of your choice. Cook for 2 minutes, or until bubbly. Serve warm. Makes 1 cup.

Dried Fruit Syrup. In a small saucepan, combine ¾ cup maple syrup, ¼ cup dried tart cherries or cranberries, and ¼ cup finely chopped dried figs. Cook, stirring occasionally, over low heat for 5 minutes, or until the fruit is warmed through and plumped. Makes 1 cup.

Never-Too-Early-for-Chocolate Sauce. In a small saucepan, combine 1 can (12 ounces) fat-free evaporated milk, ½ cup cocoa powder, and ¼ cup packed brown sugar. Whisk until smooth. Cook, whisking constantly, over low heat for 4 to 5 minutes, or until the mixture boils. Add ½ teaspoon vanilla extract. Stir to mix. Serve warm or at room temperature. Makes 1 cup.

Peach Sauce. In a medium saucepan, melt ½ cup peach jam over low heat. Add 1 tablespoon lemon juice and 2½ cups peeled and sliced peaches. Stir gently to combine. Cook for 3 to 5 minutes, or until the peaches soften. Serve warm or at room temperature. Makes 2 cups.

Pearfect Sauce. In a medium saucepan, combine ¼ cup water, 2 tablespoons sugar, a pinch of ground cinnamon, and a dash of ground cloves. Cook over medium heat for 2 to 3 minutes, or until the mixture boils. Add 6 peeled and thinly sliced ripe Bartlett pears. Reduce the heat to medium-low. Cook, stirring occasionally, for 15 to 20 minutes, or until the pears are very soft. Serve warm or at room temperature. Makes 4 cups.

Tropical Twister. In a medium saucepan, combine ½ cup unsweetened pineapple juice, 2 tablespoons lime juice, ¼ cup sugar, and 2 teaspoons cornstarch. Cook, stirring often, over medium heat for 3 to 4 minutes, or until thickened. Add 4 cups chopped tropical fruits such as kiwifruit, mango, pineapple, papaya, or banana. Cover and reduce the heat to low. Cook, stirring often, for 8 to 10 minutes, or until the fruit cooks down into a thick sauce. Remove from the heat and continue to stir as it cools to prevent lumps. Serve warm or at room temperature. Makes 3 cups.

Multigrain Blueberry Waffles

Hands-on time: 15 minutes
Total time: 1 hour

1 cup unbleached or all-purpose flour

1/2 cup whole-wheat flour

1/2 cup oats

1/2 teaspoon baking powder

1/2 teaspoon baking soda

1/2 teaspoon salt

1 2/3 cups fat-free milk

2 egg whites

3 tablespoons packed light brown sugar

1 tablespoon vegetable oil

1 1/2 cups blueberries

1/2 cup maple syrup

Preheat the oven to 200°F. Coat a baking sheet with nonstick spray.

In a large bowl, combine the unbleached or all-purpose flour, whole-wheat flour, oats, baking powder, baking soda, and salt.

In a medium bowl, combine the milk, egg whites, brown sugar, and oil. Add to the flour mixture. Whisk until a smooth batter forms. Fold in the blueberries.

Coat a nonstick waffle iron with nonstick spray. Preheat the iron.

Pour 1/2 cup of the batter onto the center of the iron. Cook for 5 to 6 minutes, or until steam no longer escapes from under the waffle-iron lid and the waffle is golden. Transfer the waffles to the prepared baking sheet. Place in the oven to keep warm. Repeat with the remaining batter to make a total of 8 waffles. Serve drizzled with maple syrup.

Makes 8

Per waffle

Calories 232	*Sodium 301 mg.*
Total fat 3 g.	*Dietary fiber 2 g.*
Saturated fat 0 g.	*Protein 6 g.*
Cholesterol 1 mg.	*Carbohydrates 47 g.*

Cooking Note

This batter also makes excellent pancakes. To create your own nutritious convenience mix, double or triple the recipe for the dry ingredients and store in an airtight container in a cool cupboard. To make pancakes, measure 2 cups of the dry mix into a bowl and then add the liquid ingredients from the recipe.

Good for You

DRINK TO YOUR HEALTH'S DESIRE

Our bodies need 8 cups of water per day to replace the fluid that we lose through perspiration, breathing, and waste removal. So be sure to drink plenty of water. Not only will you feel better, but drinking plenty of water aids in weight loss, too. We often perceive dehydration as hunger, so if you are hungry between meals, first have a large glass of water. If you are still hungry after 15 minutes, then eat your snack.

Apricot-Pecan Scones

Hands-on time: 15 minutes
Total time: 35 minutes

- 2 cups unbleached or all-purpose flour
- 3 tablespoons + 2 teaspoons sugar
- 2 teaspoons baking powder
- 1/2 teaspoon baking soda
- 1/4 teaspoon salt
- 2 tablespoons cold butter or margarine, cut into small pieces
- 1 1/4 cups chopped dried apricots
- 1/4 cup chopped toasted pecans
- 3/4 cup buttermilk or low-fat plain yogurt
- 1 egg white
- 1/4 teaspoon ground cinnamon

Makes 12

Per scone

Calories 178	Sodium 228 mg.
Total fat 4 g.	Dietary fiber 2 g.
Saturated fat 1 g.	Protein 4 g.
Cholesterol 1 mg.	Carbohydrates 32 g.

A New Twist

DESIGNER SCONES

Using the same proportions of dried fruits and nuts as in the Apricot-Pecan Scones, try these variations.

- Dried peaches and almonds. Add 1/4 cup chopped candied ginger.
- Dried cranberries and walnuts. Add 2 teaspoons grated orange peel
- Dried sour cherries. Substitute semisweet chocolate chips for the nuts
- Dried pineapple or papaya. Substitute toasted coconut for the nuts.

Preheat the oven to 400°F. Coat a baking sheet with nonstick spray.

In a large bowl, combine the flour, 3 tablespoons of the sugar, baking powder, baking soda, and salt. Using a pastry blender or a fork, cut the butter or margarine into the flour mixture until evenly dispersed. Add the apricots and pecans. Stir to mix.

In a medium bowl, combine the buttermilk or yogurt and egg white. Beat with a fork to mix. Add to the flour mixture. Stir with a fork until the dough comes together.

Spoon onto the prepared baking sheet in 12 equal portions. In a small bowl, combine the remaining 2 teaspoons sugar and the cinnamon. Sprinkle over the scones.

Bake for 15 minutes, or until lightly browned. Remove to a rack to cool for 5 minutes.

Quick Cinnamon Rolls

Hands-on time: 20 minutes
Total time: 40 minutes

- 1/2 cup packed light brown sugar
- 1/2 cup raisins, finely chopped
- 2 tablespoons toasted and finely chopped walnuts
- 3 tablespoons wheat-and-barley nuggets cereal, such as *Grape-Nuts*
- 2 teaspoons ground cinnamon
- 2 tubes (11 ounces each) refrigerated bread dough
- 1 1/2 tablespoons butter or margarine, melted
- 1 egg white, lightly beaten with 1 tablespoon water
- 1/3 cup confectioners' sugar
- 1 tablespoon fat-free milk
- 1/2 teaspoon vanilla extract

Preheat the oven to 375°F. Lightly coat a 13" × 9" baking dish with nonstick spray.

In a medium bowl, combine the brown sugar, raisins, walnuts, cereal, and cinnamon.

Unroll the dough pieces on a lightly floured surface. Place 1 piece on top of the other. Pinch the edges to seal. Roll into an 18" × 12" rectangle. Brush the surface with 1 tablespoon of the butter or margarine. Sprinkle evenly with the brown-sugar mixture. Press the filling lightly into the dough. Starting with 1 long side, roll the dough into a tube, brushing the outside of the dough with egg white as you roll. Pinch the seam to seal. Cut into 12 slices. Arrange the slices, cut side up, in the prepared baking dish. Brush the tops with the remaining 1/2 tablespoon butter or margarine.

Bake for 18 to 20 minutes, or until golden brown. Remove to a rack to cool slightly.

Meanwhile, in a small bowl, combine the confectioners' sugar, milk, and vanilla extract. Drizzle over the rolls.

Makes 12

Per roll

Calories 243	*Sodium 425 mg.*
Total fat 6 g.	*Dietary fiber 1 g.*
Saturated fat 1 g.	*Protein 5 g.*
Cholesterol 0 mg.	*Carbohydrates 44 g.*

Try it — ON A NEW ROLL

As a self-proclaimed sweets addict, Elaine Ullman was at first hesitant to try this lean version of cinnamon rolls. She couldn't imagine parting with the high-fat version that she had been making for many years. But the easy preparation using ready-made dough caught her attention as a great time-saver for a Sunday-morning brunch. After trying the recipe on her family, she knew she had a winner.

Ginger-Date Muffins

Hands-on time: 15 minutes
Total time: 35 minutes

2¹/₂ cups unbleached or all-purpose flour

1 teaspoon baking soda

1 teaspoon ground cinnamon

¹/₄ teaspoon salt

1 cup shredded bran cereal

¹/₂ cup boiling water

1 cup buttermilk

²/₃ cup molasses

¹/₄ cup vegetable oil

1 egg

1 tablespoon grated fresh ginger

1¹/₂ cups chopped pitted dates

¹/₃ cup chopped toasted walnuts

Makes 18

Per muffin

Calories 198	Sodium 170 mg.
Total fat 5 g.	Dietary fiber 3 g.
Saturated fat 1 g.	Protein 4 g.
Cholesterol 12 mg.	Carbohydrates 37 g.

Preheat the oven to 350°F. Coat 18 muffin cups with nonstick spray.

In a large bowl, combine the flour, baking soda, cinnamon, and salt.

In a medium bowl, combine the cereal and water. Stir until the cereal is soft. Add the buttermilk, molasses, oil, egg, and ginger. Stir to blend. Add to the flour mixture. Stir just until blended. Add the dates and walnuts. Stir to mix. Spoon into the prepared muffin cups.

Bake for 15 to 18 minutes, or until a wooden pick inserted in the center of 1 muffin comes out clean. Cool in the pan on a rack for 5 minutes. Remove to the rack to cool completely.

Appetizers and Snacks

Snacks can actually benefit your overall nutrition when you make smart eating choices. Nutritional surveys have shown that snackers—those who eat five or six smaller meals throughout the day—have more nutritionally complete diets than nonsnackers.

Snacks can give you that boost of energy you need at times of the day when you feel your stamina waning. They also prevent you from getting too hungry for main meals, eliminating the possibility of overeating at those meals.

Snack times provide an opportunity to incorporate fresh fruits and vegetables, thus increasing fiber and other important nutrients. Snacks can also include dairy foods like yogurt or a glass of fat-free milk. Baked chips provide complex carbohydrates full of energy and B vitamins. So packing nutrition into your snacks can be just as easy and convenient as eating junk food.

Planning is essential for smart snacking. Be sure to stock up on healthful shelf-stable or refrigerated foods—such as fat-free yogurt, ready-cut vegetables, fresh or dried fruits, whole-grain cereals, pretzels, and popcorn—that are ready to grab and eat on busy days. Be sure to include foods that provide a variety of textures, including chewy, crunchy, and smooth.

For more advanced snacking, mini-meals of appetizer snacks spaced evenly throughout the day provide constant energy and nutrients. Whole-grain baked chips or breads with vegetable spreads or dips provide excellent nutrition and are convenient to have on hand.

Good snacks equal good times as well. When planning a party, be sure to include plenty of nutrient-rich appetizers and snacks.

Recipes

Nachos

Hands-on time: 10 minutes
Total time: 20 minutes

1 small onion, chopped

3 cloves garlic, chopped

1 can (19 ounces) cannellini beans, rinsed and drained

1 teaspoon ground cumin

1/4 teaspoon salt

2 roasted red peppers, chopped

4 plum tomatoes, chopped

1/2 cup frozen corn kernels, thawed

2 scallions, sliced

2 tablespoons chopped fresh cilantro or parsley

1 tablespoon lime juice

6 ounces small baked tortilla chips

1 1/2 cups (6 ounces) shredded low-fat Monterey Jack cheese

Preheat the oven to 350°F. Coat a 13" × 9" baking dish with nonstick spray.

Coat a medium nonstick skillet with nonstick spray. Set over medium heat. Add the onion and garlic. Cook, stirring often, for 5 minutes, or until soft. Add the beans, cumin, and salt. With the back of a spoon, coarsely mash the beans. Remove from the heat.

Meanwhile, in a medium bowl, combine the peppers, tomatoes, corn, scallions, cilantro or parsley, and lime juice.

Spread the chips in the prepared baking dish. Dot with dollops of the bean mixture and the pepper mixture. Sprinkle with the Monterey Jack.

Bake for 5 to 7 minutes, or until the cheese has melted.

Makes 8 servings

Per serving
Calories 227   *Sodium 604 mg.*
Total fat 5 g.   *Dietary fiber 5 g.*
Saturated fat 3 g. *Protein 13 g.*
Cholesterol 15 mg. *Carbohydrates 34 g.*

CALCIUM FROM PLANTS

We all know the importance of calcium in our diets, but did you know that calcium is available in sources other than dairy products? Some favorite foods that provide calcium include broccoli, apricots, bok choy, kale, almonds, and oranges. In addition, some foods such as breakfast cereals, tofu, soy milk, orange juice, white rice, and cereal bars are fortified with calcium by food manufacturers.

Italian Salsa and Chips

Photograph on page 61
Hands-on time: 15 minutes
Total time: 25 minutes

Makes 6 servings

Per serving
Calories 210
Total fat 6 g.
Saturated fat 1 g.
Cholesterol 3 mg.
Sodium 498 mg.
Dietary fiber 2 g.
Protein 7 g.
Carbohydrates 33 g.

CHIPS

1 package (10 ounces) pitas (6" diameter)

1/4 cup (1 ounce) grated Parmesan cheese

1 1/2 teaspoons Italian seasoning

SALSA

5 plum tomatoes, chopped

1 small onion, chopped

3/4 cup chopped fresh basil

3 tablespoons balsamic or wine vinegar

2 tablespoons chopped Kalamata olives

1 tablespoon olive oil

2 cloves garlic, chopped

1/4 teaspoon salt

1/4 teaspoon ground black pepper

To make the chips: Preheat the oven to 375°F. Cover a baking sheet with foil.

Cut the pitas into quarters. Separate each wedge into 2 pieces. Place on the baking sheet. Lightly coat the pitas with nonstick spray.

In a small bowl, combine the Parmesan and Italian seasoning. Sprinkle over the pitas. Bake for 8 to 10 minutes, or until golden and crisp. Transfer to a platter or serving basket.

To make the salsa: Meanwhile, in a medium bowl, combine the tomatoes, onion, basil, vinegar, olives, oil, garlic, salt, and pepper. Serve with the chips.

QUICK NACHOS

In a medium nonstick skillet, cook 3/4 pound extra-lean ground round beef or ground turkey breast for 5 minutes, or until no longer pink. Place the Italian chips in a baking dish coated with non-stick spray. Sprinkle the beef or turkey over the chips. Top with dollops of the salsa. Sprinkle with 1 cup (4 ounces) shredded low-fat mozzarella cheese. Bake at 375°F for 4 to 7 minutes, or until the cheese melts. Serve with fat-free sour cream or Guacamole (page 78).

Mushroom Spread

Hands-on time: 15 minutes
Total time: 55 minutes

1 ounce dried mushrooms

2¹⁄₂ cups boiling water

¹⁄₂ cup brown lentils, picked over and rinsed

1 large onion, finely chopped

8 ounces button mushrooms, finely chopped

4 cloves garlic, chopped

¹⁄₂ teaspoon dried thyme leaves

¹⁄₄ cup finely chopped toasted walnuts

¹⁄₄ teaspoon salt

2 tablespoons chopped fresh parsley

In a small bowl, combine the dried mushrooms and water. Let stand for 15 minutes.

Line a fine sieve with a coffee filter or paper towels. Set over a medium saucepan. Pour the mushroom liquid through the sieve. Set the mushrooms aside. Add the lentils to the pan. Bring to a boil over high heat. Reduce the heat to medium-low. Cover the pan and simmer, stirring occasionally, for 20 minutes, or until tender and all the liquid has been absorbed.

Meanwhile, coat a medium nonstick skillet with nonstick spray. Set over medium heat. Add the onion, button mushrooms, reconstituted mushrooms, garlic, and thyme. Cook, stirring occasionally, for 18 to 20 minutes, or until golden brown and very soft.

Transfer the lentils to a food processor. Puree until smooth. Add the mushroom mixture, walnuts, and salt. Pulse briefly just until com-

bined. Spoon into a serving bowl. Sprinkle with the parsley.

Makes 16 servings

Per serving
Calories 52	Sodium 47 mg.
Total fat 1 g.	Dietary fiber 2 g.
Saturated fat 0 g.	Protein 3 g.
Cholesterol 0 mg.	Carbohydrates 8 g.

Cooking Note

Serve the Mushroom Spread with crackers, bread slices, or raw vegetables. Or stuff it into Belgian endive leaves or hollowed cherry tomatoes.

Hard Facts about Fats

Trans-fatty acids are formed in certain liquid fats during the process of hardening them, which is called hydrogenation. Trans-fatty acids also occur naturally in beef, pork, lamb, butter, and milk. Research has shown that these fats may raise cholesterol levels similarly to saturated fat. Foods that often contain hydrogenated oils include snack foods such as crackers and cookies as well as prepared bakery items. Read labels and look for alternatives that don't contain hydrogenated oils. When you must use the ones that do, be sure to consume these products in moderation. Also, cook with healthful oils such as olive or canola instead of lard or shortening.

Greek-Style Appetizer Cheesecake

Hands-on time: 15 minutes
Total time: 1 hour and 15 minutes

1 ounce dry-pack sun-dried tomatoes

1 bunch scallions, sliced

2 cloves garlic, chopped

1 can (14 ounces) water-packed artichoke hearts, rinsed, drained, and coarsely chopped

1 teaspoon dried oregano

2 cups (16 ounces) fat-free ricotta cheese

3/4 cup (6 ounces) fat-free sour cream

1 egg

2 egg whites

2 tablespoons unbleached or all-purpose flour

1/3 cup (1 1/2 ounces) grated Parmesan cheese

1/2 cup (2 ounces) crumbled feta cheese

1/4 teaspoon salt

Preheat the oven to 325°F. Lightly coat a 9" springform pan with nonstick spray.

Place the sun-dried tomatoes in a small bowl. Cover with boiling water. Soak for 10 minutes, or until very soft. Drain and coarsely chop.

Meanwhile, coat a medium nonstick skillet with nonstick spray. Add the scallions and garlic. Cook, stirring occasionally, over medium heat for 2 to 3 minutes, or until tender. Add the artichokes and oregano. Cook for 2 minutes to evaporate any liquid.

In a blender or food processor, combine the ricotta, sour cream, egg, egg whites, and flour.

Puree until smooth. Transfer to a medium mixing bowl. Add the artichoke mixture, Parmesan, feta, sun-dried tomatoes, and salt. Stir to mix. Pour into the prepared pan.

Bake for 50 to 60 minutes, or until a wooden pick inserted in the center comes out clean. Remove to a rack to cool completely. Cover and refrigerate for at least 3 hours. To serve, bring to room temperature. Remove the ring from the pan and cut into wedges.

Makes 16 servings

Per serving
Calories 80
Total fat 2 g.
Saturated fat 1 g.
Cholesterol 27 mg.
Sodium 210 mg.
Dietary fiber 2 g.
Protein 7 g.
Carbohydrates 9 g.

Cooking Note
Serve the cheesecake with toasted pita chips or toasted slices of French baguette.

A New Twist

Party Finery

For a special presentation, bake the cheesecake in a prebaked flaky phyllo crust. To prebake, coat the springform pan with nonstick spray. Cut 6 sheets of thawed phyllo dough (17" × 11" each) into 12" rounds. Place the rounds, one at a time, in the pan in a slightly off-center pattern so that they extend 2½" up the sides. Coat each round lightly with butter- or olive oil–flavored nonstick spray. Make 3 small slits in the center. Bake at 375°F for 10 minutes, or until lightly golden.

Pumped-Up Popcorn

Some brands of microwave popcorn contain as much fat as potato chips. By tossing your own plain popped corn with seasoning combinations, such as Chinese five-spice powder or Cajun seasoning, you can enjoy this great snack without excess fat. Or make your own seasoning mixes from this selection.

To make a batch of flavored popcorn, place 6 cups of plain popped popcorn (popped in an air popper or microwave oven) in a large bowl. Toss while coating with nonstick spray. Sprinkle with the selected seasoning. Toss to mix. Spread onto 2 foil-lined baking sheets coated with nonstick spray. Lightly coat the popcorn with nonstick spray. Bake at 300°F for 3 to 5 minutes, or until it looks dry.

Harvest. ½ teaspoon each ground cinnamon and ground ginger with ¼ cup each dried apples and raisins

Indian. ½ teaspoon each curry powder, dry mustard, turmeric, ground coriander, and ground cumin

Italian. ½ teaspoon each dried basil and oregano, ⅛ teaspoon dried red-pepper flakes, and ¼ cup (1 ounce) grated Parmesan cheese

Jamaican. ½ teaspoon each onion powder, allspice, jerk seasoning, and ground cinnamon

Mediterranean. ½ teaspoon each thyme, sage, marjoram, and grated lemon peel

Mexican. ½ teaspoon each ground cumin and ground coriander, with ¼ teaspoon each chili powder and ground red pepper

Deviled Eggs

Hands-on time: 5 minutes
Total time: 20 minutes

1¹⁄₂ cups (12 ounces) 1% cottage cheese

12 hard-cooked eggs, peeled and chilled

¹⁄₄ cup (2 ounces) fat-free sour cream

1¹⁄₂ tablespoons sweet pickle relish

1 tablespoon Dijon mustard

¹⁄₄ teaspoon salt

¹⁄₄ teaspoon ground black pepper

1 tablespoon chopped parsley

Line a fine sieve with a coffee filter. Spoon in the cottage cheese. Set over a bowl and allow to drain for 15 minutes. Discard the liquid.

Meanwhile, slice the eggs in half lengthwise. Reserve the egg whites and 6 yolk halves. Discard the remaining yolks.

In a food processor, combine the cottage cheese, sour cream, and egg yolks. Process until smooth. Add the relish, mustard, salt, and pepper. Pulse until well-mixed.

Spoon into the hollows of the egg whites. Sprinkle with the parsley.

Makes 24 servings

Per serving
Calories 30	*Sodium 133 mg.*
Total fat 1 g.	*Dietary fiber 0 g.*
Saturated fat 0 g.	*Protein 4 g.*
Cholesterol 28 mg.	*Carbohydrates 2 g.*

DEVILED EGG SANDWICHES

Leftover deviled eggs make heavenly egg salad sandwiches that are low in fat and high in protein. For each sandwich, lightly toast 2 thin slices whole-wheat bread. In a small bowl, coarsely mash 4 deviled eggs with the back of a fork. Stir in 1 to 1½ tablespoons low-fat mayonnaise. Spread over 1 slice of the toast. Top with a lettuce leaf and the remaining toast. Cut in half diagonally.

Spring Rolls

Hands-on time: 20 minutes
Total time: 20 minutes

- 2 ounces thin rice-flour noodles (see note)
- 1/2 pound large shrimp, cooked, peeled, and deveined
- 3 ounces snow peas, cut into thin matchsticks
- 6 rice papers (12" diameter); see note
- 1 cup mung bean sprouts
- 2 carrots, shredded
- 1 small red bell pepper, cut into thin matchsticks
- 3 scallions, shredded
- 1 small bunch mint leaves

Bring a small pot of water to a boil. Add the noodles. Cook for 2 to 3 minutes, or until tender but still firm. Drain. Rinse with cold water and drain.

Slice the shrimp in half lengthwise. Soak the snow peas in hot water for 2 minutes and drain.

Fill a large pan with hot water. Immerse 1 sheet of the rice papers in the water for 1 minute, or until soft and pliable. Remove to a work surface and pat dry. Leaving a 2" border on each side, arrange 6 shrimp halves in a row down the center. Top with some of the rice noodles, snow peas, bean sprouts, carrots, bell peppers, scallions, and mint. Fold the bottom and side edges of the rice paper over the filling, then fold the top toward the center to make a tight cylinder. Repeat with the remaining ingredients to make a total of 6 spring rolls. Slice the rolls in half diagonally.

Makes 6 servings

Per serving

Calories 164	Sodium 51 mg.
Total fat 1 g.	Dietary fiber 2 g.
Saturated fat 0 g.	Protein 9 g.
Cholesterol 32 mg.	Carbohydrates 32 g.

Cooking Note

Thin rice-flour noodles (dried, thin, round rice noodles sometimes called rice sticks) and rice papers (dried translucent sheets made from rice flour, salt, and water) are sold in Asian food stores and some supermarkets.

Hoisin Dipping Sauce

For a dipping sauce to accompany the spring rolls, in a small bowl, combine 1/2 cup hoisin sauce, 1/4 cup water, 4 tablespoons lime juice, 1 teaspoon chopped garlic, and crushed red-pepper flakes to taste. Makes about 1 cup.

Baked Potato Skins

Photograph on page 62
Hands-on time: 5 minutes
Total time: 1 hour and 20 minutes

- 1 large russet potato
- 2 large sweet potatoes
- ¹/₂ cup (2 ounces) grated Parmesan cheese
- 1 tablespoon chopped parsley
- 1 teaspoon dried basil leaves
- ¹/₂ teaspoon garlic powder
- ¹/₂ teaspoon salt
- ¹/₂ cup (4 ounces) fat-free sour cream
- 2 tablespoons chopped fresh chives or scallion greens

Preheat the oven to 425°F. Line a baking sheet with foil. Pierce the potatoes a few times with a fork. Place on the prepared baking sheet. Bake for 50 to 60 minutes, or until easily pierced with a fork. Remove and allow to cool slightly.

Meanwhile, in a small bowl, combine the Parmesan, parsley, basil, garlic powder, and salt.

When the potatoes are cool enough to handle, quarter them lengthwise. Scoop out the flesh, leaving a ¼"-thick shell. Reserve the flesh for another use. Cut the strips in half crosswise. You should have 24 wedges. Place on the foil-lined baking sheet. Coat both sides with nonstick spray. Sprinkle with the Parmesan mixture.

Bake for 10 to 12 minutes, or until golden brown. To serve, top with dollops of sour cream. Sprinkle with the chives or scallions.

Makes 8 servings

Per serving

Calories 114	Sodium 280 mg.
Total fat 2 g.	Dietary fiber 3 g.
Saturated fat 1 g.	Protein 5 g.
Cholesterol 5 mg.	Carbohydrates 19 g.

CLASSIC STAR

FAT-FREE DAIRY

Fat-free dairy products have flooded the market and have become a major part of low-fat cooking. Most of these dairy products are fat-free milk versions of their higher-fat counterparts and are therefore a much healthier alternative. Do be aware, however, that often, the sodium content will be higher in these lower-fat foods. In most cases, the reduction of total fat and saturated fat in the diet is a benefit that far outweighs the additional sodium.

~Apple Skillet Cake (page 36)~

❤Florentine Omelette (page 30) and Smoked Turkey Hash (page 34)❤

~Cranberry-Orange Coffee Cake (page 38)~

❧ Cornmeal Flapjacks (page 39) ❧

❤ Sesame Chicken Fingers (page 76) ❤

❤ Baked Potato Skins (page 54) ❤

♥ The New Classic Reuben (page 89) ♥

64 ❤ New York–Style Roast Beef Sandwich (page 94) ❤

~Club Sandwich (page 88)~

65

66

Tuna Salad Pockets (page 83)

❤Barbecue Chicken and Cheddar Calzones (page 108)❤

~ Classic Tomato Pizza (page 98) ~

❤ Double-Crust Pizza (page 110) ❤

Snacks for Health

Snacking is a great way to maintain a healthy diet because it prevents you from getting too hungry between meals. And choosing snacks with an eye toward complete nutrition is an even better idea. Here are some delicious and nutritious ideas to get you started.

Baked tortilla chips and salsa (10 chips and ½ cup salsa) are an excellent source of vitamin C and a good source of fiber and vitamin A.
Calories: 135. *Fat:* 1 gram.

Cheese and crackers (6 fat-free whole-wheat crackers and 2 ounces low-fat cheese) are an excellent source of calcium and a good source of fiber, vitamins A, B_2, and B_{12}, and zinc.
Calories: 161. *Fat:* 3 grams.

Chili and crackers (¾ cup vegetable chili with 6 whole-wheat saltines) are an excellent source of fiber and vitamins A and C and a good source of iron.
Calories: 260. *Fat:* 2 grams.

Hummus with a pita (¼ cup hummus with 1 whole-wheat pita, 6" diameter) is an excellent source of fiber and vitamin B_6 and a good source of vitamins B_1 and B_3, folic acid, copper, iron, magnesium, and zinc.
Calories: 275. *Fat:* 7 grams.

Shredded wheat cereal with fat-free milk (1 cup cereal with ½ cup milk) is a good source of fiber, vitamins B_1, B_2, B_3, and D, calcium, copper, iron, magnesium, potassium, and zinc.
Calories: 195. *Fat:* 1 gram.

Vegetables and dip (1 cup assorted bell pepper strips and ½ cup fat-free sour cream combined with ½ packet reduced-calorie ranch dressing mix) are an excellent source of vitamins A and C and a good source of vitamins B_1 and B_6, calcium, and potassium.
Calories: 258. *Fat:* 1 gram.

Yogurt with granola (1 cup fat-free plain yogurt and 2 tablespoons low-fat granola) is an excellent source of vitamins B_2, B_{12}, and C, calcium, and zinc and a good source of vitamins B_1, B_3, B_6, and E, folate, pantothenic acid, magnesium, and potassium.
Calories: 167. *Fat:* 1 gram.

Grilled Vegetable Quesadillas

Hands-on time: 15 minutes
Total time: 20 minutes

2 medium zucchini or yellow squash, cut lengthwise into ¼"-thick slices

1 small onion, cut into ¼"-thick slices

1 small red bell pepper, cut into thick strips

2 ounces fat-free cream cheese, softened

1 tablespoon chopped parsley or fresh cilantro

2 teaspoons lime juice

¼ teaspoon ground cumin

Hot-pepper sauce

1 cup (4 ounces) shredded low-fat Cheddar cheese

8 corn tortillas (6" diameter)

Coat a grill rack or broiler pan with nonstick spray. Preheat the grill or broiler. Grill or broil the vegetables 6" from the heat for 3 to 4 minutes, or until tender. Remove and cut into bite-size pieces.

Meanwhile, in a medium bowl, combine the cream cheese, parsley or cilantro, lime juice, and cumin. Season with a few drops of hot-pepper sauce to taste. Add the vegetables and Cheddar. Stir to mix.

Place 4 tortillas on a work surface. Spread ⅓ cup filling over each tortilla. Cover with the remaining tortillas. Press lightly to adhere. Coat lightly with nonstick spray. Grill or broil 6" from the heat for 1 to 2 minutes per side, or until the tortillas are golden and the filling is heated through. Cut each quesadilla into 4 wedges.

Makes 4 servings

Per serving
Calories 207   *Sodium 320 mg.*
Total fat 4 g.   *Dietary fiber 4 g.*
Saturated fat 2 g.   *Protein 13 g.*
Cholesterol 7 mg.   *Carbohydrates 32 g.*

Good for You

TOSS THE PEELER

Leave edible skins on fruits and vegetables for an enhanced fiber-rich diet. Whether you are eating fruits and vegetables raw or you plan to cook them as part of a recipe, the skins and the flesh just below the skin often contain the majority of the nutrients and should be left on whenever possible. Be sure to scrub the produce before cooking with the skin on.

Tomato-Basil Tartlets

Photograph on page 59
Hands-on time: 15 minutes
Total Time: 30 minutes

1¹⁄2 ounces dry-pack sun-dried tomatoes

8 sheets (17" × 11") frozen phyllo dough, thawed

³⁄4 cup (6 ounces) 1% cottage cheese

3 tablespoons (1¹⁄2 ounces) crumbled goat cheese or feta cheese

1 egg white

1 scallion, chopped

2 tablespoons chopped fresh basil

2 cloves garlic, chopped

Preheat the oven to 375°F. Coat 24 miniature muffin cups with nonstick spray.

Place the sun-dried tomatoes in a small bowl. Cover with boiling water. Soak for 10 minutes, or until very soft. Drain and chop.

Meanwhile, place 1 phyllo sheet on a work surface. Coat with nonstick spray. Top with 3 more sheets, coating each sheet with nonstick spray.

Cut the sheets in thirds lengthwise and then in quarters crosswise to get 12 squares. Press each square into a muffin cup to form a shell with jagged edges.

Repeat with the remaining sheets to line the remaining muffin cups. Bake for 5 to 7 minutes, or until golden.

Meanwhile in a food processor, combine the cottage cheese, goat cheese or feta cheese, and egg white. Process until smooth. Add the scallion, basil, garlic, and tomatoes. Pulse briefly to mix. Spoon into the tart shells. Bake for 5 to 7 minutes, or until lightly puffed and heated through.

Makes 24

Per tartlet

Calories 71	*Sodium 231 mg.*
Total fat 2 g.	*Dietary fiber 1 g.*
Saturated fat 1 g.	*Protein 4 g.*
Cholesterol 5 mg.	*Carbohydrates 10 g.*

Cooking Note

The tartlet shells can be made ahead and stored in an airtight container for up to 2 days before filling and baking. Or, look for prepared phyllo tart shells in the freezer section of your supermarket.

Good for You

SMALL STEPS LEAD TO BIG STRIDES

As you begin to implement positive healthful changes in your diet, always make sure that you set a realistic goal with each change that you desire. Start with small steps and work at it for a period of time. Remember that you are not perfect, and allow for occasional slipups. You will be more likely to make a lifelong change if you take it one day at a time.

Stuffed Mushrooms

Hands-on time: 15 minutes
Total time: 45 minutes

16 large mushroom caps

3 scallions, sliced

2 ounces (1 packed cup) spinach leaves

2 cloves garlic, chopped

1 can (16 ounces) water-packed artichoke hearts, rinsed and drained

1/2 cup (2 ounces) grated Parmesan cheese

1/3 cup seasoned bread crumbs

3 tablespoons low-fat mayonnaise

1 teaspoon grated lemon peel

1/4 teaspoon ground red pepper

Preheat the oven to 400°F. Coat a 13" × 9" baking dish with nonstick spray.

Scoop out a small hollow in the bottom of each mushroom cap. Set aside. (Reserve the trimmings for another use.)

Coat a medium nonstick skillet with nonstick spray. Set over medium heat. Add the scallions. Cook for 1 minute, or until they start to soften. Add the spinach and garlic. Cook for 2 minutes, or until the spinach is wilted.

Meanwhile, place the artichoke hearts in the center of a clean kitchen towel. Gather up the ends and twist firmly to extract all the moisture. Place in a food processor along with the spinach mixture. Pulse until finely chopped. Add the Parmesan, bread crumbs, mayonnaise, lemon peel, and pepper. Pulse briefly to combine.

Spoon into the reserved mushroom caps. Arrange in the prepared baking dish. Coat lightly with nonstick spray. Cover loosely with foil.

Bake for 20 minutes. Remove the foil. Bake for 10 minutes longer, or until the mushrooms are tender when pierced with a knife.

Makes 16

Per mushroom
Calories 50   *Sodium 170 mg.*
Total fat 1 g.   *Dietary fiber 2 g.*
Saturated fat 1 g.   *Protein 3 g.*
Cholesterol 3 mg.   *Carbohydrates 7 g.*

MUSHROOMS IN THE MIDDLE

Stuffed mushrooms caps can be made into a wonderful savory surprise for meat loaf–lovers. Coarsely chop any leftover cooked stuffed mushrooms and place in a small bowl. Fill a loaf pan with half the meat-loaf mixture. Sprinkle with a layer of the chopped stuffed mushrooms and cover with the remaining meat-loaf mixture. Pat down to shape and bake according to recipe directions.

Sizzling Jumbo Shrimp

Hands-on time: 5 minutes
Total time: 30 minutes

SHRIMP

16 jumbo shrimp, peeled and deveined

2$\frac{1}{2}$ teaspoons olive oil

CILANTRO-LIME SAUCE

2 teaspoons Cajun seasoning

1 cup packed fresh cilantro leaves

1 cup packed fresh parsley leaves

$\frac{1}{2}$ cup (4 ounces) fat-free sour cream

Juice of 1 lime

2 cloves garlic, chopped

1 tablespoon seeded and finely
chopped jalapeño chile pepper
(wear plastic gloves when handling)

To make the shrimp: Preheat the oven to 375°F.

Place the shrimp in an 8" × 8" baking dish. Add the oil and Cajun seasoning. Toss to mix. Let sit at room temperature for 15 minutes.

To make the cilantro-lime sauce: Meanwhile, in a food processor, combine the cilantro, parsley, sour cream, lime juice, garlic, and chile pepper. Process until pureed. Transfer to a serving dish.

Bake the shrimp for 10 minutes, or until opaque. Transfer to a serving platter. Pass with wooden picks and the cilantro-lime sauce.

Makes 16

Per shrimp
Calories 39	*Sodium 142 mg.*
Total fat 1 g.	*Dietary fiber 0 g.*
Saturated fat 0 g.	*Protein 10 g.*
Cholesterol 81 mg.	*Carbohydrates 5 g.*

SIZZLING SHRIMP PASTA SALAD

Play it Again!

Use any leftover shrimp and sauce to create a refreshing luncheon salad. In a large bowl, combine 2½ cups cooked cooled pasta (such as penne or shells); 5 of the shrimp, halved lengthwise; 1 cup cooked fresh or frozen broccoli florets; ½ red bell pepper, cut into strips; and ½ cup of cilantro-lime sauce. Toss to mix. Makes 2 servings.

Sesame Chicken Fingers

Photograph on page 60
Hands-on time: 15 minutes
Total time: 1 hour and 15 minutes

SAUCE

2/3 cup soy sauce

6 tablespoons rice wine vinegar or white wine vinegar

6 tablespoons water

3 scallions, sliced

2 1/2 tablespoons sugar

1 tablespoon grated fresh ginger

1 1/2 teaspoons toasted sesame oil

1/2 teaspoon crushed red-pepper flakes

CHICKEN

1 1/2 pounds boneless, skinless chicken breasts, cut into 3/4"-wide strips

2 egg whites

1 tablespoon water

3/4 cup unbleached or all-purpose flour

3 tablespoons sesame seeds, toasted

To make the sauce: In a medium bowl, combine the soy sauce, vinegar, water, scallions, sugar, ginger, oil, and red-pepper flakes. Transfer 1/3 cup of the sauce to a large bowl. Cover and refrigerate the remaining sauce.

To make the chicken: Place the chicken in the large bowl with the sauce. Toss well to coat. Allow to marinate for 15 minutes.

Line a baking sheet with foil. Coat with nonstick spray.

Meanwhile, in a shallow bowl, combine the egg whites and water. Beat lightly with a fork.

In another shallow bowl, combine the flour and sesame seeds.

Dip the chicken strips, one at a time, first into the egg-white mixture and then into the flour mixture, shaking off any excess. Place on the prepared baking sheet. Cover loosely with plastic wrap. Refrigerate for 30 minutes.

Meanwhile, preheat the oven to 350°F.

Remove the plastic wrap from the baking sheet. Coat the chicken with nonstick spray. Bake for 5 minutes. Remove from the oven. Turn the chicken strips over. Coat with nonstick spray. Bake for 5 minutes longer, or until golden and cooked through.

Serve on a platter with the sauce on the side.

Makes 10 servings

Per serving
Calories 159   *Sodium 615 mg.*
Total fat 4 g.   *Dietary fiber 1 g.*
Saturated fat 1 g.   *Protein 16 g.*
Cholesterol 38 mg.   *Carbohydrates 14 g.*

MEAT THE CHALLENGE

Fat and cholesterol are found within even the leanest of meats, but with careful selection of meat cuts, you can minimize the amounts that you eat. When shopping for red meat, pick select grade. The words *round* or *loin* in the name—for example, eye of round, top round, sirloin, and tenderloin—are the lowest-fat choices. Buy cuts of pork with *loin* in the name, such as pork tenderloin. If the package lists trim size, choose 1/4" trim or less.

Buffalo Chicken with Blue Cheese Dressing

Hands-on time: 5 minutes
Total time: 20 minutes

24 chicken drummettes, skinned

 4 tablespoons hot sauce

 2 teaspoons vinegar

$1/4$ teaspoon garlic powder

$1/3$ cup ($1^1/2$ ounces) crumbled blue
    cheese

 1 cup (8 ounces) fat-free sour cream

 1 scallion, chopped

 1 tablespoon white wine vinegar

 1 teaspoon sugar

 2 large ribs celery, cut into sticks

Preheat the oven to 400°F. Line a baking sheet with foil. Coat with nonstick spray.

In a large bowl, combine the chicken, 2 tablespoons of the hot sauce, 1 teaspoon of the vinegar, and garlic powder. Toss to coat evenly. Arrange on the prepared baking sheet. Bake for 12 to 15 minutes, or until the juices run clear.

Meanwhile, in a medium bowl, combine the blue cheese, sour cream, scallion, vinegar, and sugar. Stir to mix, mashing the cheese with the back of a spoon.

Remove the chicken from the oven. Drizzle with the remaining 2 tablespoons hot sauce and 1 teaspoon vinegar. Toss to mix. Arrange on a serving platter. Drizzle with any sauce left on the foil. Serve with the blue cheese dressing and celery sticks.

Makes 24 servings

Per serving
Calories 29
Total fat 1 g.
Saturated fat 0 g.
Cholesterol 10 mg.
Sodium 129 mg.
Dietary fiber 0 g.
Protein 3 g.
Carbohydrates 2 g.

Hot Chicken Salad

Play it Again!

Remove the meat from half of the cooked chicken. Place in a medium bowl with 4 cups sliced romaine lettuce. Add ¼ cup baked croutons, ½ cup cherry tomato halves, 1 sliced celery rib, and 1 coarsely grated carrot. Toss with ⅓ cup of the blue cheese dressing. Makes 2 servings.

Guacamole

Hands-on time: 10 minutes
Total time: 10 minutes

1 avocado, peeled and pitted

3 cups frozen baby peas, thawed

1$\frac{1}{2}$ cups (12 ounces) fat-free ricotta cheese

4 tablespoons lime juice

3 cloves garlic, chopped

$\frac{3}{4}$ teaspoon ground cumin

1 cup spicy green salsa, drained

1 small onion, chopped

4 tablespoons chopped fresh cilantro

Hot-pepper sauce

In a food processor or blender, combine the avocado, peas, ricotta, lime juice, garlic, and cumin. Process until pureed. Transfer to a bowl. Stir in the salsa, onion, and cilantro. Season with hot-pepper sauce to taste. Stir to mix.

Makes 12 servings

Per serving
Calories 94
Total fat 3 g.
Saturated fat 0 g.
Cholesterol 2 mg.
Sodium 348 mg.
Dietary fiber 3 g.
Protein 5 g.
Carbohydrates 13 g.

AVOCADO

Avocados are exceptionally high in fat, but it is primarily monounsaturated fat. Research has linked this healthier fat to lower blood cholesterol levels when it's substituted for saturated fat in the diet. In addition, this fruit is rich in nutrients, providing beta-carotene, potassium, and fiber.

Y ou can pack a sandwich with just about any good food—vegeta-bles, meats, salads—to create a portable, satisfying meal. The best part about a sandwich is that you can make it any way you want it, and you can make it as healthy as you want it.

"The sandwich is the essence of variety. It brings together a wonderful blending of foods for a meal full of texture, color, and nutrition," says Nelda Mercer, R.D., co-author of *The M-Fit Grocery Shopping Guide.*

Building the Best

The making of a sandwich can be quite an adventure. Follow these guidelines for constructing a hearty, healthy one.

Breads. Pitas, English muffins, tortillas, foccacia, rye bread, sour-dough bread—all make an interesting base of complex carbohydrates. When you choose whole-grain bread, you get the benefit of fiber, too.

Fillers. Lean meats, vegetables, salads, and cheeses are just a few of the most common sandwich centers. Fish, bean spreads or patties, and fruits are a few more unique choices. Whatever you decide, choose the leanest of proteins and make sure that any mayonnaise-based salads are made with low-fat mayonnaise or yogurt cheese as a healthy alternative. Fillers add protein as well as essential vitamins and minerals.

Toppers. Most sandwiches are amenable to extra vegetables for texture, color, and nutrition. Red and green bell pepper slices, cucumbers, lettuce, tomato slices, onion slices, shredded carrots, and sliced mushrooms are just a few of the many choices you have. These colorful additions contribute fiber, vitamins, and other beneficial nutrients.

Spreads. Crown your creation sensibly with low-fat mayonnaise, mustard, a dab of barbecue sauce, prepared horseradish, or even drained salsa.

In today's fast-paced world, a quick sandwich is more indispensable than ever. For breakfast, lunch, snack, or dinner, a healthy sandwich fits any eating occasion.

Recipes

Uptown Vegetable Melts

Hands-on time: 5 minutes
Total time: 20 minutes

2   zucchini, cut lengthwise into
    $1/4$"-thick slices

1   small red onion, cut crosswise into
    $1/4$"-thick slices

2   yellow and/or red bell peppers,
    quartered

$1/4$ teaspoon salt

$1^1/2$ tablespoons balsamic vinegar

8   slices (8 ounces) Italian bread,
    lightly toasted

    Basil Spread (at right)

4   slices (4 ounces) low-fat Jarlsberg
    cheese

Coat a grill rack or broiler pan with nonstick spray. Preheat the grill or broiler.

Arrange the zucchini, onion, and bell peppers in a single layer on the prepared rack or pan. Coat lightly with nonstick spray. Sprinkle with the salt. Grill or broil 6" from the heat for 8 to 10 minutes, turning once, or until lightly browned. Transfer to a medium bowl. Cover and allow to steam for 3 to 4 minutes. Add the vinegar and toss to mix.

Arrange 4 of the bread slices on the grill rack or broiler pan. Spread with the Basil Spread. Top with layers of zucchini, onion, bell pepper, and Jarlsberg. Grill or broil for 1 minute, or until the cheese melts. Top with the remaining bread slices.

Makes 4 servings

Per serving
Calories 341   *Sodium 825 mg.*
Total fat 10 g.   *Dietary fiber 6 g.*
Saturated fat 5 g. *Protein 20 g.*
Cholesterol 19 mg. *Carbohydrates 45 g.*

A New Twist

BASIL SPREAD

In a food processor, combine 1 cup packed fresh basil leaves, 2 tablespoons grated Parmesan cheese, 1 tablespoon toasted walnuts, and 1 clove garlic. Process to puree. Add ¼ cup fat-free cream cheese or sour cream. Process to mix. Makes 4 servings.

Santa Fe Stuffed Sandwiches

Hands-on time: 10 minutes
Total time: 15 minutes

- 1 unsliced round (12 ounces) sourdough or multigrain bread
- 1 can (19 ounces) black beans, rinsed and drained
- 2 scallions, sliced
- 2 tablespoons chopped fresh cilantro or parsley
- 1/4 cup barbecue sauce
- 1/2–1 teaspoon hot-pepper sauce
- 5 large leaves lettuce
- 1 cup (4 ounces) shredded low-fat Monterey Jack cheese
- 1 tomato, thinly sliced
- 2 roasted red peppers

With a serrated knife, slice off the top third of the loaf. Set aside. Hollow out the bottom, leaving a ½"-thick shell. Reserve the bread pieces for another use.

In a medium bowl, coarsely mash half the beans. Add the scallions, cilantro or parsley, barbecue sauce, and the remaining beans. Stir to mix. Add ½ teaspoon hot-pepper sauce. Taste and add up to ½ teaspoon more hot-pepper sauce, if desired.

Line the hollowed bread with the lettuce. Cover with the bean mixture. Sprinkle with the Monterey Jack. Cover with the tomato and peppers. Cover with the reserved bread top and press firmly. Cut into 6 wedges.

Makes 6 servings

Per serving

Calories 261	Sodium 729 mg.
Total fat 5 g.	Dietary fiber 7 g.
Saturated fat 3 g.	Protein 15 g.
Cholesterol 13 mg.	Carbohydrates 39 g.

A New Twist

SALSA VERDE

This salsa adds a piquant note when layered into Santa Fe Stuffed Sandwiches. In a bowl, combine 6 husked and chopped tomatillos, 1 small finely chopped onion, 1 jar (4 ounces) chopped green chile peppers, 1 chopped clove garlic, 3 tablespoons chopped fresh cilantro, ½ teaspoon sugar, and a dash of salt.

Tuna Salad Pockets

Photograph on page 66
Hands-on time: 10 minutes
Total time: 20 minutes

DRESSING

1/2 cup balsamic or cider vinegar

2 teaspoons olive oil

1 teaspoon Dijon mustard

1 teaspoon Italian seasoning

1 clove garlic, chopped

SANDWICHES

3/4 pound red potatoes, cut into 1/4"-thick slices

1/4 pound small green beans

1 can (6 ounces) water-packed white tuna, drained and flaked

1/4 red onion, thinly sliced

2 hard-cooked egg whites, coarsely chopped

1/4 cup coarsely chopped niçoise olives

4 leaves lettuce, chopped

4 pitas

To make the dressing: In a medium bowl, combine the vinegar, oil, mustard, Italian seasoning, and garlic.

To make the sandwiches: Set a vegetable steamer in a medium saucepan filled with 2" of water. Cover and bring to a boil. Steam the potatoes and beans for 6 to 8 minutes, or until tender. Remove to a colander and rinse with cold water. Pat dry.

To the bowl with the dressing, add the potatoes, beans, tuna, onion, egg whites, olives, and lettuce. Toss gently to combine.

Cut each pita in half crosswise. Spoon the tuna mixture into each pocket. Drizzle lightly with any dressing left in the bowl.

Makes 4 servings

Per serving
Calories 353	*Sodium 627 mg.*
Total fat 6 g.	*Dietary fiber 5 g.*
Saturated fat 1 g.	*Protein 20 g.*
Cholesterol 18 mg.	*Carbohydrates 54 g.*

TUNA BURGER

To make burgers, marinate 4 tuna steaks (4 ounces each) in half the dressing for 1 hour. Omit the potatoes from the recipe. Marinate the beans, onion, egg whites, and olives in the remaining dressing. Preheat the broiler. Coat a broiler pan with nonstick spray. Broil the tuna for 3 to 4 minutes per side, or until the fish is just opaque. Place on toasted sandwich buns lined with lettuce leaves. Top with the marinated vegetables. Cover with the top half of the sandwich buns.

Spreads Sheet

Try any of these delightful spreads to enliven your next sandwich.

Asian Spread. Combine equal parts ketchup and hoisin sauce with hot-pepper sauce to taste. You can even add a dash of Chinese five-spice powder for an interesting edge. Serve on lean roasted pork in a sandwich roll.

Creamy Herb Spread. For every 1/2 cup reduced-fat cream cheese or homemade yogurt cheese, mix in 3 tablespoons chopped fresh herbs, such as basil or tarragon. Spread on flour tortillas. Top with roasted turkey breast and low-fat Swiss cheese and roll up.

Creamy Vegetable Spread. Combine 2 tablespoons reduced-fat cream cheese or homemade yogurt cheese with 1 tablespoon grated vegetables such as carrots, radishes, peppers, or zucchini. Spread on bagels.

Horseradish Spread. Combine 2 tablespoons low-fat mayonnaise, 1 teaspoon drained prepared horseradish, and 1 teaspoon Dijon mustard. For added interest, use beet horseradish. Wonderful on a roast beef sandwich.

Roasted Garlic Spread. Combine 1 tablespoon fat-free sour cream, 1 tablespoon chopped reconstituted dry-pack sun-dried tomatoes, and 1 tablespoon roasted garlic until smooth. Spread on French or Italian country-style bread for a grilled chicken breast sandwich.

Sweet-and-Spicy Ketchup. Combine 2 tablespoons ketchup, 1 1/2 teaspoons honey, and hot-pepper sauce to taste. Use as a sandwich spread for lean hot dogs and hamburgers or as a glaze for lean roasted meats.

Sweet-and-Spicy Spread. Combine equal parts bottled spicy chutney, Dijon mustard, and reduced-fat cream cheese or homemade yogurt cheese. Terrific on a roasted turkey or chicken sandwich.

Tex-Mex Mayonnaise. Mix 1/4 cup low-fat mayonnaise, 1 tablespoon chopped scallions, 1 tablespoon chopped cilantro, 1/2 teaspoon ground cumin, and hot-pepper sauce to taste. Great for eating on the run in a tortilla with roasted chicken and vegetables.

Grilled Cheese Sandwiches

Hands-on time: 10 minutes
Total time: 15 minutes

8 slices semolina or sourdough bread
   (8 ounces), sliced diagonally

4 slices (4 ounces) low-fat mozzarella
   or Jarlsberg cheese

1 large tomato, cut into 8 slices

2 roasted red peppers, halved

12 large leaves fresh basil

Coat both sides of the bread with olive oil fla-vored nonstick spray. In a large nonstick skillet, cook the bread on 1 side over medium heat for 1 to 2 minutes, or until lightly toasted. Do this in batches, if necessary. Remove from the pan.

Arrange 4 of the slices, toasted side up, on a work surface. Top with the mozzarella or Jarls-berg, tomatoes, peppers, and basil. Top with the remaining bread slices, toasted sided down.

Carefully place the sandwiches in the skillet. Cook for 2 to 3 minutes per side, or until toasted and the cheese melts. Cut in half diag-onally.

Makes 4 servings

Per serving
Calories 268   *Sodium 567 mg.*
Total fat 8 g.   *Dietary fiber 3 g.*
Saturated fat 4 g.   *Protein 15 g.*
Cholesterol 15 mg.   *Carbohydrates 36 g.*

Curry Shrimp Pitas

Hands-on time: 10 minutes
Total time: 10 minutes

$1/2$ cup low-fat mayonnaise

$1/4$ cup hot mango chutney

1 tablespoon soy sauce

1 tablespoon curry powder

$3/4$ pound cold peeled and cooked
   shrimp

2 ribs celery, chopped

2 nectarines, chopped

$1/4$ cup slivered almonds, toasted

6 pitas

2 cups shredded romaine lettuce

In a large bowl, combine the mayonnaise, chutney, soy sauce, and curry powder. Add the shrimp, celery, nectarines, and almonds. Toss to coat. Cut each pita in half crosswise. Stuff each half with ½ cup of the shrimp salad and some of the lettuce.

Makes 6 servings

Per serving
Calories 358   *Sodium 940 mg.*
Total fat 7 g.   *Dietary fiber 4 g.*
Saturated fat 1 g.   *Protein 22 g.*
Cholesterol 104 mg.   *Carbohydrates 52 g.*

CURRY SHRIMP SALAD

For an easy luncheon entrée that serves 4, omit the pitas. Add 4 cups assorted salad greens and 1 finely chopped red bell pepper.

Smoked Salmon 'n' Bagels

Hands-on time: 10 minutes
Total time: 10 minutes

6   ounces fat-free cream cheese, at
     room temperature

2   tablespoons chopped fresh dill

2   teaspoons drained capers, chopped

4   pumpernickel bagels, halved

3   ounces smoked salmon

$\frac{1}{2}$ small red onion, thinly sliced

$\frac{1}{3}$ English cucumber, sliced

1   tomato, cut into 8 thin slices

4   leaves lettuce

In a small bowl, combine the cream cheese,
dill, and capers. Spread 4 bagel halves with 1
tablespoon of the cream-cheese mixture. Top
with layers of salmon, onion, cucumber,
tomato, and lettuce. Cover with the remaining
bagel halves. Cut each sandwich in half.

Makes 4 servings

Per serving
Calories 274   *Sodium 1,021 mg.*
Total fat 6 g.   *Dietary fiber 6 g.*
Saturated fat 3 g.   *Protein 19 g.*
Cholesterol 20 mg.   *Carbohydrates 39 g.*

A New Twist

LEMON-MUSTARD DILL SPREAD

The flavors of salmon and dill have always been
a classic pairing. For an easy-to-make-ahead
accompaniment to this sandwich, in a small
bowl, combine $\frac{1}{3}$ cup low-fat mayonnaise,
2 tablespoons chopped fresh dill, 1 tablespoon
chopped fresh parsley, 2 teaspoons Dijon mustard, 1 teaspoon lemon juice, $\frac{1}{2}$ teaspoon grated
lemon peel, and ground black pepper to taste.

Chicken Salad Roll-Ups

Hands-on time: 15 minutes
Total time: 15 minutes

1   can (8 ounces) mandarin oranges
1/4 cup Asian plum sauce
1   tablespoon rice wine vinegar or
    wine vinegar
1   teaspoon grated fresh ginger
1/2 pound cold cooked boneless, skinless
    chicken breast, cut into small strips
1   red bell pepper, chopped
1/2 cup chopped seeded cucumber
2   scallions, thinly sliced
2 1/2 cups packed chopped romaine
    lettuce
4   whole-wheat tortillas (8" diameter)

Drain the oranges, reserving 2 tablespoons of the juice.

In a large bowl, combine the plum sauce, vinegar, ginger, and reserved orange juice. Add the chicken, bell pepper, cucumber, scallions, lettuce, and oranges. Toss to coat.

Place the tortillas on a work surface. Divide the salad evenly on top. Roll into cylinders. Slice in half diagonally.

Makes 4 servings

Per serving
Calories 331   *Sodium 416 mg.*
Total fat 6 g.   *Dietary fiber 6 g.*
Saturated fat 1 g.   *Protein 22 g.*
Cholesterol 50 mg.   *Carbohydrates 48 g.*

Good for You

LUNCH PLANS

If preparing your lunch in the morning is too much of a hassle, consider making lunch the evening before when you have a few extra minutes. By preparing a sandwich, salad, yogurt, and fresh fruits and vegetables, you can eat sensibly and decrease the amount of calories, fat, and cholesterol that are so easily consumed when you dine out on fast food.

Club Sandwiches

Photograph on page 65
Hands-on time: 15 minutes
Total time: 15 minutes

LEMON-CAPER MAYONNAISE

$1/2$ cup low-fat mayonnaise

1 teaspoon lemon juice

2 teaspoons drained capers, coarsely chopped

SANDWICHES

12 thin slices multigrain bread, toasted

$1/2$ pound cooked skinless chicken breast, sliced

2 ounces alfalfa sprouts

$1/3$ English cucumber, thinly sliced

1 large tomato, cut into 8 slices

8 slices turkey bacon, cooked

4 leaves lettuce

To make the lemon-caper mayonnaise: In a small bowl, combine the mayonnaise, lemon juice, and capers.

To make the sandwiches: Place 4 of the bread slices on a work surface. Spread 2 teaspoons of the lemon-caper mayonnaise on each slice. Top with layers of chicken, alfalfa sprouts, and cucumber.

Spread 4 of the remaining bread slices each with 2 teaspoons of lemon-caper mayonnaise. Place, mayonnaise side up, on the 4 sandwiches. Top with layers of tomato, bacon, and lettuce.

Spread the remaining 4 bread slices with the remaining lemon-caper mayonnaise. Place, mayonnaise side down, on top of the sandwiches. Cut in half diagonally. Secure with toothpicks.

Makes 4 servings

Per serving
Calories 349
Total fat 9 g.
Saturated fat 2 g.
Cholesterol 79 mg.
Sodium 1,060 mg.
Dietary fiber 10 g.
Protein 29 g.
Carbohydrates 41 g.

Cooking Note

Although this sandwich is relatively high in sodium, traditional club sandwiches can contain up to three times as much sodium in a serving. If sodium is a concern for you, omit the bacon and use only 2 slices of bread per sandwich. For further fat reduction, replace the turkey bacon with Canadian bacon or a soy-based imitation bacon.

Good for you

THE RIGHT SIDES

Simple side dishes that can accompany any quick sandwich are fresh fruit chunks, raw vegetables with fat-free dressing, a baked potato with fat-free sour cream and cheese, a bowl of low-fat soup, or coleslaw mix tossed with fat-free dressing. Side dishes to avoid are potato chips, coleslaw, potato salad, and macaroni salad.

The New Classic Reuben

Photograph on page 63
Hands-on time: 15 minutes
Total time: 15 minutes

8 slices soft rye bread

6 tablespoons fat-free Thousand Island dressing (at right)

³⁄4 pound very thinly sliced cooked turkey breast

1 cup sauerkraut, rinsed and drained

4 slices (4 ounces) low-fat, reduced-sodium Swiss or Jarlsberg cheese

Place 4 slices of the bread on a work surface. Spread evenly with the dressing. Top with layers of the turkey, sauerkraut, and Swiss or Jarlsberg. Cover with the remaining bread slices. Coat the tops with nonstick spray.

Set a large nonstick skillet over medium heat. Place the sandwiches, coated side down, in the skillet. Cover and cook for 3 to 4 minutes, or until the bottoms are golden brown. Coat the tops of the sandwiches with nonstick spray. Carefully turn the sandwiches over. Cover and cook for 3 to 4 minutes, or until the bottoms are golden and the cheese is melted. Cut each sandwich in half.

Makes 4 servings

Per serving

Calories 417	*Sodium 836 mg.*
Total fat 9 g.	*Dietary fiber 5 g.*
Saturated fat 5 g.	*Protein 40 g.*
Cholesterol 91 mg.	*Carbohydrates 42 g.*

Cooking Note

Although the fat and sodium in this sandwich are relatively high, the overall nutritional profile is profoundly better than the original Reuben, which contains around 30 grams of fat and 2,000 milligrams of sodium.

A New Twist

Thousand Island Dressing

It's easy to make your own fat-free Thousand Island dressing, and it will stay fresh for up to a week, covered, in the refrigerator. In a medium bowl, combine ½ cup low-fat mayonnaise, ½ cup fat-free sour cream, ¼ cup chili sauce, 2 tablespoons pickle relish, 1 small finely chopped onion, and 1 tablespoon chopped fresh parsley. Season with ground black pepper to taste. Makes about 1¼ cups.

Sloppy Joes

Hands-on time: 10 minutes
Total time: 20 minutes

1 onion, chopped

1 green bell pepper, chopped

1 rib celery, chopped

2 cloves garlic, chopped

1 pound extra-lean ground round beef

1 bottle (12 ounces) chili sauce

$^{1}/_{2}$ cup fat-free reduced-sodium beef broth

2 tablespoons packed light brown sugar

2 teaspoons Worcestershire sauce

1 teaspoon dried oregano

4 whole-wheat sandwich buns

Coat a large nonstick skillet with nonstick spray. Set over medium heat. Add the onion, bell pepper, celery, and garlic. Cook for 5 to 7 minutes, or until soft. Add the beef. Cook for 5 minutes, breaking the meat up with a spoon, or until no longer pink. Add the chili sauce, broth, brown sugar, Worcestershire sauce, and oregano. Cook, stirring occasionally, for 5 minutes, or until hot and bubbly. Spoon into the buns.

Makes 4 servings

Per serving
Calories 530	*Sodium 942 mg.*
Total fat 15 g.	*Dietary fiber 6 g.*
Saturated fat 5 g.	*Protein 33 g.*
Cholesterol 41 mg.	*Carbohydrates 67 g.*

A New Twist

SLOPPY SUBSTITUTES

You can replace the ground beef with lean ground turkey breast, lean ground chicken breast, or 1 cup textured vegetable protein (reconstituted)—a compressed soy flaked protein that swells to twice its volume and resembles the texture of ground meat when mixed with a liquid.

Mile-High Burgers

Hands-on time: 15 minutes
Total time: 20 minutes

1 1/2 ounces dry-pack sun-dried tomatoes

2 tablespoons low-fat mayonnaise

1/3 cup packed fresh basil leaves

1 clove garlic

1 1/4 pounds extra-lean ground round beef

1 roasted red pepper, quartered

2 slices (2 ounces) low-fat mozzarella cheese, halved

4 large leaves lettuce

4 Italian-style sandwich buns

Place the sun-dried tomatoes in a small bowl. Cover with boiling water. Soak for 10 minutes, or until very soft. Drain and discard the liquid. In a food processor, combine the tomatoes, mayonnaise, basil, and garlic. Process until smooth.

In a medium bowl, combine the beef and tomato mixture. Mix to blend evenly. Shape into 4 patties.

Coat a grill rack or broiler pan with nonstick spray. Preheat the grill or broiler. Place the burgers on the rack or pan. Cook 4" from the heat for 4 minutes per side, or until a thermometer inserted in the center registers 160°F and the meat is no longer pink. Top each burger with a slice of pepper and mozzarella. Cook for 30 to 40 seconds, or until the cheese melts.

Divide the lettuce among the buns. Top each with a burger.

Makes 4 servings

Per serving
Calories 591
Total fat 16 g.
Saturated fat 8 g.
Cholesterol 135 mg.
Sodium 840 mg.
Dietary fiber 3 g.
Protein 64 g.
Carbohydrates 45 g.

A New Twist

GARDEN MAYONNAISE

Try topping plain burgers with this spread. In a food processor, combine ¾ cup lightly packed fresh parsley leaves, 1½ cups lightly packed basil leaves, 1 clove garlic, and 1 small onion, quartered. Process until very finely chopped. Mix in ½ cup low-fat mayonnaise and 2 teaspoons wine vinegar. Pulse to mix. Season with salt and ground black pepper to taste. Makes about 1 cup.

Lean on Protein

After water, protein is the largest component of the human body. Protein helps build skin, muscles, bones, and organs. It assists in functions as diverse as blood clotting, water balance, hormone production, and immunity.

Because protein is so important to a healthy body, it's natural that many people trying to eat more vegetables, fruits, and grains are concerned that they may not get enough protein. The reality is quite the opposite.

Most health experts recommend that the average person consume between 12 and 15 percent of their calories from protein. For example, a person eating 2,000 calories daily would consume 60 to 75 grams of protein. Just one 3-ounce serving of lean beef, chicken, or fish (about the size of a deck of cards) would supply one-third of that minimum amount—21 grams of protein.

When protein comes from an animal source—beef, pork, chicken, fish, eggs, milk, cheese, or yogurt—it contains the nine essential amino acids to make it a "complete" protein. These amino acids are called essential because our bodies cannot manufacture them. They must come from food sources.

Although you'll want to get some of your protein through animal sources, in order to limit your intake of saturated fat and cholesterol, it is desirable to also get protein through a wide variety of plant foods.

Protein also comes from plant foods but is generally not as concentrated as animal sources. Foods such as legumes (beans, peas, and lentils), nuts, seeds, grains, and vegetables all contain protein.

Plant proteins, with the important exception of soy, are missing one or more essential amino acid. As a result, these proteins are often called complementary or incomplete. But various vegetables, grains, nuts, and legumes can be combined to create the essential amino acids necessary for the body to function properly. Foods can be consumed over the course of a day to provide the total amount of protein needed.

By choosing moderate portions of lean meats, poultry, and fish balanced with a variety of grains, vegetables, and legumes, you'll be sure to take in the proper amount of protein while keeping cholesterol and saturated fat in check.

Grilled Portobello Burgers

Hands-on time: 15 minutes
Total time: 45 minutes

¹/2 cup balsamic vinegar

¹/4 cup soy sauce

1 tablespoon dried oregano

2 cloves garlic, chopped

2 teaspoons olive oil

4 large portobello mushroom caps

4 slices (¹/4" thick) sweet onion

4 slices (2 ounces) fontina cheese

4 Kaiser rolls, halved

4 leaves lettuce

2 roasted red peppers, halved

In a 13" × 9" baking dish, combine the vinegar, soy sauce, oregano, garlic, and oil. Add the mushroom caps, turning to coat. Set aside, turning occasionally, for 30 minutes.

Coat a grill rack or broiler pan with nonstick spray. Preheat the grill or broiler. Remove the mushroom caps. Reserve the marinade. Grill or broil the mushroom caps and onion 6" from the heat for 3 minutes per side, or until golden. Top the mushrooms with the fontina. Cook for 1 to 2 minutes, or until the cheese melts.

Meanwhile, toast the cut side of the rolls on the grill or under the broiler for 1 minute, or until golden. Remove and place the lettuce on the bottoms of the rolls. Top each with a pepper half, an onion slice, and a mushroom cap. Drizzle with a bit of the reserved marinade. Cover with the tops of the rolls. Cut in half.

Makes 4 servings

Per serving

Calories 366	*Sodium 995 mg.*
Total fat 10 g.	*Dietary fiber 6 g.*
Saturated fat 4 g.	*Protein 16 g.*
Cholesterol 16 mg.	*Carbohydrates 58 g.*

Good for You

SPREAD YOURSELF THIN

When ordering a sandwich in a restaurant, order the bun or bread without butter or mayonnaise. Often, the restaurant will put these condiments on your selection without asking you. Ask for prepared horseradish, mustard, or ketchup instead.

New York–Style Roast Beef Sandwiches

Photograph on page 64
Hands-on time: 10 minutes
Total time: 10 minutes

1/4 cup buttermilk or fat-free plain yogurt

2 tablespoons low-fat mayonnaise

1/4 cup (1 ounce) crumbled blue cheese

2 tablespoons chopped fresh chives or scallion greens

4 small plum tomatoes, halved lengthwise

1 small red onion, cut into 4 slices

4 onion sandwich buns, toasted

3/4 pound thinly sliced cooked lean roast beef

4 leaves lettuce

In a small bowl, combine the buttermilk or yogurt, mayonnaise, blue cheese, and chives or scallion greens.

Coat a large nonstick skillet with nonstick spray. Set over medium-high heat until hot. Place the tomatoes and onion in the skillet. Cook for 2 to 3 minutes per side, or until lightly charred.

Layer the roast beef, onion, tomatoes, and lettuce on the bottoms of the buns. Drizzle with the blue cheese dressing. Cover with the bun tops.

Makes 4 servings

Per serving
Calories 353
Total fat 10 g.
Saturated fat 5 g.
Cholesterol 65 mg.
Sodium 503 mg.
Dietary fiber 2 g.
Protein 32 g.
Carbohydrates 33 g.

Teriyaki Tuna Burgers

Hands-on time: 10 minutes
Total time: 15 minutes

1 1/4 pounds tuna steak, skin and dark edges trimmed

4 tablespoons teriyaki sauce

1 scallion, chopped

2 teaspoons grated fresh ginger

2 cloves garlic, chopped

1 can (6 ounces) unsweetened pineapple slices

2 slices (2 ounces) low-fat mozzarella cheese, halved

4 leaves lettuce

4 sesame seed sandwich buns

Coat a grill rack or broiler pan with nonstick spray. Preheat the grill or broiler.

Finely chop the tuna to the consistency of ground meat. Transfer to a bowl. Add 3 tablespoons of the teriyaki sauce, the scallion, ginger, and garlic. Stir to mix. Shape into 4 patties. Coat lightly with nonstick spray.

Grill or broil the patties 6" from the heat for 3 minutes, or until the edges appear cooked about halfway up the burger. Turn. Drizzle with the remaining 1 tablespoon teriyaki sauce. Top each with a slice of pineapple and a slice of mozzarella. Cook for 2 to 3 minutes longer, or until the burgers are opaque in the center.

Divide the lettuce among the buns. Top each with a burger.

Makes 4 servings

Per serving
Calories 478
Total fat 8 g.
Saturated fat 2 g.
Cholesterol 89 mg.
Sodium 665 mg.
Dietary fiber 3 g.
Protein 53 g.
Carbohydrates 48 g.

With the annual per capita pizza consumption at 23 pounds a year, Americans consume more than 11 *billion* slices of pizza every year. That represents a lot of opportunities for healthier eating. Healthy pizza? Yes.

Pizza is a fine candidate for a nutritious meal. The crust contributes complex carbohydrates. If you use whole-wheat flour, you will add B vitamins and fiber. Cheese gives you calcium and protein. The sauce and vegetable toppings add vitamins. Lean meat toppings contribute protein. So you can easily wrap up a wealth of nutrition in every bite.

A serving of hearty Double-Crust Pizza (with three cheeses and ground beef) contains 315 calories and 6 grams of fat. Contrast that with a slice of carryout deep-dish pizza that can contain as much as 700 calories and more than 30 grams of fat.

With the easy master recipe for Basic Pizza Dough, you can have the base for satisfying homemade pizza always on hand in the freezer. Choose from roasted vegetables, fresh herbs, chile peppers, cooked bean purees, shrimp, strips of cooked lean beef, chicken, or pork, and moderate amounts of high-flavor cheeses such as Romano, Parmesan, and sharp Cheddar for toppings that make pizzas exciting and healthier.

If making your own homemade pizza isn't possible all the time, you can still have your health and enjoy pizza, too. "With smart ordering and creative preparation, the fat and calories in your pizza of choice can be in line with your goals for optimal health," says Evelyn Tribole, R.D., consulting nutritionist in Beverly Hills, California, and author of *Healthy Homestyle Cooking* and *Stealth Health*.

Remember, it is generally the cheese that sends the calories and fat skyrocketing, so extra cheese is not the healthiest way to go. "Health-conscious Californians are incredibly aware of the fat content of cheese," says Tribole. "At a Beverly Hills restaurant, the waiter asked if I even wanted cheese on my pizza."

Eliminating cheese altogether may be a bit extreme for some, but by asking for smaller amounts and more vegetable toppings, you can get by with smaller amounts of high-fat cheese. When you order your next pizza, try asking for half the amount of cheese.

Whether you order carryout pizza or prepare it yourself, whether you eat pizza for breakfast, lunch, dinner, or dessert, the possibilities for fun and healthy eating are endless.

Recipes

Basic Pizza Dough

Hands-on time: 15 minutes
Total time: 1 hour and 15 minutes

1 cup lukewarm water (105°-115°F)

1 teaspoon sugar

1 package active dry yeast

3¹⁄₂ cups unbleached or all-purpose flour

1 teaspoon salt

1 tablespoon olive oil

Lightly coat a large bowl with nonstick spray.

In a glass measuring cup, combine the water, sugar, and yeast. Let stand for 5 minutes, or until foamy.

In a food processor or bowl of an electric mixer fitted with a dough hook, combine 3¼ cups of the flour and the salt. With the machine running, add the yeast mixture and oil through the feed tube. Process just until the dough comes together in a slightly sticky mass. If using an electric mixer, mix on low speed for 2 minutes, or until the dough comes together in a slightly sticky mass.

Turn onto a lightly floured work surface. Knead for 4 to 7 minutes, adding the remaining ¼ cup flour, if necessary, to prevent sticking, until smooth and elastic. Shape into a ball.

Place in the prepared bowl. Cover tightly with plastic wrap. Let rise in a warm place for 1 hour, or until doubled.

Punch the dough down. Shape into two balls. To store the dough, place each ball in a resealable plastic bag, pressing out excess air. Refrigerate overnight or freeze for up to 3 weeks. Bring the dough to room temperature before shaping.

Makes 2 crusts (12" diameter); 8 servings per crust

Per serving
Calories 113	*Sodium 147 mg.*
Total fat 1 g.	*Dietary fiber 0 g.*
Saturated fat 0 g.	*Protein 3 g.*
Cholesterol 0 mg.	*Carbohydrates 22 g.*

Cooking Note
This recipe can also be divided into 4 small crusts (6" diameter) or 2 thicker crusts (9" diameter).

Good for You

THE TRUTH ABOUT CARBS

The myth persists that carbohydrates like pasta, bread, and potatoes are fattening. Nothing could be further from the truth. Carbohydrate sources, such as grains, fruits, and vegetables, fuel the body while supplying valuable vitamins, minerals, and fiber necessary for bodily functions. Depending upon your calorie needs, experts recommend at least 6 to 11 servings of carbohydrate-rich foods a day.

Classic Tomato Pizza

Photograph on page 69
Hands-on time: 10 minutes
Total time: 30 minutes

1 tablespoon cornmeal

1 teaspoon olive oil

3 cloves garlic, minced

6 plum tomatoes, chopped

¼ cup chopped fresh basil

¼ teaspoon salt

½ recipe Basic Pizza Dough (page 97) or 1 tube (10 ounces) refrigerated pizza dough

¾ cup (3 ounces) shredded low-fat mozzarella cheese

Preheat the oven to 450°F. Coat a large round pizza pan with nonstick spray. Sprinkle with the cornmeal.

In a medium nonstick skillet over medium heat, combine the oil and garlic. Cook, stirring occasionally, for 2 to 3 minutes, or until fragrant. Add the tomatoes, basil, and salt. Cover and cook, stirring occasionally, for 5 minutes, or until the tomatoes are soft. Remove from the heat.

Turn the dough out onto a lightly floured work surface. Roll into a 12" circle. Place on the prepared pan. Spread the tomato sauce over the dough to within ¼" of the edge. Sprinkle with the mozzarella.

Bake for 10 to 12 minutes, or until the crust is golden brown.

Makes 8 servings

Per serving
Calories 162
Total fat 4 g.
Saturated fat 1 g.
Cholesterol 6 mg.
Sodium 280 mg.
Dietary fiber 2 g.
Protein 7 g.
Carbohydrates 26 g.

Tex-Mex Pizza with Chili Crust

Hands-on time: 5 minutes
Total time: 20 minutes

1 tablespoon cornmeal

½ recipe Basic Pizza Dough (page 97) or 1 tube (10 ounces) refrigerated pizza dough

Chili powder

1 can (15 ounces) Mexican-style tomatoes, drained and finely chopped

1 can (15 ounces) black beans, rinsed and drained

1 cup frozen corn kernels, thawed

2 scallions, chopped

¾ cup (3 ounces) shredded low-fat pepper Jack cheese or Monterey Jack cheese

¾ cup (3 ounces) shredded low-fat sharp Cheddar cheese

Preheat the oven to 450°F. Coat a large round pizza pan with nonstick spray. Sprinkle with the cornmeal.

Turn the dough out onto a lightly floured work surface. Roll into a 12" circle. Place on the prepared pan. Dust lightly with chili powder. Spread evenly with the tomatoes, beans, corn, and scallions. Sprinkle with the pepper Jack or Monterey Jack and Cheddar.

Bake for 12 to 15 minutes, or until the crust is golden brown.

Makes 8 servings

Per serving
Calories 237
Total fat 6 g.
Saturated fat 4 g.
Cholesterol 19 mg.
Sodium 498 mg.
Dietary fiber 4 g.
Protein 12 g.
Carbohydrates 34 g.

Upper Crusts

Creative crusts can give a pizza real personality. Crusts range from cracker-thin to thick, and they can harbor zesty flavorings such as cheese, herbs, olives, and sun-dried tomatoes. With the master recipe for Basic Pizza Dough on page 97, you can create your own convenience crusts for the freezer and customize them with the flavors you like.

I use unbleached or all-purpose flour in my pizza dough, which makes for a tender yet crisp crust. Try adding a few tablespoons of whole-wheat flour for a slightly nutty accent. Or, for a crispier crust, replace a few tablespoons of all-purpose flour with cornmeal or semolina flour. Adding whole grains and flours such as rye, oat bran, and triticale to the pizza dough will add flavor and increase the nutritional value. Add any dry or semi-dry flavorings to the flour before adding the yeast water.

When selecting these added grains for your crust, consider the toppings that will go on the pizza. Make sure that they will complement each other and allow you to layer flavors for the best results.

For an Italian crust, try adding Italian seasoning or minced fresh basil leaves. Minced or roasted garlic adds a new dimension. Grated Parmesan or Romano cheeses are terrific flavor-enhancers. Chopped olives or reconstituted sun-dried tomatoes, finely chopped and patted dry, are robust additions.

If you like it hot, try adding crushed red-pepper flakes or even minced fresh chile peppers (wear plastic gloves when handling). Extend the Latin influence with cumin, chili powder, or minced fresh cilantro.

Stromboli

Hands-on time: 15 minutes
Total time: 30 minutes

- 1 tablespoon cornmeal
- 1 small green bell pepper, chopped
- 1 onion, chopped
- 1 recipe Basic Pizza Dough (page 97) or 2 tubes (10 ounces each) refrigerated pizza dough
- 1/2 pound reduced-fat, reduced-sodium turkey salami and/or turkey pastrami
- 1/4 pound reduced-fat, reduced-sodium baked ham
- 2 ounces sliced pepperoni
- 3/4 cup (3 ounces) shredded low-fat mozzarella cheese
- 1 egg white, lightly beaten with 1 teaspoon water

Preheat the oven to 375°F. Coat a baking sheet with nonstick spray. Lightly dust with the cornmeal.

Coat a medium nonstick skillet with nonstick spray. Add the bell pepper and onion. Cook, stirring, over medium heat for 5 to 7 minutes, or until soft.

Meanwhile, turn the dough out onto a lightly floured work surface. Roll into a 16" × 6" rectangle. Layer the salami and/or pastrami, ham, and pepperoni down the center, leaving a 1" border on all sides. Top with the bell pepper, onion, and mozzarella.

With a pair of kitchen scissors, make eight 1" cuts every 2" into each edge of the long side of the dough. Starting at a narrow end, fold the 1" edge of dough over the filling. Repeat on the opposite narrow end. Pull two opposite cut edges of dough together. Twist to seal at the middle of the loaf. Repeat with the remaining cut edges. Lightly brush the dough with the egg-white mixture. Transfer to the prepared baking sheet.

Bake for 20 minutes, or until golden brown and the crust sounds hollow when tapped. Place on a cutting board and allow to cool slightly before cutting into 10 slices.

Makes 10 servings

Per serving

Calories 290	*Sodium 706 mg.*
Total fat 9 g.	*Dietary fiber 2 g.*
Saturated fat 3 g.	*Protein 15 g.*
Cholesterol 31 mg.	*Carbohydrates 38 g.*

Mushroom-Sage Pizza

Hands-on time: 20 minutes
Total time: 35 minutes

1 tablespoon cornmeal

1 cup 1% milk

1 1/2 tablespoons unbleached or all-purpose flour

1 clove garlic, halved

1/4 teaspoon ground nutmeg

1/4 teaspoon salt

1/2 pound button and/or portobello or shiitake mushrooms, stems removed and thinly sliced

2 tablespoons Madeira wine or fat-free reduced-sodium chicken broth

1 1/2 tablespoons chopped fresh sage

1/2 recipe Basic Pizza Dough (page 97) or 1 tube (10 ounces) refrigerated pizza dough

1 cup (4 ounces) shredded Parmesan and/or provolone cheese

Preheat the oven to 450°F. Coat a large round pizza pan with nonstick spray. Sprinkle with the cornmeal.

In a small saucepan, whisk the milk with the flour to dissolve. Add the garlic. Cook, whisking constantly, over medium heat for 5 to 7 minutes, or until thickened. Season with the nutmeg and salt. Remove from the heat. Remove and discard the garlic.

Meanwhile, in a medium nonstick skillet set over medium heat, combine the mushrooms, wine or broth, and sage. Cook, stirring occasionally, for 5 to 7 minutes, or until the mushrooms are soft and the liquid has evaporated. Remove from the heat.

Turn the dough out onto a lightly floured work surface. Roll into a 12" circle. Place on the prepared pan. Spread with the milk mixture, leaving a 1/4" border. Top with the mushrooms in an even layer. Sprinkle with the Parmesan and/or provolone.

Bake for 10 to 12 minutes, or until the crust is golden brown.

Makes 8 servings

Per serving
Calories 209 *Sodium 328 mg.*
Total fat 6 g. *Dietary fiber 1 g.*
Saturated fat 3 g. *Protein 9 g.*
Cholesterol 13 mg. *Carbohydrates 30 g.*

A New Twist

MUSHROOM FETTUCCINE

To make mushroom fettuccine, double the amount of white sauce and mushrooms. Cook 12 ounces fettuccine according to package directions. Drain. Place in a large bowl and toss with the white sauce, mushrooms, and 1/3 cup grated Parmesan cheese. Makes 6 servings.

Onion-Rosemary Focaccia

Photograph on page 67
Hands-on time: 10 minutes
Total time: 35 minutes

1 tablespoon cornmeal

1 tablespoon olive oil

1 red onion, halved and thinly sliced

2 teaspoons dried rosemary, crushed

1/4 teaspoon salt

1 recipe Basic Pizza Dough (page 97) or 2 tubes (10 ounces each) refrigerated pizza dough

1 teaspoon dried basil

Preheat the oven to 450°F. Coat a baking sheet with nonstick spray. Sprinkle with the cornmeal.

Warm the oil in a medium nonstick skillet set over medium heat. Add the onion, rosemary, and salt. Cover and cook, stirring occasionally, for 15 to 20 minutes, or until very soft. Remove from the heat and allow to cool slightly.

Turn the dough out onto a lightly floured work surface. Roll into a 12" × 6" rectangle. Place on the prepared baking sheet. Sprinkle with the basil. With your fingertips, press the basil into the dough. Top with the onion mixture.

Bake for 12 to 15 minutes, or until the crust is browned.

Makes 10 servings

Per serving
Calories 164   Sodium 179 mg.
Total fat 2 g.   Dietary fiber 1 g.
Saturated fat 0 g.   Protein 4 g.
Cholesterol 0 mg.   Carbohydrates 33 g.

A New Twist

BALSAMIC GLAZE

For a sweet-tart touch, make this glaze to serve over the focaccia. Place 1/2 cup balsamic vinegar in a small saucepan set over medium-high heat. Cook, swirling the pan often, at a gentle simmer for 5 to 6 minutes, or until it reaches a syrupy consistency. Drizzle over the baked focaccia just before serving.

Ratatouille Pizza

Hands-on time: 15 minutes
Total time: 30 minutes

1 tablespoon cornmeal

$1/2$ small onion, chopped

1 small eggplant, peeled and cut into small chunks

1 small zucchini, cut into small chunks

2 cloves garlic, chopped

2 plum tomatoes, chopped

$1/4$ cup chopped fresh basil

1 teaspoon drained capers

$1/4$ teaspoon salt

$1/2$ recipe Basic Pizza Dough (page 97) or 1 tube (10 ounces) refrigerated pizza dough

$1 1/4$ cups (5 ounces) shredded low-fat mozzarella cheese

$1/4$ cup (1 ounce) grated Parmesan cheese

Preheat the oven to 450°F. Coat a large round pizza pan with nonstick spray. Sprinkle with the cornmeal.

Coat a medium nonstick skillet with nonstick spray. Set over medium heat. Add the onion, eggplant, zucchini, and garlic. Cook, stirring occasionally, for 5 to 7 minutes, or until soft. Add the tomatoes, basil, capers, and salt. Cook for 3 minutes, or until the tomatoes are soft. Remove from the heat to cool slightly.

Turn the dough out onto a lightly floured work surface. Roll into a 12" circle. Place on the prepared pan. Spread evenly with the ratatouille. Top with the mozzarella and Parmesan.

Bake for 10 to 12 minutes, or until the crust is golden brown.

Makes 8 servings

Per serving
Calories 192
Total fat 5 g.
Saturated fat 3 g.
Cholesterol 12 mg.
Sodium 386 mg.
Dietary fiber 2 g.
Protein 10 g.
Carbohydrates 26 g.

READY WITH RATATOUILLE

Play it Again!

The French summer vegetable stew called ratatouille is a very versatile dish. Use as a filling for omelets with a little shredded mozzarella cheese. Or, toss with cooked pasta and a little grated Parmesan cheese. It also makes a wonderful chunky topping for grilled or baked fish.

Fettuccine Alfredo Pizza

Hands-on time: 20 minutes
Total time: 35 minutes

1 tablespoon cornmeal

1 small onion, chopped

2 cloves garlic, finely chopped

1 cup 1% milk

1 tablespoon unbleached or all-purpose flour

3 tablespoons chopped fresh basil or 1 teaspoon dried

1/4 teaspoon salt

1/4 teaspoon ground nutmeg

4 ounces fettuccine, cooked and drained

1/2 recipe Basic Pizza Dough (page 97) or 1 tube (10 ounces) refrigerated pizza dough

3/4 cup (3 ounces) shredded low-fat mozzarella cheese

1/2 cup (2 ounces) grated Parmesan cheese

Preheat the oven to 450°F. Coat a large round pizza pan with nonstick spray. Sprinkle with the cornmeal.

Meanwhile, coat a medium saucepan with nonstick spray. Set over medium heat. Add the onion and garlic. Cook, stirring often, for 3 minutes, or until soft.

In a small bowl, whisk together the milk and flour until well-blended. Add to the pan with the onion. Cook, whisking often, for 4 minutes, or until thickened. Remove from the heat. Add the basil, salt, and nutmeg. Add the fettuccine. Toss to coat.

Turn the dough out onto a lightly floured work surface. Roll into a 12" circle. Place on the prepared pan. Spread evenly with the fettuccine mixture, leaving a 1/4" border. Sprinkle with the mozzarella and Parmesan.

Bake for 10 to 12 minutes, or until the crust is golden brown.

Makes 8 servings

Per serving
Calories 235
Total fat 6 g.
Saturated fat 3 g.
Cholesterol 12 mg.

Sodium 433 mg.
Dietary fiber 2 g.
Protein 11 g.
Carbohydrates 35 g.

GARLIC GOODNESS

Fresh garlic is good for you, so you'll want to eat plenty of it. No need to spend money on fancy gadgets to quickly peel garlic. Just use the flat side of a knife or cleaver. Smack the cloves to lightly crush them and break the skins. The skins will come away easily. Also, look for heads of garlic with large cloves, which are easier to peel.

Greek Pizza

Hands-on time: 10 minutes
Total time: 25 minutes

1 tablespoon cornmeal

4 tablespoons dry-pack sun-dried tomato bits

1 bunch scallions, chopped

10 ounces fresh baby spinach or 1 box (10 ounces) frozen chopped spinach, thawed and squeezed dry

1/2 cup (2 ounces) crumbled feta cheese

1/2 recipe Basic Pizza Dough (page 97) or 1 tube (10 ounces) refrigerated pizza dough

1 cup rinsed and drained water-packed canned artichoke hearts, patted dry and quartered

1/2 cup (2 ounces) grated provolone cheese

Preheat the oven to 450°F. Coat a large round pizza pan with nonstick spray. Sprinkle with the cornmeal.

Place the sun-dried tomato bits in a small bowl. Cover with boiling water. Allow to soak for 10 minutes, or until soft. Drain and discard the liquid.

Coat a medium nonstick skillet with nonstick spray. Set over medium heat. Add the scallions. Cook for 2 minutes, or until almost soft. Add the spinach and cook, stirring often, for 2 minutes, or until wilted and/or heated through. Remove from the heat. Stir in the feta. Set aside to cool.

Turn the dough out onto a lightly floured work surface. Roll into a 12" circle. Place on the pre-pared pan. Spread with the spinach mixture, leaving a 1/4" border. Sprinkle evenly with the tomato bits. Arrange the artichokes on top. Sprinkle with the provolone.

Bake for 10 to 12 minutes, or until the crust is golden brown.

Makes 8 servings

Per serving
Calories 187
Total fat 5 g.
Saturated fat 3 g.
Cholesterol 11 mg.
Sodium 352 mg.
Dietary fiber 4 g.
Protein 8 g.
Carbohydrates 29 g.

A New Twist

SPINACH STRUDEL

To make spinach strudel, omit the pizza dough and double the remaining ingredients. In a large bowl, combine the cooked spinach, feta, artichoke hearts, and provolone with 15 ounces fat-free ricotta and 1 lightly beaten egg. Season with salt and pepper to taste. One at a time, lightly coat 6 sheets of phyllo dough (17" × 11") with nonstick spray before stacking them atop one another. Spoon the spinach mixture down the center. Roll into a tight cylinder. Make several small slashes across the top. Transfer to a baking sheet coated with nonstick spray. Coat the strudel with nonstick spray. Bake in a 375°F oven for 15 to 20 minutes, or until the phyllo is golden brown. Makes 6 servings.

Time for an Oil Change

Are you fed up with fats and oils? Do you wonder what fat is most beneficial for healthy cooking? How much should you use? When should you use it? Just picking a cooking oil can be a very confusing task.

Your healthiest fat choices are oils that are predominantly monounsaturated, such as canola oil, olive oil, and peanut oil. Be aware, however, that just because you choose a healthier cooking oil does not mean that you can use it with abandon. In general, smaller quantities of fat are best. Remember that just one tablespoon of oil, regardless of the type, contains about 14 grams of fat and about 120 calories.

Look for ways to limit the amount of fat in cooking by using nonstick sprays and low-fat and fat-free dairy products and selecting the leanest poultry and meat cuts. Also, by never using solid vegetable shortening and by eliminating processed snack foods, crackers, and cookies from your eating plan, you will eliminate most of the manmade trans-fatty acids, which may raise total cholesterol levels.

Ginger Shrimp Pizza

Hands-on time: 10 minutes
Total time: 20 minutes

 1 tablespoon cornmeal
 1/2 recipe Basic Pizza Dough (page 97) or 1 tube (10 ounces) refrigerated pizza dough
 1 recipe Ginger Sauce (at right)
 1/4 pound peeled and deveined cooked shrimp
 1 small red or yellow bell pepper, cut into matchsticks
 1 1/2 ounces snow peas, halved diagonally
 1 tablespoon chopped peanuts
 1 cup (4 ounces) shredded low-fat mozzarella cheese

Preheat the oven to 450°F. Coat a large round pizza pan with nonstick spray. Sprinkle with the cornmeal.

Turn the dough out onto a lightly floured work surface. Roll into a 12" circle. Place on the prepared pan. Spread evenly with the Ginger Sauce, leaving a ¼" border. Scatter the shrimp, bell pepper, snow peas, and peanuts on top. Sprinkle with the mozzarella.

Bake for 10 to 12 minutes, or until the crust is golden brown.

Makes 8 servings

Per serving
Calories 242	Sodium 741 mg.
Total fat 4 g.	Dietary fiber 1 g.
Saturated fat 2 g.	Protein 10 g.
Cholesterol 28 mg.	Carbohydrates 40 g.

A New Twist

GINGER SAUCE

This sauce can be tightly covered and refrigerated for up to 1 week for use with pizza, stir-fries, or pasta. In a small cup, dissolve 1 tablespoon cornstarch in 1 tablespoon water.

In a small saucepan, combine ½ cup soy sauce, ¼ cup + 2 tablespoons packed light brown sugar, ¼ cup white wine or fat-free reduced-sodium chicken broth, 1 tablespoon chopped garlic, 1 tablespoon grated fresh ginger, and 1½ teaspoons chili powder. Bring to a boil over medium-high heat. Reduce the heat to medium-low. Cook, stirring occasionally, for 10 minutes. Add the cornstarch mixture. Cook, stirring, for 1 to 2 minutes, or until thickened. Makes about 1 cup.

Barbecue Chicken and Cheddar Calzones

Photograph on page 68
Hands-on time: 25 minutes
Total time: 50 minutes

- 1 tablespoon cornmeal
- 1 large onion, halved and thinly sliced
- 3/4 pound boneless, skinless chicken breasts, cooked and shredded (see note)
- 1 cup barbecue sauce
- 1 recipe Basic Pizza Dough (page 97) or 2 tubes (10 ounces each) refrigerated pizza dough
- 1 cup (4 ounces) shredded low-fat Cheddar cheese
- 1 egg white, lightly beaten with 1 teaspoon water

Preheat the oven to 375°F. Coat a baking sheet with nonstick spray. Sprinkle with the cornmeal.

Coat a medium nonstick skillet with nonstick spray. Set over medium heat. Add the onion. Cook, stirring occasionally, for 5 to 7 minutes, or until soft. Add the chicken and barbecue sauce. Stir to mix.

Turn the dough out onto a lightly floured work surface. Divide into 4 equal pieces. Roll 1 piece of dough into a 7" circle. Place ½ cup of the chicken mixture on 1 side of the circle, spreading to within 1" of the edge. Sprinkle with ¼ cup of the Cheddar. Brush the edges of the crust with some of the egg-white mixture. Fold the circle in half. Pinch the edges to seal. Repeat with the remaining dough and filling to make a total of 4 calzones.

Transfer to the prepared baking sheet. Brush the calzones with the remaining egg-white mixture. With a sharp knife, make 3 small slashes in the tops of each calzone.

Bake for 20 to 25 minutes, or until the crusts are golden brown. To serve, cut each calzone in half.

Makes 8 servings

Per serving
Calories 357	Sodium 673 mg.
Total fat 5 g.	Dietary fiber 3 g.
Saturated fat 2 g.	Protein 24 g.
Cholesterol 39 mg.	Carbohydrates 51 g.

Cooking Note

Cook the chicken in a broiler or in a large nonstick skillet coated with nonstick spray. Broil or cook over medium-high heat for 5 to 7 minutes per side, or until a thermometer inserted in the thickest portion registers 160°F and the juices run clear. Remove the chicken to a plate. Set aside for 5 minutes. Pull into shreds with a fork.

Good for You

WHOLE GRAINS

The best way to choose a healthy bread or cereal is to make sure that the label identifies the first ingredient as a "whole" grain. For example, breads that list "whole wheat" as the first ingredient are sure to be a healthy choice.

Chicken Pesto Pizza

Hands-on time: 10 minutes
Total time 20 minutes

- 1 tablespoon cornmeal
- $\frac{1}{2}$ recipe Basic Pizza Dough (page 97) or 1 tube (10 ounces) refrigerated pizza dough
- $\frac{1}{3}$ cup Pesto (see page 137) or low-fat prepared pesto
- $\frac{1}{4}$ pound cooked boneless, skinless chicken breasts, cut into small strips
- 1 roasted red pepper, cut into small strips
- $\frac{1}{2}$ cup rinsed and drained water-packed canned artichoke hearts, patted dry and quartered
- $\frac{1}{2}$ cup (2 ounces) crumbled low-fat goat cheese or shredded low-fat Jarlsberg

Preheat the oven to 450°F. Coat a large round pizza pan with nonstick spray. Sprinkle with the cornmeal.

Turn the dough out onto a lightly floured work surface. Roll into a 12" circle. Place on the prepared pan. Spread with the pesto, leaving a $\frac{1}{4}$" border. Arrange the chicken, pepper strips, and artichokes over the top. Dot with the goat cheese or sprinkle with Jarlsberg.

Bake for 10 to 12 minutes, or until the crust is golden brown.

Makes 8 servings

Per serving
Calories 196	*Sodium 234 mg.*
Total fat 6 g.	*Dietary fiber 2 g.*
Saturated fat 2 g.	*Protein 10 g.*
Cholesterol 18 mg.	*Carbohydrates 26 g.*

Good for You

It's Worth Noting

If weight loss is your goal, a log of your daily nutrient intake could be very enlightening. Track fat, calories, and fiber, which all impact your weight and your health. In general, women should consume between 1,200 and 1,800 calories each day, while men can take in up to 2,200 calories, depending on their healthy body weight and exercise level. Fat should account for no more than 30 percent of daily caloric intake. Keep fiber at 20 to 35 grams each day. Make sure you choose nutrient-dense foods that are filling and satisfying. Consult your physician or a registered dietitian to assess your individual needs. Remember that regular exercise completes the equation.

Double-Crust Pizza

Photograph on page 70
Hands-on time: 20 minutes
Total time: 45 minutes

1 tablespoon cornmeal

2 egg whites

1 onion, chopped

2 cloves garlic, chopped

1/2 pound extra-lean ground round beef

1 1/2 cups pasta sauce

1/4 cup chopped fresh parsley and/or basil or oregano or 2 teaspoons dried

2 cups (16 ounces) fat-free ricotta cheese

1 cup (4 ounces) shredded low-fat mozzarella cheese

1/4 teaspoon ground nutmeg

1 recipe Basic Pizza Dough (page 97) or 2 tubes (10 ounces each) refrigerated pizza dough

2 tablespoons (1/2 ounce) grated Parmesan cheese

Preheat the oven to 400°F. Coat a large round pizza pan with nonstick spray. Sprinkle with the cornmeal.

Place 1 egg white in a small bowl. Beat lightly with a fork.

Coat a medium nonstick skillet with nonstick spray. Set over medium heat. Cook the onion and garlic, stirring often, for 3 minutes, or until almost soft. Add the beef and cook, stirring occasionally, for 3 to 5 minutes, or until no longer pink. Stir in the pasta sauce and parsley and/or basil or oregano.

Meanwhile, in a medium bowl, combine the ricotta, 1/2 cup of the mozzarella, the nutmeg, and the remaining egg white.

Turn the dough out onto a lightly floured work surface. Divide the dough into 2 balls. Roll 1 ball into a 12" circle. Place on the prepared pan. Spread the ricotta mixture evenly over the dough, leaving a 1" border. Top with the beef mixture and the remaining 1/2 cup mozzarella. Sprinkle with the Parmesan.

On a lightly floured work surface, roll the remaining dough ball into a 12" circle. Place over the filling. Fold in the edges of the bottom crust. Pinch the crusts to seal. Brush the top and sides of the pie with the egg-white mixture. With a sharp knife, make several small slashes in the top crust.

Bake for 20 to 25 minutes, or until golden brown.

Makes 10 servings

Per serving
Calories 315	Sodium 492 mg.
Total fat 6 g.	Dietary fiber 2 g.
Saturated fat 3 g.	Protein 21 g.
Cholesterol 30 mg.	Carbohydrates 42 g.

Mexican Stuffed Pizza

Replace the pasta sauce with 1 can (15 ounces) Mexican-style tomatoes. Chop the tomatoes finely and add to the cooked beef along with 1 jar (4 ounces) chopped green chile peppers. Cook for 2 to 3 minutes, or until thickened. Replace the chopped parsley and/or basil or oregano with chopped parsley and cilantro. Omit the nutmeg. Add 1/2 teaspoon ground cumin. Substitute low-fat shredded Monterey Jack cheese for the mozzarella.

Caramelized Pear Pizza

Hands-on time: 10 minutes
Total time: 20 minutes

1 tablespoon cornmeal

2 teaspoons + 3 tablespoons sugar

$^1/4$ teaspoon ground cinnamon

2 cups (16 ounces) fat-free ricotta cheese

2 teaspoons butter or margarine

1 large pear, cut into $^1/2$"-thick slices

$^1/4$ cup dried cranberries, softened (see note)

$^1/2$ recipe Basic Pizza Dough (page 97) or 1 tube (10 ounces) refrigerated pizza dough

$^1/3$ cup apricot preserves

2 tablespoons slivered almonds

Preheat the oven to 450°F. Coat a large round pizza pan with nonstick spray. Sprinkle with the cornmeal.

In a small cup, mix 2 teaspoons of the sugar with the cinnamon.

In a small bowl, mix the ricotta with 2 tablespoons of the remaining sugar.

Melt the butter or margarine in a medium nonstick skillet set over medium heat. Add the pear and the remaining 1 tablespoon sugar. Cook for 4 minutes, or until the pear is soft. Add the cranberries. Remove from the heat.

Turn the dough out onto a lightly floured work surface. Roll into a 12" circle. Place on the prepared pan. Spread evenly with the ricotta. Scatter evenly with the pear and cranberries. Dollop the preserves on top. Sprinkle with the almonds. Dust with the cinnamon sugar.

Bake for 8 to 10 minutes, or until the crust is golden brown.

Makes 8 servings

Per serving
Calories 253	*Sodium 206 mg.*
Total fat 3 g.	*Dietary fiber 2 g.*
Saturated fat 1 g.	*Protein 11 g.*
Cholesterol 20 mg.	*Carbohydrates 47 g.*

Cooking Note

To soften dried cranberries, place in a glass measuring cup. Cover with boiling water. Allow to soak for 3 to 5 minutes. Drain.

A New Twist

PIZZA FOR DESSERT

Sweet pizza makes a unique dessert or side dish for brunch. To vary this recipe, try apples, peaches, plums, or bananas in place of the pear. Experiment with various types of dried fruits, berries, or nuts, as well as different flavors of jam to invent your own combinations.

Pasta and More Pasta

Southern Italians have lower rates of heart disease than Americans. Researchers believe that part of the reason may be their low-fat diet that focuses on foods, like pasta, that are high in complex carbohydrates. Southern Italians consume close to 60 pounds of pasta per person per year, compared with only 19 pounds for Americans.

Contrary to the myth that pasta and other carbohydrates make you fat, the reality is that carbohydrates—preferably in the form of whole-grain foods—should form the base of a healthy diet. Pasta fits the bill as a healthy food for those interested in maintaining and improving the health of their heart.

By incorporating pasta—a naturally low-fat complex carbohydrate—into a dish with higher-fat protein, you can cut the fat significantly. Two ounces of dry pasta (approximately 1 cup cooked) have less than 1 gram of fat, 0 milligrams of cholesterol, 0 milligrams of sodium, and just over 200 calories. In addition, pasta provides iron, calcium, and B vitamins.

Good Company

"It is important to watch what you add to pasta because the toppings can change the nutrient profile significantly," says Diana Armstrong, certified culinary professional and instructor for the University Hospitals of Cleveland Synergy Culinary School in Ohio. "Just two tablespoons of olive oil added to one cup of cooked pasta more than doubles the calories.

"We teach our students that one cup of cooked pasta served with chopped fresh herbs and one teaspoon of highly flavored grated Parmesan cheese has just over 200 calories and just under two grams of fat. The same amount of pasta served with two tablespoons of olive oil has about 436 calories and 30 grams of fat," Armstrong says.

Fortunately, pasta's neutral flavor makes it easy to pair with a variety of lean and healthful foods: beans, lentils, vegetables, seafood, lean poultry, lean pork, lean beef, and moderate amounts of highly flavored cheeses. Add because pasta is so versatile, it can go into soups, salads, main dishes, and side dishes.

Recipes

Turkey Tetrazzini

Hands-on time: 15 minutes
Total time: 50 minutes

$1/4$ pound mushrooms, sliced

1 onion, chopped

1 large rib celery, thinly sliced

1 jar (2 ounces) diced pimientos, drained

$1 1/2$ teaspoons Italian seasoning

$1/3$ cup unbleached or all-purpose flour

$2 1/2$ cups 1% milk

$1/3$ cup ($1 1/2$ ounces) grated Parmesan cheese

$1/2$ pound cooked skinless turkey breasts, cut into $1/2$" cubes

$1/4$ teaspoon salt

8 ounces spaghetti, cooked and drained

Preheat the oven to 350°F. Coat a medium baking dish with nonstick spray.

Coat a large nonstick skillet with nonstick spray. Add the mushrooms, onion, and celery. Coat with nonstick spray. Cook, stirring occasionally, over medium-high heat for 4 to 5 minutes, or until soft. Stir in the pimientos and Italian seasoning. Set aside.

Place the flour in a large saucepan. Gradually add the milk, whisking constantly, until smooth. Cook, whisking constantly, over medium heat for 6 to 8 minutes, or until slightly thickened and bubbling.

Remove from the heat. Add the Parmesan. Stir until smooth. Add the turkey, salt, the reserved mushroom mixture, and the spaghetti. Toss to mix. Pour into the prepared baking dish.

Cover and bake for 20 minutes. Uncover and bake for 10 minutes longer, or until bubbly. Remove and let stand for 5 minutes before serving.

Makes 6 servings

Per serving
Calories 335	*Sodium 290 mg.*
Total fat 6 g.	*Dietary fiber 4 g.*
Saturated fat 2 g.	*Protein 24 g.*
Cholesterol 40 mg.	*Carbohydrates 45 g.*

HEALTHFUL HERBS

When you add fresh herbs to food, you are not only adding flavor and color but nutrition as well. Because herbs are plants, they provide us with vitamins A and C, calcium, iron, and other nutrients.

Spicy Shrimp Linguine

Hands-on time: 25 minutes
Total time: 35 minutes

8 ounces linguine

1 onion, chopped

1 small green bell pepper, chopped

1 rib celery, chopped

2 cloves garlic, minced

1 teaspoon Cajun seasoning

3/4 teaspoon dried thyme leaves

1 can (15 ounces) chopped tomatoes

1 cup fat-free reduced-sodium chicken broth

1/2 teaspoon hot-pepper sauce

3/4 pound medium shrimp, peeled and deveined

Cook the pasta according to package directions.

Meanwhile, coat a medium saucepan with nonstick spray. Set over medium heat. Add the onion, bell pepper, celery, garlic, Cajun seasoning, and thyme. Coat with nonstick spray. Cook, stirring often, for 7 minutes, or until soft. Add the tomatoes (with juice), broth, and hot-pepper sauce. Stir to combine. Reduce the heat to low. Cook for 20 minutes.

Add the shrimp. Cook for 2 to 3 minutes, or until opaque.

Place the pasta in a serving bowl. Top with the sauce.

Makes 4 servings

Per serving
Calories 309
Total fat 4 g.
Saturated fat 1 g.
Cholesterol 129 mg.
Sodium 522 mg.
Dietary fiber 4 g.
Protein 26 g.
Carbohydrates 43 g.

Good for You

SELF SERVICE

Many restaurants offer edible freebies—bread with butter or olive oil, chips and salsa—to keep you satisfied while you're waiting for your meal. In reality, these snacks often wreak havoc on your healthy eating plans. Next time you're dining out, try serving yourself a reasonable portion of the snack, then have the rest removed from the table. You'll enjoy your dinner much more knowing that you haven't overindulged beforehand.

Vegetable Lasagna

Hands-on time: 20 minutes
Total time: 1 hour and 15 minutes

1 teaspoon olive oil

1 large zucchini or yellow squash, halved lengthwise and thinly sliced

2 onions, chopped

1 clove garlic, minced

1 teaspoon Italian seasoning

3 cups (1 1/2 pounds) fat-free ricotta cheese

1 box (10 ounces) frozen chopped spinach, thawed and squeezed dry

1 egg white

1/4 teaspoon salt

1 jar (48 ounces) pasta sauce

10 ounces no-boil lasagna noodles

2 cups (8 ounces) shredded low-fat mozzarella cheese

4 tablespoons (1 ounce) grated Parmesan cheese

Preheat the oven to 375°F.

Warm the oil in a large nonstick skillet set over medium-high heat. Add the zucchini or yellow squash, onions, garlic, and Italian seasoning. Cook, stirring often, for 8 to 10 minutes, or until soft.

Meanwhile, in a medium bowl, combine the ricotta, spinach, egg white, and salt.

Pour 2 cups of the pasta sauce into a 13" × 9" baking dish. Spread to cover the bottom. Top with a single layer of the lasagna noodles. Spread with half of the ricotta mixture. Top with half of the vegetables. Sprinkle with 2/3 cup of the mozzarella and 2 tablespoons of the Parmesan. Top with 1 cup of the remaining pasta sauce.

Cover with a single layer of lasagna noodles, the remaining ricotta mixture, and the remaining vegetables. Sprinkle with 2/3 cup of mozzarella and the remaining 2 tablespoons Parmesan. Top with 1 cup of the remaining pasta sauce.

Cover with the remaining lasagna noodles, the remaining 2 cups pasta sauce, and the remaining 2/3 cup mozzarella.

Bake for 45 minutes, or until bubbling. Remove and allow to rest for 10 minutes before cutting.

Makes 10 servings

Per serving

Calories 288	Sodium 664 mg.
Total fat 6 g.	Dietary fiber 6 g.
Saturated fat 3 g.	Protein 24 g.
Cholesterol 38 mg.	Carbohydrates 35 g.

SPINACH

Spinach is a powerhouse vegetable, packing beta-carotene, vitamin C, iron, calcium, and potassium. This dark green leafy vegetable is also high in folic acid. Folic acid, along with a balanced, low-fat eating plan and healthy lifestyle, is a nutrient that is being researched for its possible role in reducing the risk of cardiovascular disease.

Spaghetti with Meatballs

Photograph on opposite page
Hands-on time: 20 minutes
Total time: 55 minutes

MEATBALLS

2 onions, chopped

1/4 cup chopped parsley

3 cloves garlic, minced

2/3 cup fresh bread crumbs

1/4 cup fat-free milk

1 egg, lightly beaten

2 teaspoons Italian seasoning

1/4 teaspoon salt

1/2 pound extra-lean ground round beef

1/2 pound ground turkey breast

2 teaspoons olive oil

SAUCE

2 cans (28 ounces each) tomato sauce

1 can (15 ounces) diced tomatoes

2 tablespoons sugar

2 tablespoons Italian seasoning

12 ounces spaghetti

To make the meatballs: Coat a Dutch oven with nonstick spray. Warm over medium heat. Add the onions, parsley, and garlic. Cook, stirring often, for 8 to 10 minutes, or until the onions are soft. Add a few tablespoons water, if necessary, to prevent the onions from sticking. Remove 1/4 cup of the onion mixture to a large bowl. Set the remainder aside.

To the bowl, add the bread crumbs, milk, egg, Italian seasoning, and salt. Stir to mix. Stir in the beef and turkey. Shape into 12 meatballs, each 2" in diameter.

Return the Dutch oven to the stove top. Warm the oil over medium-high heat. Add the meatballs. Cook, turning often, for 5 minutes, or until well-browned.

To make the sauce: To the Dutch oven, add the tomato sauce, diced tomatoes (with juice), sugar, Italian seasoning, and the reserved onion mixture. Bring to a boil over high heat. Reduce the heat to low. Cover and simmer, stirring occasionally, for 20 to 25 minutes, or until the meatballs are cooked through.

Meanwhile, cook the pasta according to package directions. Place in a serving bowl. Top with the sauce and meatballs.

Makes 6 servings

Per serving
Calories 541 *Sodium 417 mg.*
Total fat 10 g. *Dietary fiber 11 g.*
Saturated fat 3 g. *Protein 29 g.*
Cholesterol 72 mg. *Carbohydrates 87 g.*

CHOOSE LEANER MEATS

Meats are an essential source of protein, iron, and minerals, but they can also be a major source of saturated fat unless you choose the leanest grades and cuts. Look for meats that are labeled "select;" these contain the least fat. The leanest cuts are generally "round" or "loin." Keep in mind that ground beef is often made from the higher-fat cuts of meat. You can ask the butcher to trim and grind a round steak, which yields the leanest form of ground beef. Don't hesitate to ask your butcher to trim the fat for any meat purchase that you choose.

~Spaghetti with Meatballs (page 118)~

119

❤Pasta with Beans and Cajun Salmon (page 143)❤

~Pork Chops with Sauerkraut and Potatoes (page 157)~ 121

❤ Bow-Ties with Chicken and Asparagus (page 146) ❤

❤ Seafood Potpie (page 166) ❤

❤ Mediterranean Penne with Sausage (page 147) ❤

❤ Tortellini Corn Chowder (page 164) ❤

126 ❧Chicken Stew with Dumplings (page 151)❧

❤Potato Salad with Warm Bacon Dressing (page 173)❤

❤ Spaghetti Squash Casserole (page 194) ❤

♥ New Green Bean Casserole (page 187) ♥

❤ Potato Pancakes and Smoked Salmon with Chive Cream (page 172) ❤

♥ Stuffed Acorn Squash (page 195) ♥

132 ❧ Autumn Turkey Salad (page 233) ❧

♥ Fiesta Pasta Salad (page 203) ♥

❧Chinese Chicken Salad (page 232)❧

Ziti with Mushroom Sauce

Hands-on time: 10 minutes
Total time: 45 minutes

$3/4$ pound button and/or cremini mushrooms, sliced

1 small red onion, chopped

2 cloves garlic, minced

$3/4$ cup Madeira or nonalcoholic white wine

1 can ($14\frac{1}{2}$ ounces) fat-free reduced-sodium chicken broth

1 can (15 ounces) diced tomatoes

$1/2$ teaspoon dried rosemary, crumbled

$1/4$ teaspoon salt

8 ounces ziti

$1/2$ cup (2 ounces) grated Parmesan cheese

Coat a large nonstick skillet with nonstick spray. Add the mushrooms, onion, and garlic. Cook, stirring occasionally, for 10 to 12 minutes, or until the onion is soft and the mushrooms start to brown. Add the wine. Cook for 3 to 5 minutes, or until reduced to ¼ cup. Add the broth, tomatoes (with juice), rosemary, and salt. Simmer for 10 to 12 minutes.

Meanwhile, cook the pasta according to package directions. Place in a serving bowl. Add the sauce and Parmesan.

Makes 4 servings

Per serving
Calories 389
Total fat 6 g.
Saturated fat 3 g.
Cholesterol 10 mg.
Sodium 655 mg.
Dietary fiber 7 g.
Protein 21 g.
Carbohydrates 64 g.

SAUCE SOME MORE

Play it Again!

This versatile mushroom sauce can dress up a variety of dishes, not just pasta. You can make a batch and refrigerate it for 1 to 2 days—it actually improves in flavor. Try these tasty ideas.

• Use the mushroom sauce as an omelette filling.

• Spoon warmed mushroom sauce on a baked potato.

• Mix some of the cold mushroom sauce with softened reduced-fat cream cheese for an appetizer or bagel spread.

• Top a reduced-fat Swiss cheeseburger (made with lean ground round beef) with warm mushroom sauce.

• Add slightly warmed mushroom sauce to a savory soufflé batter.

Chinese Pasta Salad

Hands-on time: 10 minutes
Total time: 10 minutes

- 8 ounces angel hair pasta
- 1/2 cup lime juice
- 1/4 cup chopped fresh cilantro
- 1/4 cup rice wine vinegar or white wine vinegar
- 3 tablespoons sugar
- 2 teaspoons toasted sesame oil
- 1/4–1/2 teaspoon crushed red-pepper flakes
- 1/4 English cucumber, halved lengthwise and thinly sliced crosswise
- 5 scallions, cut into 2"-long matchsticks
- 1 small carrot, grated
- 2 tablespoons chopped salted peanuts

Cook the pasta according to package directions. Rinse and drain.

In a large bowl, combine the lime juice, cilantro, vinegar, sugar, oil, and ¼ teaspoon red-pepper flakes. Whisk until the sugar is dissolved. Add the pasta, cucumber, scallions, carrot, and peanuts. Toss to mix. Taste and add up to ¼ teaspoon more red-pepper flakes, if desired.

Makes 6 servings

Per serving

Calories 180	*Sodium 148 mg.*
Total fat 4 g.	*Dietary fiber 2 g.*
Saturated fat 1 g.	*Protein 6 g.*
Cholesterol 0 mg.	*Carbohydrates 32 g.*

SUMMER FARE

"I doubled this fast and easy pasta recipe for a summer gathering of friends," says attorney Susan Margulies. "This light, cool, and tangy dish went well with side dishes of fruit and salad and a dessert of fortune cookies. The cilantro in the oil added great flavor and made this pasta salad more unusual than other cold noodle dishes."

Potatoes, Pasta, and Green Beans with Pesto

Hands-on time: 5 minutes
Total time: 20 minutes

³⁄₄	pound small red potatoes, sliced ¹⁄₄" thick
¹⁄₈	teaspoon salt
¹⁄₈	teaspoon ground black pepper
8	ounces linguine
6	ounces green beans, trimmed and cut into 2" to 3" pieces
¹⁄₂	cup Pesto (at right) or ¹⁄₂ cup low-fat prepared pesto

Preheat the oven to 425°F. Coat a baking sheet with nonstick spray.

Place the potatoes in a single layer on the prepared baking sheet. Coat lightly with nonstick spray. Season with the salt and pepper. Bake for 20 minutes, or until golden and tender.

Meanwhile, cook the pasta according to package directions; add the beans during the last 4 minutes of cooking time. Reserve ¼ cup of the cooking water.

Place the pasta, beans, and potatoes in a serving bowl. Add the pesto. Toss to coat, adding up to ¼ cup of the reserved cooking water, if necessary.

Makes 4 servings

Per serving
Calories 286	*Sodium 280 mg.*
Total fat 7 g.	*Dietary fiber 6 g.*
Saturated fat 1 g.	*Protein 11 g.*
Cholesterol 2 mg.	*Carbohydrates 47 g.*

A New Twist

PESTO

This pesto can be frozen for up to 3 months in an airtight container. To use, spoon out the required amount of frozen pesto needed to add to pizza, soup, pasta, or a sandwich. In the bowl of a food processor or blender, combine 2½ cups packed fresh basil leaves, ¾ cup packed fresh parsley leaves, 2 tablespoons olive oil, 3 cloves garlic, 2 tablespoons toasted pine nuts or walnuts, and a pinch each of salt and ground black pepper. Pulse to finely chop. Sprinkle with ¼ cup grated Parmesan cheese. With the machine running, add ¼ cup fat-free reduced-sodium chicken broth, 1 tablespoon at a time, until the mixture is the consistency of prepared mustard. Makes 1 cup.

The World's Easiest Sauces

Pesto originated in Genoa, Italy, as an easy, no-cook fresh basil and olive oil sauce for pasta. But the basic method lends itself to many variations that can be made lower in fat. To use the following pestos as a pasta sauce, cook 16 ounces of pasta according to package directions. Reserve ¼ cup of the cooking water. Place the pasta in a serving bowl. Add the pesto and about 2 tablespoons of the reserved cooking water. Toss and add up to 2 tablespoons more water to make the pesto cling nicely to the pasta.

Asian Pesto. In a blender or food processor, combine 1 can (16 ounces) rinsed and drained water chestnuts, 1 tablespoon peanut butter, ½ cup soy sauce, ¼ cup honey, ⅓ cup rice wine vinegar or white wine vinegar, 3 large cloves garlic, and 1 tablespoon toasted sesame oil. Process until pureed. Makes 1½ cups.

Olive Pesto. In a blender or food processor, combine 1 tablespoon olive oil, ¼ cup fat-free reduced-sodium chicken broth, 2 large cloves garlic, ½ cup chopped fresh or drained canned tomatoes, 3 tablespoons pitted olives, 1½ cups loosely packed fresh basil leaves, 1 tablespoon balsamic vinegar, and a pinch each of salt and ground black pepper. Process until pureed. Makes 1 cup.

Roasted Red Pepper Pesto. In a blender or food processor, combine 1⅓ cups diced roasted red peppers (patted dry), ¾ cup fresh parsley, ⅓ cup toasted pine nuts, 2 large cloves garlic, 1 tablespoon wine vinegar, 1 tablespoon grated Parmesan cheese, and a pinch each of salt and ground black pepper. Process until pureed. Makes 1 cup.

South-of-the-Border Pesto. In a blender or food processor, combine 1 can (19 ounces) rinsed and drained black beans, 1 seeded jalapeño chile pepper (wear plastic gloves when handling), 2 cloves garlic, ½ cup loosely packed fresh cilantro leaves, 1 teaspoon chili powder, and 2 tablespoons fat-free sour cream. Process until coarsely pureed. Makes 1½ cups.

Sun-Dried Tomato Pesto. In a blender or food processor, combine ⅔ cup reconstituted dry-pack sun-dried tomatoes, 1 cup fresh oregano leaves, 1 tablespoon olive oil, 1 tablespoon reduced-sodium vegetable broth, 1 small onion, 2 large cloves garlic, 1 tablespoon wine vinegar, and a pinch each of salt and ground black pepper. Process until pureed. Makes 1 cup.

Orzo Milanese

Hands-on time: 20 minutes
Total time: 20 minutes

- 1 teaspoon olive oil
- 1 small onion, minced
- 1 clove garlic, minced
- ³/₄ cup orzo pasta
- 3 cups fat-free reduced-sodium chicken broth
- ¹/₂ cup frozen peas
- ¹/₈ teaspoon crushed saffron threads
- 2 tablespoons (¹/₂ ounce) grated Parmesan cheese

Warm the oil in a medium saucepan set over medium heat. Add the onion and garlic. Cook, stirring often, for 3 minutes, or until soft. Add the orzo. Cook, stirring constantly, for 2 minutes, or until the orzo is well-coated. Stir in the broth, peas, and saffron. Increase the heat to high. Bring to a boil. Reduce the heat to medium-low. Cover and simmer, stirring occasionally, for 10 minutes, or until the orzo is tender but still holds its shape. Remove from the heat and allow to rest for 3 minutes. Stir in the Parmesan.

Makes 6 servings

Per serving
Calories 147	*Sodium 145 mg.*
Total fat 2 g.	*Dietary fiber 1 g.*
Saturated fat 1 g.	*Protein 8 g.*
Cholesterol 2 mg.	*Carbohydrates 23 g.*

The Good, the Bad, and the Balanced

Don't think of individual foods as being "good" for you or "bad" for you, but look at what you eat for a day or a week as a whole. Just as a puzzle isn't complete without all the pieces, a healthy eating plan requires many different foods to complete the picture.

Cheesy Rotelle with Broccoli

Hands-on time: 10 minutes
Total time: 20 minutes

10 ounces rotelle pasta

 1 box (10 ounces) frozen broccoli
    spears, thawed and cut into
    1" pieces

 2 tablespoons unbleached or
    all-purpose flour

 2 cups 1% milk

 3 tablespoons (³⁄4 ounce) crumbled
    Gorgonzola or blue cheese

¹⁄3 cup (1¹⁄2 ounces) grated Parmesan
    cheese

¹⁄8 teaspoon salt

¹⁄4 cup chopped walnuts, toasted

Cook the pasta according to package directions; add the broccoli during the last 4 minutes of cooking time.

Meanwhile, place the flour in a medium saucepan. Gradually whisk in the milk until smooth. Cook, stirring often, over medium heat for 5 minutes, or until the mixture boils and thickens. Add the Gorgonzola or blue cheese, Parmesan, and salt. Stir until smooth. Place the pasta, broccoli, and walnuts in a serving bowl. Add the milk mixture. Toss to coat.

Makes 4 servings

Per serving
Calories 416   *Sodium 412 mg.*
Total fat 11 g.   *Dietary fiber 5 g.*
Saturated fat 4 g.   *Protein 21 g.*
Cholesterol 16 mg.   *Carbohydrates 60 g.*

Good for You

LESS IS MORE FLAVOR

By choosing small amounts of full-flavored cheeses to garnish a dish rather than melting large measures of bland-tasting cheeses in a sauce, you can cut down significantly on calories, fat, and saturated fat. For greatest flavor impact, turn to feta, Parmesan, Jarlsberg, Gorgonzola, Cheddar, and aged Gruyère.

Macaroni and Cheese

Hands-on time: 15 minutes
Total time: 35 minutes

- 1/4 cup unbleached or all-purpose flour
- 2 1/2 cups 1% milk
- 1 clove garlic, halved
- 1/2 teaspoon dry mustard
- 1/4 teaspoon salt
- 1/4 teaspoon ground red pepper
- 1 1/3 cups (5 1/2 ounces) shredded low-fat extra-sharp Cheddar cheese
- 1/2 pound macaroni, cooked and drained
- 2 tablespoons dry bread crumbs
- 2 tablespoons (1/2 ounce) grated Parmesan cheese

Preheat the oven to 350°F. Coat a medium baking dish with nonstick spray.

Place the flour in a medium saucepan. Gradually add the milk, whisking constantly, until smooth. Add the garlic, mustard, salt, and pepper. Place over medium heat. Cook, whisking constantly, for 7 to 8 minutes, or until thickened. Remove from the heat. Remove the garlic and discard. Add the Cheddar. Stir until smooth. Add the macaroni. Stir to mix. Pour into the prepared baking dish.

In a small bowl, combine the bread crumbs and Parmesan. Sprinkle over the casserole. Bake for 15 to 20 minutes, or until bubbling and lightly browned.

Makes 6 servings

Per serving

Calories 303	*Sodium 423 mg.*
Total fat 8 g.	*Dietary fiber 1 g.*
Saturated fat 5 g.	*Protein 16 g.*
Cholesterol 23 mg.	*Carbohydrates 39 g.*

A New Twist

BACON AND TOMATO MACARONI

Pat dry and crumble 3 strips of turkey bacon. Core a large tomato and cut it in half through the middle. With your finger, push out and discard the seeds. Cut each half into 6 slices. Pour half the macaroni and cheese mixture into the prepared baking dish. Cover with a single layer of tomato slices. Sprinkle with the bacon pieces. Top with the remaining macaroni and cheese mixture, bread crumbs, and Parmesan.

Stir-Fried Linguine with Shrimp

Hands-on time: 20 minutes
Total time: 30 minutes

STIR-FRY SAUCE

3 tablespoons fat-free reduced-sodium chicken broth

3 tablespoons soy sauce

2 tablespoons sugar

1 serrano chile pepper, seeded and minced (optional); wear plastic gloves when handling

2 large cloves garlic, minced

1 1/2 tablespoons grated fresh ginger

1 teaspoon cornstarch

STIR-FRY

2 teaspoons vegetable oil

3/4 pound large shrimp, peeled, deveined, and halved lengthwise

1 bunch scallions, sliced diagonally into 1" pieces

1 cup snow peas, cut into matchsticks

1 red bell pepper, thinly sliced

1 carrot, cut into matchsticks

1/2 pound linguine, cooked and drained

To make the stir-fry sauce: In a medium bowl, combine the broth, soy sauce, sugar, chile pepper (if desired), garlic, ginger, and cornstarch. Whisk to mix. Set aside.

To make the stir-fry: Warm the oil in a large non-stick skillet set over medium-high heat. Add the shrimp. Cook for 1 minute. Add the scallions, snow peas, bell pepper, and carrot. Cook, stirring often, for 2 minutes.

Stir the sauce and add to the pan. Cook for 2 to 3 minutes, or until slightly thickened. Add the linguine. Cook, tossing, for 1 to 2 minutes longer, or until warmed through.

Makes 4 servings

Per serving
Calories 315
Total fat 4 g.
Saturated fat 1 g.
Cholesterol 121 mg.
Sodium 712 mg.
Dietary fiber 4 g.
Protein 22 g.
Carbohydrates 48 g.

Good for You

STORED RIGHT

Keep unused fruits and vegetables nutritious by properly storing them. When cut fruits and vegetables are exposed to air, they dry out and lose valuable vitamins and minerals. So try to cut fruits and vegetables just before using whenever possible. Refrigerate produce in vented resealable plastic bags made especially for fruit and vegetable storage.

Pasta with Beans and Cajun Salmon

Photograph on page 120
Hands-on time: 15 minutes
Total time: 30 minutes

8 ounces penne pasta

1 onion, chopped

2 cloves garlic, minced

6 plum tomatoes, chopped

$1/3$ cup chopped fresh basil

1 can (15 ounces) cannellini beans, rinsed and drained

$1^1/2$ cups fat-free reduced-sodium chicken broth

4 salmon fillets (4 ounces each), skin removed

$1/2$ teaspoon Cajun seasoning

Cook the pasta according to package directions. Drain and return to the pot.

Meanwhile, coat a large nonstick skillet with nonstick spray. Set over medium heat. Add the onion and garlic. Cook, stirring often, for 5 to 7 minutes, or until soft. Add the tomatoes and basil. Cook, stirring occasionally, for 4 to 5 minutes, or until the tomatoes are soft. Add the beans and broth. Simmer for 3 to 4 minutes, or until slightly reduced. Stir into the pasta and cover partially.

Rinse the skillet and wipe dry with paper towels. Set over medium-high heat until hot. Coat both sides of the salmon with nonstick spray. Sprinkle with Cajun seasoning. Place the salmon in the pan. Cook for 4 to 5 minutes per side, or until the fish flakes easily.

To serve, spoon the pasta mixture onto 4 plates. Top each serving with a salmon fillet.

Makes 4 servings

Per serving
Calories 509   *Sodium 382 mg.*
Total fat 14 g.   *Dietary fiber 7 g.*
Saturated fat 3 g.   *Protein 36 g.*
Cholesterol 67 mg.   *Carbohydrates 57 g.*

FISH WISH

Heart-healthy omega-3 fatty acids, which work to lower harmful fat and cholesterol levels in the bloodstream, are highest in dark-fleshed fish such as salmon, mackerel, and herring. Health experts recommend eating 8 ounces of fish weekly not only to increase beneficial omega-3 fatty acids but also to decrease the consumption of saturated fat from eating meat.

Spaghetti with Meat Sauce

Hands-on time: 15 minutes
Total time: 40 minutes

2 teaspoons olive oil

1 onion, chopped

1 rib celery, minced

1 carrot, chopped

2 cloves garlic, minced

³/4 pound extra-lean ground round beef

1 cup dry red wine or nonalcoholic red wine

1¹/2 tablespoons unbleached or all-purpose flour

1¹/2 cups fat-free milk

1 can (28 ounces) crushed tomatoes

1 can (8 ounces) tomato sauce

2 tablespoons chopped parsley

1 teaspoon dried basil or oregano

12 ounces spaghetti

Warm the oil in a large nonstick skillet set over medium-high heat. Add the onion, celery, carrot, and garlic. Cook, stirring often, for 7 to 10 minutes, or until tender. Add the beef. Cook for 3 minutes, or until no longer pink. Add the wine. Cook for 2 minutes, or until the wine is almost evaporated.

Place the flour in a small bowl. Gradually add the milk, whisking constantly, until blended. Add to the skillet. Cook, stirring constantly, for 2 minutes, or until the sauce is thickened and reduced by one-third. Add the crushed tomatoes, tomato sauce, parsley, and basil or oregano. Simmer for 15 minutes.

Meanwhile, cook the pasta according to package directions. Place in a serving bowl. Top with the sauce.

Makes 6 servings

Per serving
Calories 450	*Sodium 495 mg.*
Total fat 8 g.	*Dietary fiber 9 g.*
Saturated fat 3 g.	*Protein 26 g.*
Cholesterol 22 mg.	*Carbohydrates 70 g.*

WINE NOT?

For individuals who choose to abstain from alcohol but still want to enjoy the flavor and potential health benefits of a fine wine, nonalcoholic wine is the beverage of choice. An added bonus is that it reduces the calories by up to 50 percent. For finest flavor, choose de-alcoholized wines made from premium varietal grapes that are fermented to dryness. Look for the phrase "cold filtration process" on the label to guarantee that the de-alcoholized wine was not heated to remove the alcohol.

Carbohydrates: Fuel for Life

Carbohydrates are your body's primary source of energy. Once thought of as fattening, complex carbohydrates are now hailed as the foundation for a healthy diet, providing not only energy but vitamins, minerals, and fiber as well.

Health experts recommend that up to 60 percent of your total caloric intake should come from carbohydrate sources, with the emphasis on the complex variety contained in whole grains, beans, and vegetables. So if your goal is 2,000 calories a day, about 1,200 should come from carbohydrate sources.

The U.S. Department of Agriculture Food Guide Pyramid identifies the foods that contain these important complex carbohydrates. The base of the pyramid recommends 6 to 11 servings a day of whole grains, cereals, pasta, and rice, 3 to 5 servings of vegetables, and 2 to 3 servings from the meat group (in which the complex carbohydrates beans and legumes are included.)

With the exception of fruit and fruit juices—which can contain fiber, vitamins, and minerals— the simple carbohydrates should be eaten far more sparingly than complex carbohydrates. Simple carbohydrate foods fuel the body but contain mostly empty calories that are devoid of nutrients. Examples include sodas, candies, cookies, and desserts. Also limit intake of processed foods that contain large amounts of sweeteners such as corn syrup, high-fructose corn syrup, honey, sugar, turbinado sugar, maple syrup, brown sugar, and dextrose.

Bow-Ties with Chicken and Asparagus

Photograph on page 122
Hands-on time: 25 minutes
Total time: 35 minutes

8 ounces bow-tie pasta (farfalle)

³/₄ pound asparagus, ends trimmed, cut into 1¹/₂" pieces

2 teaspoons olive oil

2 large onions, quartered and thinly sliced

¹/₂ cup white wine or nonalcoholic white wine

3 cloves garlic, minced

2 teaspoons minced fresh rosemary or 1 teaspoon dried, crushed

¹/₂ pound boneless, skinless smoked chicken breasts, cut into 2" strips

1 cup fat-free reduced-sodium chicken broth

¹/₃ cup (1¹/₂ ounces) grated Parmesan cheese

Cook the pasta according to package directions; add the asparagus during the last 3 minutes of cooking time.

Meanwhile, warm the oil in a large nonstick skillet over medium heat. Add the onions. Cover and cook, stirring often, for 20 to 25 minutes, or until very soft.

Increase the heat to medium-high. Add the wine, garlic, and rosemary. Stir to combine. Cook for 5 minutes, or until the wine is almost evaporated. Add the chicken and broth. Cook for 5 minutes, or until the broth is reduced by one-third.

Place the pasta and asparagus in a serving bowl. Top with the sauce. Sprinkle with the Parmesan.

Makes 4 servings

Per serving
Calories 383   *Sodium 934 mg.*
Total fat 8 g.   *Dietary fiber 4 g.*
Saturated fat 2 g.   *Protein 24 g.*
Cholesterol 37 mg.   *Carbohydrates 51 g.*

A New Twist

CARAMELIZING ONIONS

Caramelized onions are perfectly wonderful accompaniment to many dishes. Try them as a pizza topping with crumbled blue cheese and chopped fresh rosemary, as an omelette filling, or an addition to a lean roast beef sandwich.

To make a caramelized onion relish, cook the onions in 1 tablespoon butter for 10 minutes, or until lightly browned. Add 1 tablespoon sherry vinegar or balsamic vinegar. Cook over low heat for 15 minutes. Serve with grilled fish, lamb, or chicken.

Mediterranean Penne with Sausage

Photograph on page 124
Hands-on time: 15 minutes
Total time: 45 minutes

2 red bell peppers, chopped

1 small bulb fennel, quartered lengthwise and thinly sliced

1 large onion, chopped

1 small eggplant, peeled and cut into small chunks

1 clove garlic, minced

3/4 pound Italian-style turkey sausage, casings removed

1 jar (26 ounces) pasta sauce

2 cups water

2 teaspoons fennel seeds, crushed

1/2 teaspoon crushed red-pepper flakes

8 ounces penne pasta

Coat a large nonstick skillet with nonstick spray. Add the bell peppers, fennel bulb, onion, eggplant, and garlic. Coat with nonstick spray. Cook, stirring often, over medium heat for 5 minutes, or until the fennel starts to soften. Add the sausage. Cook, breaking up the sausage with the back of a spoon, for 3 minutes, or until no longer pink.

Add the pasta sauce, water, fennel seeds, and red-pepper flakes. Stir to mix. Cover and reduce the heat to low. Cook for 20 to 25 minutes, or until the vegetables are tender.

Meanwhile, cook the pasta according to package directions. Reserve ½ cup of the cooking water. Place the pasta in a serving bowl. Top with the sauce. Add up to ½ cup of the reserved cooking water, if needed, for the sauce to coat the pasta.

Makes 6 servings

Per serving
Calories 319
Total fat 7 g.
Saturated fat 2 g.
Cholesterol 48 mg.

Sodium 654 mg.
Dietary fiber 7 g.
Protein 17 g.
Carbohydrates 46 g.

RED BELL PEPPERS

Red bell peppers are bright, beautiful, and rich in nutrients. Filled with beta-carotene and vitamin C, this colorful vegetable contains powerful substances called antioxidants, which help prevent cancer, heart disease, and other degenerative health conditions. Keep pepper slices in the refrigerator as a quick snack. Or, when peppers are in season, roast a batch to have on hand in the refrigerator or freezer.

Noodle Pudding

Hands-on time: 15 minutes
Total time: 1 hour and 10 minutes

PUDDING

2 cups (16 ounces) 1% cottage cheese

1 cup (8 ounces) fat-free sour cream

1 cup liquid egg substitute

1 cup fat-free milk

1/2 cup sugar

2 teaspoons vanilla extract

1/2 teaspoon salt

1 can (8 ounces) crushed pineapple, drained

1/2 cup raisins

1/2 pound medium egg noodles, cooked and drained

STREUSEL TOPPING

2 1/2 cups cornflakes

1/3 cup sliced almonds

1/4 cup packed light brown sugar

3/4 teaspoon ground cinnamon

To make the pudding: Preheat the oven to 350°F. Coat a 13" × 9" baking dish with nonstick spray.

In a food processor or blender, combine the cottage cheese, sour cream, egg substitute, milk, sugar, vanilla extract, and salt. Process until smooth. Transfer to a large bowl. Add the pineapple, raisins, and noodles. Stir to mix. Pour into the prepared baking dish.

To make the streusel topping: Rinse the food processor bowl or blender and wipe dry with a paper towel. Add the cornflakes, almonds,

brown sugar, and cinnamon to the bowl. Pulse until the cornflakes are crushed. Sprinkle over the pudding. Lightly press the topping into place.

Bake for 40 to 45 minutes, or until set. Remove and allow to stand for 10 minutes before serving.

Makes 12 servings

Per serving
Calories 247   *Sodium 369 mg.*
Total fat 3 g.   *Dietary fiber 1 g.*
Saturated fat 1 g.   *Protein 12 g.*
Cholesterol 20 mg.   *Carbohydrates 44 g.*

Can Care

Before you purchase canned fruits or vegetables, examine the can. While a dented can is presumably safe as long as the factory seal is still in place, be able to recognize other warning signs. Never purchase a leaking can or one with a broken seal or a rusty or dirty label. A can with bulging ends may be an indication of botulism, a potentially deadly food-borne illness.

One-Dish Meals

One-dish meals serve two masters—convenience and health—equally well. One easy recipe puts a great-tasting meal on the table. The same easy recipe provides a complete nutritional balance. What more could a busy cook ask for?

Practically speaking, eliminating the task of making multiple recipes to create a single meal can be a real time-saver. And many one-dish meals—casseroles, stews, and hearty soups—lend themselves to advance preparation. No flavor is lost if they are refrigerated and/or frozen then reheated before serving. Flexibility like this is a real plus when adapting to a new style of healthier cooking.

One-Stop Nutrition

With Americans striving to reduce the fat in their diets while upping the consumption of vegetables and grains, one-dish meals provide an ideal way to ease meat off the center of the dinner plate.

"It is a breeze to combine fresh or frozen vegetables with easy-to-prepare grains and smaller amounts of lean meats, poultry, and seafood," says Barrie Rosencrans, R.D., licensed dietitian at the University Hospitals of Cleveland Synergy Program in Ohio. "Most important, these well-balanced meals will satisfy your appetite and support your overall health since they are rich in carbohydrates, vitamins, and minerals and low in fat."

Because these recipes are complete meals, they call for a few more ingredients than the average main dish that needs two or three side dishes to make it complete. So review ingredient lists before you decide on a one-dish recipe. And by all means, be flexible. If there is an ingredient that you don't have in your cupboard or don't particularly like, don't use it.

Don't let one or more ingredients discourage you from making a dish. Be creative. If you don't like broccoli, replace it with green beans or spinach. The same principle applies to grains or protein sources. If you don't care for barley, try rice or bulgur instead. Replace canned salmon with canned tuna, and so on. You'll find that you can create personalized one-dish dinners that please those you love and make cooking enjoyable.

Recipes

Chicken Stew with Dumplings

Photograph on page 126
Hands-on time: 15 minutes
Total time: 50 minutes

STEW

2 pounds chicken parts, skinned

1/4 teaspoon salt

2 onions, chopped

2 carrots, sliced

2 ribs celery, sliced

3 cups fat-free reduced-sodium chicken broth

1 bay leaf

1 teaspoon dried thyme

1/2 cup (4 ounces) fat-free sour cream

2 tablespoons unbleached or all-purpose flour

DUMPLINGS

1 cup unbleached or all-purpose flour

1 1/2 teaspoons baking powder

1/2 cup buttermilk

1 egg white, lightly beaten

To make the stew: Pat the chicken dry. Sprinkle with 1/8 teaspoon of the salt. Coat lightly on all sides with nonstick spray.

Place the chicken in a Dutch oven set over medium-high heat. Cook, turning occasionally, for 3 to 5 minutes, or until lightly golden on all sides. Remove to a plate. Set aside.

Coat the bottom of the pot with nonstick spray. Add the onions, carrots, and celery. Cook, stirring occasionally, over medium-high heat for 5 minutes, or until the onions start to soften. Add the broth, bay leaf, thyme, the remaining 1/8 teaspoon salt, and the reserved chicken. Increase the heat to high. Bring to a boil. Reduce the heat to medium-low. Simmer for 10 minutes.

In a small bowl, combine the sour cream and flour. Whisk until smooth. Add to the chicken mixture. Stir until thickened.

To make the dumplings: In a medium bowl, combine the flour and baking powder. Add the buttermilk and egg white. Stir until just mixed. The batter will be slightly lumpy.

Evenly divide the batter into dollops and drop onto the chicken mixture. Cover the pot and cook at a gentle simmer over medium-low heat for 25 minutes, or until a thermometer inserted in the thickest portion of the chicken registers 170°F and the juices run clear.

Remove and discard the bay leaf before serving.

Makes 4 servings

Per serving

Calories 476	Sodium 668 mg.
Total fat 9 g.	Dietary fiber 4 g.
Saturated fat 2 g.	Protein 52 g.
Cholesterol 122 mg.	Carbohydrates 44 g.

Cooking Note

It is important to keep the temperature of the stew at a very gentle simmer. Otherwise, the sour cream will separate when it's added. If it does happen to separate, keep stirring vigorously for 3 to 4 minutes, and the sauce will come back together. Add the dumplings and continue with the recipe.

Last-Minute Cooking

A quick dinner from the pantry can be a tasty reality in just minutes if you stock your cupboard right. Here are top picks for a well-stocked larder.

Pasta and grains. From broad lasagna noodles to tiny couscous and all the shapes in between, pasta is *the* essential of a quick pantry. In the time that it takes to cook pasta, a variety of quick sauces can be put together. Also stock grains such as rice, quick-cooking barley, quinoa, or bulgur for terrific additions to soups and stews and as a nutrient-rich base for pilafs and stuffings.

Pizza pizzazz. Bottled pizza sauce, a thicker version of pasta sauce, can be spread onto prebaked pizza shells, pitas, tortillas, bagels, or English muffins. In small quantities, olive pastes and low-fat herb pestos add excitement to your favorite Italian pie.

Canned fish and poultry. Tuna, salmon, or chicken packed in water are perfect for quick sandwich fillings. Just combine with low-fat mayonnaise and spread on whole-grain bread, a roll, or a pita. For additional flavor, add some pimientos, pickle relish, flavored mustards, diced celery, minced fresh herbs, or onion. These shelf-stable proteins are also perfect for end-of-the-week casseroles.

Condensed soups. Choose low-fat versions of popular condensed soups such as cream of mushroom, cream of broccoli, and even cream of roasted garlic. Try them in casseroles or rice side dishes or as the base of a creamy low-fat sauce to top poultry, fish, or pasta.

Canned chili. Low-fat canned chili is a versatile item to top a baked potato, use as a sauce base for a Mexican rice dish, or serve on its own topped with low-fat cheese and reduced-fat or fat-free sour cream. Add more heat with canned diced jalapeño chile peppers or hot-pepper sauce.

Mexican products. With fat-free refried beans, salsa, diced chile peppers, rice, and tortillas close at hand, you can prepare a Mexican meal in no time.

Reduced-fat baking mixes. Meals like chicken and dumplings and hamburger pie become easier to make and a lot lower in fat and calories.

Assorted canned products. Keep on hand various kinds of tomato products, including diced tomatoes, tomato puree, assorted canned beans, baby corn, sweet potatoes, fruits packed in fruit juice, fruit juices, and nectars. To make bottled pasta sauce go from simple to spectacular, also stock up on capers, water-packed artichoke hearts, olives, and roasted red peppers. These items can be easily added to your sauce prior to heating to give it a whole new flavor.

Chicken and Mushroom Pasta Casserole

Hands-on time: 10 minutes
Total time: 40 minutes

1/2 pound boneless, skinless chicken breasts

1 large portobello mushroom cap, cut in strips

1 onion, halved and sliced

8 ounces small rigatoni pasta, cooked and drained

2 cans (10 ounces each) low-fat, reduced-sodium condensed cream of mushroom soup

2 cups water

2 roasted red peppers, coarsely chopped

1/4 cup chopped parsley

1/4 teaspoon salt

1/3 cup (1 1/2 ounces) grated Parmesan cheese

Preheat the oven to 375°F. Coat a 13" × 9" baking dish with nonstick spray.

Pat the chicken dry. Coat both sides with nonstick spray. Place in a large skillet set over medium-high heat. Cook for 3 to 4 minutes per side, or until golden. Remove the chicken and set aside.

Add the mushroom. Coat with nonstick spray. Cook, stirring, for 5 minutes, or until soft. Remove and set aside with the chicken.

Add the onion. Coat with nonstick spray. Cook, stirring, for 5 minutes, or until lightly golden.

Cut the chicken into strips. Place in a large bowl. Add the mushroom, onion, pasta, soup, water, peppers, parsley, and salt. Stir to mix. Spoon into the prepared baking dish. Sprinkle with the Parmesan.

Cover loosely with foil. Bake for 20 minutes, or until hot and bubbly.

Makes 6 servings

Per serving
Calories 271	Sodium 757 mg.
Total fat 5 g.	Dietary fiber 3 g.
Saturated fat 2 g.	Protein 17 g.
Cholesterol 29 mg.	Carbohydrates 39 g.

A New Twist

ROASTED RED PEPPERS

Fresh-roasted red bell peppers are sweeter and more flavorful than jarred roasted peppers, which are a good stand-in when you're in a hurry. To roast bell peppers, preheat the oven to 450°F. Place the peppers on a baking sheet in the upper third of the oven for 30 minutes, turning occasionally, or until they are blistered and charred. Remove to a paper bag. Allow to cool. Peel and discard the blackened skin. Remove and discard the stem and seeds. Peppers can also be roasted under a broiler, over a charcoal or gas grill, or even over a gas stove-top flame with long-handled tongs and a pot holder. Turn the peppers around as they char and blister.

Chicken Fajitas

Hands-on time: 15 minutes
Total time: 30 minutes

2 tablespoons lime juice

2 tablespoons fat-free reduced-sodium chicken broth

2 cloves garlic, minced

1/2 teaspoon dried oregano

1/8 teaspoon salt

1 pound boneless, skinless chicken breasts, cut into thin strips

8 flour tortillas (6" diameter)

1 medium red onion, sliced into thin wedges

2 green and/or yellow bell peppers, cut into 1/2"-wide strips

2 cups finely shredded green leaf lettuce

1/2 cup (2 ounces) shredded low-fat Cheddar or Monterey Jack cheese

1/2 cup salsa

1/2 cup (4 ounces) fat-free sour cream

In a medium bowl, combine the lime juice, broth, garlic, oregano, and salt. Add the chicken. Toss to coat evenly. Place in the refrigerator to marinate for 20 minutes.

Preheat the oven to 350°F. Wrap the tortillas in foil. Bake for 10 minutes, or until warmed through. Turn the oven off, but do not remove the tortillas.

Meanwhile, coat a large nonstick skillet with nonstick spray. Add the onion and bell peppers. Coat with nonstick spray. Cook, stirring occasionally, over medium-high heat for 6 to 8 minutes, or until crisp-tender. Remove to a bowl. Cover loosely with foil.

Coat the skillet with nonstick spray. Remove the chicken from the marinade. Place in the skillet. Discard the marinade. Cook, stirring, for 3 to 4 minutes until the juices run clear. Return the onion and bell peppers to the pan. Toss for 1 minute to heat through.

Arrange the tortillas on 4 plates. Spoon the chicken mixture over the tortillas. Top with lettuce, cheese, salsa, and sour cream.

Makes 4 servings

Per serving
Calories 420	Sodium 741 mg.
Total fat 7 g.	Dietary fiber 14 g.
Saturated fat 3 g.	Protein 46 g.
Cholesterol 106 mg.	Carbohydrates 40 g.

FAJITA FUTURES

Play it Again!

It's easy to double the Chicken Fajitas recipe to have the base for a future meal. For a quick breakfast, scramble some eggs and heat the leftover fajitas in a microwave oven. Wrap everything in a whole-wheat tortilla for a meal that you can take with you. For brunch, make a Southwestern omelette by adding 1/2 teaspoon ground cumin to the eggs. Fill with the fajita mixture and a couple tablespoons of shredded low-fat Monterey Jack. For an easy lunch or dinner main dish, toss the fajita mixture over some cooked pasta and top with some salsa.

Mexican Lasagna

Hands-on time: 15 minutes
Total time: 55 minutes

- 1 pound boneless, skinless chicken breasts, cut into strips
- 1 large onion, halved and cut into thin wedges
- 1 large clove garlic, minced
- 2 cups (16 ounces) fat-free ricotta cheese
- 1 cup (8 ounces) reduced-fat sour cream
- 1 jar (4 ounces) chopped green chile peppers
- $\frac{1}{2}$ cup chopped fresh cilantro (optional)
- 2 teaspoons ground cumin
- $\frac{1}{8}$ teaspoon salt
- 6 plum tomatoes, chopped
- 8 corn tortillas (6" diameter), cut in half
- $1\frac{1}{4}$ cups (5 ounces) shredded low-fat Monterey Jack cheese

Preheat the oven to 350°F. Coat a 13" × 9" baking dish with nonstick spray.

Coat a large nonstick skillet with nonstick spray. Set over medium heat. Add the chicken. Cook, turning several times, for 5 minutes, or until no longer pink. Remove to a medium bowl. Wipe the skillet with a paper towel. Coat with nonstick spray. Place over medium heat. Add the onion and garlic. Cover and cook, stirring occasionally, for 7 to 8 minutes, or until lightly browned. Add to the chicken in the bowl.

In another medium bowl, combine the ricotta, sour cream, chile peppers, cilantro (if desired), cumin, and salt.

Spread 1 cup of the tomatoes across the bottom of the prepared baking dish. Arrange half of the tortillas evenly over the tomatoes. Spread half of the ricotta mixture over the tortillas. Top with half of the chicken mixture. Top with 1 cup of the remaining tomatoes and $\frac{1}{2}$ cup of the Monterey Jack. Repeat the layering sequence with the remaining tortillas, ricotta mixture, and chicken mixture. Sprinkle with the remaining 1 cup tomatoes and $\frac{3}{4}$ cup Monterey Jack.

Bake for 30 minutes, or until heated through. Loosely cover with foil if the cheese browns too quickly.

Makes 8 servings

Per serving
Calories 259	*Sodium 333 mg.*
Total fat 5 g.	*Dietary fiber 2 g.*
Saturated fat 3 g.	*Protein 28 g.*
Cholesterol 62 mg.	*Carbohydrates 23 g.*

Baked Tamale Pie

Hands-on time: 15 minutes
Total time: 50 minutes

2 teaspoons olive oil

1 onion, chopped

1 green bell pepper, chopped

$^1/_2$ pound ground turkey breast or extra-lean ground round beef

1 can (15 ounces) tomato puree

1 can (15 ounces) red kidney beans, rinsed and drained

2 cups water

1 cup fresh or frozen corn kernels

$^1/_3$ cup coarsely chopped black olives

1 tablespoon dried oregano

1 tablespoon chili powder

1 package ($6^1/_2$ ounces) low-fat cornbread mix

1 egg white

$^1/_3$ cup fat-free milk

$^1/_2$ cup (2 ounces) shredded low-fat Monterey Jack cheese

Preheat the oven to 400°F. Coat a medium baking dish with nonstick spray.

Warm the oil in a large nonstick skillet set over medium heat. Add the onion and bell pepper. Cook, stirring, for 4 to 5 minutes, or until softened. Add the turkey or beef. Cook for 3 to 5 minutes, or until no longer pink. Add the tomato puree, beans, water, corn, olives, oregano, and chili powder. Cook for 10 minutes.

Meanwhile, in a medium bowl, combine the cornbread mix, egg white, and milk. Stir until smooth.

Pour the turkey or beef mixture into the prepared baking dish. Sprinkle with the Monterey Jack. Spread the cornbread mixture evenly over the top.

Bake for 25 minutes, or until the crust is golden brown.

Makes 6 servings

Per serving
Calories 354	*Sodium 792 mg.*
Total fat 9 g.	*Dietary fiber 8 g.*
Saturated fat 3 g.	*Protein 23 g.*
Cholesterol 38 mg.	*Carbohydrates 49 g.*

TURKEY BREAST

When purchasing ground turkey, the words "ground turkey breast" on the label are an indicator of the leanest product that you can buy, usually with only 1 gram of fat per serving. In contrast, "ground turkey" can contain as much as 17 grams of fat per serving. "Lean ground turkey" can contain about 8 grams of fat per serving and "extra-lean ground turkey" can have about 1.5 grams of fat per serving. To be sure you know what you're purchasing, always check the fat content on the Nutrition Facts label.

Pork Chops with Sauerkraut and Potatoes

Photograph on page 121
Hands-on time: 15 minutes
Total Time: 1 hour and 15 minutes

1/4 cup unbleached or all-purpose flour

1 1/2 teaspoons dried sage

4 lean pork loin chops (1 pound), trimmed of all visible fat

1 onion, halved and thinly sliced

3 Granny Smith apples, peeled and sliced

1 pound sauerkraut, rinsed, drained, and squeezed of excess moisture

1 1/2 cups frozen sliced carrots, thawed

2 cups apple cider or apple juice

3/4 pound small red potatoes, halved

1 teaspoon olive oil

1/4 teaspoon salt

Position 1 rack in the upper third of the oven. Preheat the oven to 350°F.

On a large shallow plate, combine the flour and sage. Mix with a fork. Dip both sides of each pork chop into the mixture to coat. Reserve the flour mixture. Coat a large Dutch oven with nonstick spray. Set over medium-high heat. Cook the chops for 2 minutes per side, or until browned. Remove to a plate.

Coat the pot with nonstick spray. Add the onion and apples. Cook, stirring often, for 5 minutes, or until soft. Cover with the pork chops, sauerkraut, carrots, and apple cider or apple juice. Sprinkle with the reserved flour mixture. Stir the toppings to combine.

Cover and bake in the lower third of the oven, stirring occasionally, for 1 hour, or until the pork is tender when pierced with a sharp knife.

After 20 minutes, coat a large roasting pan with nonstick spray. Place the potatoes in the pan. Drizzle with the oil. Sprinkle with the salt. Toss to combine. Bake on the upper oven rack for 40 minutes, stirring occasionally, or until golden and tender.

Makes 4 servings

Per serving
Calories 391   *Sodium 433 mg.*
Total fat 9 g.   *Dietary fiber 8 g.*
Saturated fat 2 g. *Protein 31 g.*
Cholesterol 62 mg. *Carbohydrates 48 g.*

Good for You

FIBER UP

Be sure to get your fiber needs from food, not supplements. The recommended Daily Value for dietary fiber is 25 grams per day. Just one serving of Pork Chops with Sauerkraut and Potatoes is a pleasant way to get 8 grams of dietary fiber—nearly one-third of your daily quota.

Irish Stew

Hands-on time: 15 minutes
Total time: 1 hour and 45 minutes

3/4 pound boneless leg of lamb, trimmed of all visible fat and cut into 1" cubes

3/4 pound small red potatoes, quartered

6 cups water

3 cups fat-free reduced-sodium beef or chicken broth

3 carrots, sliced

3 parsnips, sliced

1 package (8 ounces) shredded cabbage

1 large onion, halved and sliced

1 bay leaf

1 teaspoon dried thyme

1/2 teaspoon salt

1/4 cup chopped parsley

In a Dutch oven, combine the lamb, potatoes, water, broth, carrots, parsnips, cabbage, onion, bay leaf, thyme, and salt. Cover and bring to a boil over high heat. Reduce the heat to medium-low. Partially cover and simmer for 45 minutes. Stir in the parsley. Cook, uncovered, stirring occasionally, for 45 minutes, or until the lamb is fork-tender. Remove and discard the bay leaf.

Makes 4 servings

Per serving
Calories 267   *Sodium 505 mg.*
Total fat 4 g.   *Dietary fiber 8 g.*
Saturated fat 2 g.   *Protein 24 g.*
Cholesterol 50 mg.   *Carbohydrates 33 g.*

Good for You

LAMB

Lamb is a robustly flavored and versatile meat that's high in protein, B vitamins, iron, and zinc. Most of the fat on lamb is on the outside of the meat and is easy to trim. Lean lamb cuts include the leg and loin. Avoid ground lamb, unless it is trimmed and ground to order from a lean cut such as leg.

Calorie Check

One of the greatest dietary misconceptions is that you can eat as much fat-free processed food as you want and not gain weight. That's because people have gotten the message that fats are a denser source of calories than carbohydrates. While it is true that paring fat in the diet frees up some calories to eat in the form of carbohydrates, those carbohydrates should primarily be of the complex variety. That means whole grains, vegetables, and legumes.

When we overindulge in fat-free snacks and desserts, we take in far too many calories from sugar, which is a simple carbohydrate that provides energy but virtually no other nutrients. When we consistently consume too many calories from high-sugar, fat-free processed foods, the result is excess body weight. If the body receives more calories than it can burn, it stockpiles the extra as fat.

Learn to choose foods for their nutrient density as well as their caloric value. Foods naturally low in fat that are high in fiber and nutrients give you the most nutritional bang for your calorie buck.

Texas Chili Con Carne

Hands-on time: 20 minutes
Total time: 1 hour and 50 minutes

- 1 tablespoon vegetable oil
- 1$\frac{1}{2}$ pounds beef top round, trimmed of all visible fat and cut into $\frac{1}{2}$" cubes
- 2 onions, chopped
- 2 green and/or red bell peppers, chopped
- 3 serrano or jalapeño chile peppers, seeded and minced (wear plastic gloves when handling)
- 3 cloves garlic, minced
- $\frac{1}{4}$ cup chili powder
- 5 cups fat-free reduced-sodium beef broth
- 1 can (28 ounces) diced tomatoes
- 1 can (15$\frac{1}{2}$ ounces) tomato sauce
- 2 cans (15 ounces each) kidney beans and/or black beans, rinsed and drained

Warm the oil in a Dutch oven over high heat. Add the beef. Cook, turning, for 3 to 5 minutes, or until browned on all sides. Add the onions, bell peppers, chile peppers, and garlic. Reduce the heat to medium-high. Cook, stirring often, for 8 minutes, or until the vegetables are soft. Add the chili powder. Cook, stirring constantly, for 2 minutes. Add the broth, tomatoes (with juice), and tomato sauce. Stir to mix. Bring to a boil. Reduce the heat to medium-low. Simmer, stirring occasionally, for 1 hour. Add the beans. Cook for 30 minutes, or until the meat is fork-tender.

Makes 8 servings

Per serving
Calories 385	Sodium 414 mg.
Total fat 7 g.	Dietary fiber 14 g.
Saturated fat 2 g.	Protein 40 g.
Cholesterol 71 mg.	Carbohydrates 39 g.

A New Twist

CHILI GARNISHES

Zesty garnishes can really dress up a bowl of red. Try a sprinkling of chopped fresh cilantro or parsley leaves, a dollop of low-fat sour cream or low-fat plain yogurt, chopped scallions, 1 tablespoon shredded low-fat Cheddar cheese, or a squeeze of lime juice.

Shepherd's Pie

Hands-on time: 15 minutes
Total time: 55 minutes

1¹⁄₂ pounds extra-lean ground beef

1 cup fresh bread crumbs

1 small onion, finely chopped

1 small green bell pepper, finely chopped

1 egg white

3 tablespoons chili sauce or ketchup

1¹⁄₄ cups buttermilk

¹⁄₂ teaspoon salt

2¹⁄₂ pounds russet potatoes, peeled and cut into 1" cubes

1 cup (4 ounces) shredded low-fat Cheddar cheese

Preheat the oven to 350°F. Lightly coat a 9" pie pan with nonstick spray.

In a large bowl, combine the beef, bread crumbs, onion, bell pepper, egg white, chili sauce or ketchup, ¼ cup of the buttermilk, and ¼ teaspoon of the salt. Mix with a wooden spoon or your hands. Press into the bottom and up the sides of the prepared pan, creating a 1"-thick shell.

Bake for 25 minutes, or until no longer pink. Drain any accumulated juices. Pat dry with a paper towel.

Meanwhile, set a steamer rack in a large pot filled with 2" of boiling water. Place the potatoes on the rack. Cover and cook over high heat for 15 minutes, or until fork-tender. Remove to a bowl. Mash with a potato masher. Add the remaining 1 cup buttermilk and ¼ teaspoon salt. Mash until smooth.

Sprinkle ½ cup of the Cheddar over the bottom of the pie shell. Spread half of the potatoes over the top. Dollop the remaining potatoes around the edge. Sprinkle the remaining ½ cup Cheddar in the center.

Increase the oven temperature to 400°F. Bake for 15 minutes, or until heated through.

Makes 6 servings

Per serving
Calories 513
Total fat 14 g.
Saturated fat 6 g.
Cholesterol 48 mg.

Sodium 731 mg.
Dietary fiber 4 g.
Protein 37 g.
Carbohydrates 60 g.

A New Twist

GARDENER'S PIE

Although it may sound contradictory, it's easy to make a vegetarian version of Shepherd's Pie. Place about 6 cups root vegetables (such as potatoes, turnips, onions, and carrots) that are cut into 1" chunks on a baking sheet coated with nonstick spray. Bake in a 400°F oven for 30 minutes, or until golden. Place in the bottom of the pie pan. Top with 2½ pounds sweet potatoes that are cooked, mashed, and seasoned with a bit of freshly grated ginger and maple syrup. Bake for 15 minutes, or until the sweet potatoes are heated through.

Country Pot Roast

Hands-on time: 15 minutes
Total time: 3 hours and 30 minutes

  1 boneless rump roast (2 pounds), trimmed of all visible fat
 1/8 teaspoon salt
  1 large onion, halved and cut into thin wedges
2 1/2 cups fat-free reduced-sodium beef broth
  1 bay leaf
  1 teaspoon dried thyme
1 1/4 pounds small red potatoes, cut in half
 24 baby carrots
  1 large turnip, peeled, halved, and sliced into thin wedges

Preheat the oven to 325°F. Coat lightly on all sides with nonstick spray. Season with the salt.

Place the meat in a Dutch oven set over medium-high heat. Cook, turning, for 6 to 8 minutes, or until browned. Add the onion. Cook for 3 minutes, stirring often. Add the broth, bay leaf, and thyme. Cover and bake for 2 hours and 15 minutes. Turn the meat several times during the cooking time.

Add the potatoes, carrots, and turnip. Cover and bake for 45 minutes to 1 hour, or until the meat is fork-tender. Remove the meat to a cutting board. Cut in thin slices across the grain. Remove and discard the bay leaf. Serve the beef and vegetables in shallow bowls or plates topped with the sauce.

Makes 6 servings

Per serving
Calories 261	Sodium 164 mg.
Total fat 7 g.	Dietary fiber 4 g.
Saturated fat 2 g.	Protein 28 g.
Cholesterol 72 mg.	Carbohydrates 20 g.

DINNER AT THE DINER

Play it Again!

Leftover pot roast makes one of the best diner-style open-face sandwiches ever. Remove the potatoes and turnips and mash together with a fork or potato masher. Add a little buttermilk or fat-free milk to make a smooth consistency. Season with salt and black pepper. Heat the sliced meat and gravy in the microwave oven on high power. Spoon over thick slices of toasted sourdough bread and add a dollop of mashed vegetables on the side.

Peppered Beef Tenderloin and Vegetables

Hands-on time: 15 minutes
Total time: 1 hour and 20 minutes

6 red potatoes, quartered

2 leeks, cut into 2" lengths

2 carrots, cut in 2" diagonal lengths

2 teaspoons olive oil

1/4 teaspoon salt

1 1/4 pounds beef tenderloin, trimmed of all visible fat

1 tablespoon soy sauce

1 teaspoon coarsely cracked black pepper

Preheat the oven to 400°F. Coat a large roasting pan with nonstick spray.

Place the potatoes, leeks, and carrots in the prepared baking dish. Drizzle with the oil and salt. Toss to coat. Push the vegetables to the outer edge of the dish. Place the beef in the center. Sprinkle the beef with the soy sauce and pepper, rubbing in to coat evenly and pressing the pepper into the beef.

Bake for 50 to 55 minutes, or until a thermometer inserted in the center of the tenderloin registers 145°F for medium-rare or 160°F for medium doneness. Remove the tenderloin and place on a cutting board to rest for 10 minutes. Turn off the oven. Return the vegetables to the oven to keep warm.

Cut the tenderloin into thin diagonal slices. Serve with the vegetables on the side.

Makes 4 servings

Per serving

Calories 474	Sodium 667 mg.
Total fat 13 g.	Dietary fiber 10 g.
Saturated fat 5 g.	Protein 32 g.
Cholesterol 75 mg.	Carbohydrates 58 g.

A New Twist

HORSERADISH SAUCE

This sauce is a marvelous accompaniment to Peppered Beef Tenderloin and Vegetables. In a bowl, whisk 1 cup (8 ounces) fat-free sour cream with 2 to 3 tablespoons prepared horseradish.

Tortellini Corn Chowder

Photograph on page 125
Hands-on time: 10 minutes
Total time: 45 minutes

3 slices turkey bacon, coarsely chopped

1 onion, chopped

1 rib celery, chopped

1 small red bell pepper, chopped

2 cups fresh or frozen corn kernels

2 cups fat-free reduced-sodium chicken broth

$1/3$ cup unbleached or all-purpose flour

3 cups 1% milk

$1/3$ cup chopped fresh basil or 1 teaspoon dried

$1/4$ teaspoon salt

8 ounces low-fat fresh or frozen cheese tortellini, cooked and drained

Set a Dutch oven over medium heat. Add the bacon. Cook for 1 minute, or until it releases some of its moisture. Add the onion, celery, and bell pepper. Cook for 5 minutes, or until the vegetables are soft. Add the corn and broth. Bring to a boil over high heat. Reduce the heat to medium. Simmer for 15 minutes.

Place the flour in a medium bowl. Gradually add the milk, whisking until smooth. Pour into the Dutch oven. Stir until well-blended. Add the basil and salt. Cook, stirring occasionally, for 3 minutes, or until the soup thickens. Add the tortellini. Cook for 2 minutes, or until heated through.

Makes 8 servings

Per serving
Calories 213
Total fat 4 g.
Saturated fat 2 g.
Cholesterol 19 mg.
Sodium 336 mg.
Dietary fiber 2 g.
Protein 12 g.
Carbohydrates 32 g.

STOCK

Stock is a liquid resulting from simmering vegetables and/or meat or poultry bones in water to extract their flavor. Homemade stock makes an ideal ingredient for healthy cooking since it is virtually free of fat and sodium. Stock is an ideal base for soups, stews, and sauces and can be used in place of water to cook rice and grains. If homemade stock isn't an option, buy fat-free reduced-sodium canned broth as a staple for healthy meals.

Vegetable Curry

Hands-on time: 10 minutes
Total time: 25 minutes

- 1 cup quick-cooking brown rice or basmati rice
- 1 small red onion, halved and cut into thin wedges
- 1 tablespoon grated fresh ginger
- 3 cloves garlic, minced
- 3 tablespoons curry powder
- 1 tablespoon unbleached or all-purpose flour
- 1 can (14 ounces) reduced-fat coconut milk
- 1 package (10 ounces) frozen cauliflower, thawed
- 2 cans (16 ounces each) sweet potatoes, drained and cut into 1" pieces
- 1 can (15 ounces) red kidney beans, rinsed and drained
- ¹⁄3 cup raisins
- ³⁄4 pound baby spinach leaves, stems removed
- ¹⁄4 cup unsalted chopped cashews

Cook the rice according to package directions.

Meanwhile, coat a Dutch oven with nonstick spray. Add the onion, ginger, and garlic. Coat with nonstick spray. Cook, stirring often, over medium heat for 5 minutes, or until the onion is soft. Add the curry powder. Cook, stirring, for 2 minutes, or until fragrant. Sprinkle with the flour. Cook, stirring, for 2 minutes. Add the coconut milk, cauliflower, sweet potatoes, beans, and raisins. Stir to mix. Reduce the heat to low. Cook, stirring occasionally, for 10 to 12 minutes, or until heated through. Add the spinach. Cook, stirring, for 1 minute, or until wilted.

Serve over the rice. Sprinkle with the cashews.

Makes 4 servings

Per serving

Calories 648	*Sodium 200 mg.*
Total fat 12 g.	*Dietary fiber 23 g.*
Saturated fat 3 g.	*Protein 20 g.*
Cholesterol 10 mg.	*Carbohydrates 122 g.*

Coconut Milk

The amount of fat in canned reduced-fat coconut milk varies from brand to brand. Check Nutrition Facts labels for one that contains no more than 3 grams of fat per serving. Some varieties contain up to 7 grams of fat per serving.

Seafood Potpie

Photograph on page 123
Hands-on time: 20 minutes
Total time: 45 minutes

1 large leek, white part only, sliced

4 ounces mushrooms, sliced

2 teaspoons dried tarragon

1/2 cup dry sherry or nonalcoholic white wine

2 1/2 tablespoons unbleached or all-purpose flour

1 1/2 cups 1% milk

1 bottle (8 ounces) clam juice

1/2 pound bay scallops

1/4 pound small shrimp, peeled and deveined

3/4 cup frozen peas

1 jar (2 ounces) pimiento strips, drained

1 package (7 1/2 ounces) reduced-fat refrigerated biscuit dough

Preheat the oven to 400°F. Coat a medium baking dish with nonstick spray.

Coat a Dutch oven with nonstick spray. Add the leek and mushrooms. Coat with nonstick spray. Cook, stirring occasionally, over medium heat for 5 to 7 minutes, or until soft. Add the tarragon and sherry or wine. Increase the heat to medium-high. Cook for 2 to 3 minutes, or until the liquid is almost evaporated. Sprinkle with the flour. Cook, stirring constantly, for 2 minutes to coat the vegetables with the flour. Add the milk and clam juice. Stir, scraping the bottom and sides of the pan, for 4 to 5 minutes, or until thickened. Remove from the heat. Add the scallops, shrimp, peas, and pimientos.

Pour into the reserved baking dish. Arrange the biscuits over the top in a single layer.

Bake for 25 minutes, or until the filling bubbles and the biscuits are golden brown.

Makes 4 servings

Per serving
Calories 319
Total fat 4 g.
Saturated fat 1 g.
Cholesterol 78 mg.
Sodium 949 mg.
Dietary fiber 3 g.
Protein 24 g.
Carbohydrates 46 g.

Cooking Note
For a quicker preparation, place the biscuits in the mixture in the Dutch oven and bake there.

BISCUITS

When shopping for biscuit dough in the dairy aisle, check the Nutrition Facts label for brands that contain 3 grams of fat or less per 100 calories. This way, you will be assured that it is a low-fat choice.

Fish Stew with Couscous

Hands-on time: 10 minutes
Total time: 35 minutes

1 onion, halved lengthwise, quartered, and thinly sliced

2 cloves garlic, minced

1 teaspoon ground cumin

1/4 teaspoon ground cinnamon

1 can (15 ounces) chopped tomatoes

1 can (15 ounces) chickpeas, rinsed and drained

1 cup fat-free reduced-sodium chicken broth

1/3 cup chopped dates

1/4 cup pitted halved Kalamata olives

4 orange roughy or halibut fillets (4 ounces each)

1 box (10 ounces) couscous

Coat a large nonstick skillet with nonstick spray. Add the onion, garlic, cumin, and cinnamon. Coat with nonstick spray. Set over medium heat. Cook, stirring, for 7 to 8 minutes, or until soft.

Add the tomatoes, chickpeas, broth, dates, and olives. Cook, stirring occasionally, for 5 minutes. Push the mixture to the edges of the skillet. Add the fish. Spoon the chickpea mixture over the fish. Cover the pan. Reduce the heat to low. Cook for 10 minutes, or until the fish flakes easily.

Meanwhile, cook the couscous according to package directions. Fluff the couscous with a fork. Divide among 4 plates. Top with the fish and the chickpea mixture.

Makes 4 servings

Per serving

Calories 527	Sodium 598 mg.
Total fat 6 g.	Dietary fiber 10 g.
Saturated fat 1 g.	Protein 32 g.
Cholesterol 23 mg.	Carbohydrates 85 g.

Hot! Hot! Hot!

Harissa is a fiery North African condiment that goes well with stew-type dishes. To make harissa, in a small bowl, mash 2 cloves garlic and 2 coarsely chopped serrano chile peppers (wear plastic gloves when handling) with 1 teaspoon kosher or sea salt until it forms a paste. Transfer the mixture to a food processor or blender. Add 1 teaspoon crushed red-pepper flakes, 3 teaspoons caraway seeds, 1 teaspoon ground cumin, and 1 teaspoon ground coriander. Process to make a thick paste. Add 3 tablespoons olive oil. Process to mix well. Transfer to a small jar with a tight-fitting lid. Refrigerate up to 3 months. Use with caution—this red-hot sauce bites back!

Big Sur Cioppino

Hands-on time: 10 minutes
Total time: 45 minutes

2 teaspoons olive oil

1 medium onion, chopped

1 medium green bell pepper, chopped

4 cloves garlic, minced

2 teaspoons dried Italian seasoning

1/2 cup chopped parsley

1/2 cup dry red wine or nonalcoholic red wine

1 can (28 ounces) chopped tomatoes

1 bottle (8 ounces) clam juice

1/2 cup water

1/8 teaspoon crushed red-pepper flakes

12 little neck or cherrystone clams, scrubbed

1/2 pound medium shrimp, peeled and deveined

1/2 pound halibut fillet, skinned and cut into 1" chunks

Warm the oil in a Dutch oven set over medium heat. Add the onion, bell pepper, garlic, and Italian seasoning. Cook, stirring occasionally, for 5 to 7 minutes, or until soft.

Add the parsley, wine, tomatoes (with juice), clam juice, water, and red-pepper flakes. Stir to mix. Cook, stirring occasionally, for 20 minutes.

Add the clams. Cover and cook for 3 to 5 minutes, or until the clams open. Discard any clams that have cracked shells or remain closed. Add the shrimp and halibut. Cover and cook for 2 minutes, or until the shrimp are opaque and the halibut flakes easily.

Makes 4 servings

Per serving
Calories 302
Total fat 6 g.
Saturated fat 1 g.
Cholesterol 142 mg.
Sodium 809 mg.
Dietary fiber 3 g.
Protein 41 g.
Carbohydrates 19 g.

Perfecting the Potato

The average American eats about 140 pounds of potatoes each year, far more than any other vegetable. This equates to approximately one potato per person each day.

The good news is that those potatoes are high in vitamin C and potassium and are a good source of vitamin B_6 and dietary fiber.

The bad news is that around 65 percent of those potatoes are fried as chips, dehydrated, or turned into high-fat frozen items. So the manipulated spud goes from a healthy carbohydrate-rich vegetable to a fat-laden, high-calorie processed food.

The misconception that potatoes are a naturally fattening food continues to fade as health-educated consumers realize that it's the fat added to processed potatoes that makes them undesirable. Served close to their natural state, potatoes are a boon to healthy eating.

Not Just a Side Dish Anymore

"While most other vegetables have their detractors, it is probably safe to say that almost everyone likes potatoes," says Diana Shaw, author of *Essential Vegetarian Cookbook*. "With their mild flavor and agreeable texture, potatoes may be the most versatile food there is, lending themselves to such a variety of preparations that almost no one could possibly reject them."

It's this universal appeal that makes potatoes such a versatile ingredient in healthy cooking, moving back and forth from main dish to side dish with ease.

Potatoes vary, so choose the type of potato to use by considering the type of dish you are making. Lower-starch red-skin and white-skin all-purpose potatoes are best for boiling because they absorb less water when cooked, so they maintain their shape better. Use them for potato salad or scalloped potatoes.

Mashed potatoes require a high-starch potato such as russets, which are often marketed as Idaho potatoes. Yukon Gold are another good choice. Though slightly lower in starch than russets, their golden yellow flesh mimics the flavor of butter. High-starch potatoes are also the best choice for making oven-baked fries, twice-baked potatoes, and stuffed spuds.

And finally, don't peel potatoes unless you absolutely have to for appearance sake. You'll want to keep the peel for increased fiber, vitamins, and minerals as well as easier preparation.

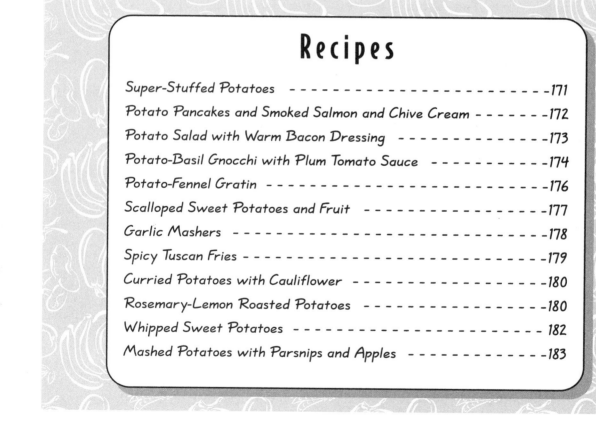

Recipes

Super-Stuffed Potatoes

Hands-on time: 15 minutes
Total time: 1 hour and 15 minutes

- 4 russet potatoes
- 1 tablespoon unbleached or all-purpose flour
- $\frac{1}{8}$ teaspoon ground nutmeg
- Pinch + $\frac{1}{4}$ teaspoon salt
- 1 cup + $\frac{2}{3}$ cup 1% milk
- 1 cup (4 ounces) shredded low-fat Cheddar cheese
- 1 package (10 ounces) frozen chopped broccoli, thawed
- 3 strips turkey bacon, chopped and cooked until crisp

Preheat the oven to 425°F. Pierce the potatoes several times with a fork. Place in the oven and bake for 1 hour, or until tender when pierced with a fork. Remove and leave the oven on.

Meanwhile, in a small saucepan, combine the flour, nutmeg, and the pinch of salt. Gradually whisk in 1 cup of milk until the flour dissolves. Cook, stirring, over medium heat for 5 minutes, or until thickened. Remove from the heat. Stir in the Cheddar until smooth. Set aside.

Holding the potatoes with an oven mitt, cut in half lengthwise. Scoop the flesh out into a bowl, leaving a ¼" shell. Place the shells on a baking sheet. Mash the flesh with a potato masher. Stir in the remaining ⅔ cup milk and ¼ teaspoon salt until smooth. Spoon the potato mixture into the reserved shells. Top with the broccoli, bacon, and cheese sauce. Bake for 10 minutes, or until heated through.

Makes 8 servings

Per serving
Calories 192	Sodium 316 mg.
Total fat 3 g.	Dietary fiber 3 g.
Saturated fat 1 g.	Protein 9 g.
Cholesterol 9 mg.	Carbohydrates 33 g.

MORE STUFF

Play it Again!

Super-Stuffed Potatoes make a wonderful omelette filling or side dish for breakfast or brunch. Scoop out the filling of 1 stuffed potato onto a small plate and break apart with a fork. Cook in the microwave oven on high power for 1 to 2 minutes, or until hot. Season with ground black pepper or hot-pepper sauce to taste.

Potato Pancakes and Smoked Salmon with Chive Cream

Photograph on page 130
Hands-on time: 15 minutes
Total time: 30 minutes

²/₃ cup fat-free sour cream

¹/₃ cup chopped fresh chives or
     scallion greens

2 pounds russet potatoes, peeled

1 onion

2 tablespoons unbleached or
   all-purpose flour

1 egg, separated

¹/₂ teaspoon salt

1 egg white

5 ounces thinly sliced smoked salmon

Preheat the oven to 300°F. Coat 2 large baking sheets with nonstick spray.

In a small bowl, combine the sour cream and chives or scallions. Cover and refrigerate.

In a food processor with the shredding disk or on a 4-sided vegetable grater, shred the potatoes and onion. Working in batches, squeeze out excess liquid and pat dry with paper towels. Place in a large bowl. Add the flour, egg yolk, and salt. Stir to mix.

Place the egg whites in a medium bowl. With an electric mixer, beat until stiff peaks form. Fold into the potato mixture.

Coat a large nonstick skillet or griddle with nonstick spray. Place over medium-high heat. Drop the batter in ¼ cupfuls onto the pan or griddle. With the back of a spoon, spread each pancake into a 4" circle. Cook for 3 to 4 min-

utes, or until browned on the bottom. Coat the tops with nonstick spray and turn over. Cook for 3 to 4 minutes, or until browned on the bottom. Remove to one of the prepared baking sheets. Place in the oven to keep warm. Repeat with the remaining batter to make a total of 15 pancakes. Serve the pancakes topped with the salmon and a dollop of the chive cream.

Makes 5 servings

Per serving
Calories 281   *Sodium 862 mg.*
Total fat 5 g.   *Dietary fiber 3 g.*
Saturated fat 1 g. *Protein 13 g.*
Cholesterol 50 mg. *Carbohydrates 48 g.*

Potato Salad with Warm Bacon Dressing

Photograph on page 127
Hands-on time: 5 minutes
Total time: 30 minutes

2 pounds red potatoes, cut into large chunks

2 strips bacon, chopped

1 small red onion, chopped

1 clove garlic, chopped

3 tablespoons cider vinegar

3 tablespoons apple juice

1 tablespoon stone-ground mustard

1/4 cup chopped parsley

1/8 teaspoon salt

Set a vegetable steamer in a medium saucepan. Fill with water to just below the steamer. Place the potatoes on the steamer. Cover and bring to a boil over high heat. Reduce the heat to medium-high. Cook for 15 to 20 minutes, or until tender. Transfer to a large bowl and allow to cool for 10 minutes.

Meanwhile, in a medium nonstick skillet set over medium heat, cook the bacon for 3 minutes. Add the onion and garlic. Cook, stirring, for 3 minutes, or until the onion is soft and the bacon is crisp. Reduce the heat to low. Add the vinegar, apple juice, mustard, parsley, and salt. Cook for 2 minutes, or until heated through. Pour over the potatoes. Toss to evenly coat.

Makes 6 servings

Per serving
Calories 153
Total fat 4 g.
Saturated fat 1 g.
Cholesterol 5 mg.
Sodium 192 mg.
Dietary fiber 4 g.
Protein 7 g.
Carbohydrates 24 g.

CLASSIC STAR

POWERFUL ONIONS

Onions add more than great flavor to your recipes. Use this versatile vegetable frequently to help decrease the risk of cancer, lower blood pressure, raise beneficial HDL (high-density lipoprotein) cholesterol, relieve congestion, and reduce inflammation.

Potato-Basil Gnocchi with Plum Tomato Sauce

Hands-on time: 30 minutes
Total time: 1 hour and 30 minutes

  2 large russet potatoes
1¼ cups unbleached or all-purpose flour
⅓ cup (3 ounces) fat-free ricotta cheese
¼ cup chopped fresh basil or
     2 teaspoons dried
  1 egg white
¼ teaspoon salt
⅛ teaspoon ground nutmeg
  1 recipe Plum Tomato Sauce (at
     right)
  3 tablespoons (¾ ounce) grated
     Parmesan cheese

Preheat the oven to 400°F. Pierce the potatoes several times with a fork. Place in the oven. Bake for 1 hour, or until tender when pierced with a fork. Remove and allow to cool slightly. Scoop the flesh into a large bowl, reserving the shells for another use. Mash with a potato masher. Set aside.

Reduce the oven temperature to 250°F. Dust a baking sheet with flour. Coat a 13" × 9" baking dish with nonstick spray. Set a large pot of water over high heat. Cover.

To the bowl with the potatoes, add 1 cup of the flour, the ricotta, basil, egg white, salt, and nutmeg. Mix to form a soft dough. Turn onto a floured work surface. Knead, working in up to ¼ cup of the remaining flour, for 3 to 4 minutes, or until pliable and no longer sticky. Divide into 4 portions.

One at a time, roll each portion of dough with your palms into a 14" rope. Cut each rope into 1" pieces. Drag the tines of a fork through one side of each piece to form a concave shape. Place on the floured baking sheet.

Bring the water to a boil. Add half of the gnocchi and stir gently. After the gnocchi float to the surface, cook for 1 to 2 minutes, or until cooked through. Check by cutting one in half. Remove with a slotted spoon or small strainer to the prepared baking dish. Cover loosely with foil. Place in the oven to keep warm. Repeat with the remaining gnocchi.

To serve, spoon the gnocchi into shallow bowls. Top with the tomato sauce. Sprinkle with the Parmesan.

Makes 4 servings

Per serving
Calories 353   *Sodium 434 mg.*
Total fat 5 g.   *Dietary fiber 6 g.*
Saturated fat 2 g.   *Protein 13 g.*
Cholesterol 15 mg.   *Carbohydrates 66 g.*

PLUM TOMATO SAUCE

While the potatoes are baking, it takes just minutes to make this fresh sauce. Coat a medium nonstick skillet with nonstick spray. Then add 1 chopped small onion and 1 minced clove garlic. Coat with nonstick spray. Cook, stirring often, for 3 to 5 minutes, or until soft. Add 8 finely chopped plum tomatoes. Cook, stirring often, for 3 to 5 minutes, or until soft. Stir in 2 teaspoons butter and ¼ teaspoon salt. Makes 4 servings.

Calcium

Most of us know that calcium helps the body build and maintain bones.

But are you also aware that this mineral is involved in helping your muscles contract and your heart beat? And scientific studies are pointing to a link between calcium intake and lower blood pressure.

Calcium needs change depending on your stage of life. The revised Recommended Dietary Allowance for most younger adults is 1,000 milligrams a day. For most adults over age 51, it is 1,200 milligrams a day.

Calcium is found in many foods. Dairy foods such as milk, yogurt, and cheese are excellent sources. And, if you select fat-free or reduced-fat dairy products, in some cases you actually benefit by taking in slightly more calcium than you would with their full-fat counterparts.

Other sources of calcium include bok choy, kale, almonds, oranges, and salmon and other fish with edible bones. With the heightened awareness of daily calcium needs, foods such as breakfast cereals, tofu, soy milk, orange juice, white rice, and cereal bars have been fortified with calcium by food manufacturers.

When evaluating a Nutrition Facts food label for calcium content, use this handy trick. (This will only work for computing calcium, however, not for other vitamins or minerals). Locate the entry with "% of Daily Value" for calcium. Replace the "%" sign with a "0." For example, an 8-ounce container of fat-free yogurt lists 40% calcium. Replace the "%" with a "0," and you get 400, which is the approximate number of milligrams of calcium that it contains. Remember, the daily recommendation for most individuals is approximately 1,000 milligrams a day. So, by eating just one carton of yogurt, you're more than one-third of the way to your daily intake.

To make sure that calcium is absorbed readily by your body, be sure to also eat foods rich in vitamin D. Milk is an excellent source, but if you don't drink milk regularly, you may want to consider eating other vitamin D–rich foods such as fortified cereals, eggs, and canned salmon with bones.

Potato-Fennel Gratin

Hands-on time: 15 minutes
Total time: 1 hour and 15 minutes

1 tablespoon olive oil

1 bulb fennel, quartered and thinly sliced

1 onion, halved and thinly sliced

2 cloves garlic, chopped

1 1/2 pounds potatoes, sliced 1/8" thick

1/2 cup (2 ounces) shredded low-fat Gruyère or Jarlsberg cheese

1 1/2 tablespoons unbleached or all-purpose flour

1/4 teaspoon salt

1 can (14 1/2 ounces) fat-free reduced-sodium chicken broth

1 cup fat-free milk

1 cup fresh bread crumbs

Preheat the oven to 375°F. Coat a medium baking dish with nonstick spray.

Warm the oil in a large nonstick skillet over medium heat. Add the fennel, onion, and garlic. Cook, stirring often, for 10 minutes, or until tender. Remove from the heat.

Spread one-third of the potatoes in an even layer in the prepared baking dish. Top with half of the fennel mixture and 1/4 cup of the Gruyère or Jarlsberg. Repeat with another layer of one-third of the potatoes, the remaining fennel mixture, and the remaining 1/4 cup cheese. Cover with the remaining potatoes.

Place the flour and salt in a bowl. Gradually whisk in about 1/4 cup of the broth until the flour dissolves. Add the remaining broth and the milk. Whisk to blend. Pour into the baking dish. Cover loosely with foil.

Bake for 40 minutes. Remove the foil. Sprinkle the top with the bread crumbs. Coat lightly with nonstick spray. Bake for 20 minutes, or until the potatoes are tender and the top is golden brown. Remove and allow to rest for 10 minutes before serving.

Makes 8 servings

Per serving
Calories 205
Total fat 3 g.
Saturated fat 1 g.
Cholesterol 3 mg.

Sodium 290 mg.
Dietary fiber 3 g.
Protein 9 g.
Carbohydrates 34 g.

POTATOES

Whenever possible, leave the peel on the potatoes. Nutrients are concentrated just below the skin surface. For the least amount of nutrient loss, bake potatoes or cook them in their skins. To minimize nutrient loss of water-soluble vitamins, prepare potatoes in a small amount of liquid and incorporate the liquid into the dish, such as a casserole.

Scalloped Sweet Potatoes and Fruit

Hands-on time: 20 minutes
Total time: 1 hour and 20 minutes

- 1 tablespoon butter or margarine
- 3 tart apples, cut into $1/2$" pieces
- 2 tablespoons packed light brown sugar
- 2 pounds sweet potatoes, cut into $3/4$" pieces
- $1/2$ cup dried sweet cherries or golden raisins
- $1 1/2$ tablespoons unbleached or all-purpose flour
- $1/4$ teaspoon ground cinnamon
- 1 cup fat-free reduced-sodium chicken broth
- $1/4$ cup finely chopped pecans

Preheat the oven to 350°F. Coat a 13" × 9" baking dish with nonstick spray.

Melt the butter or margarine in a medium non-stick skillet over medium heat. Add the apples. Cook, stirring, for 1 to 2 minutes, or until they release some of their juices. Add the brown sugar. Cook for 2 minutes, or until the apples are partially softened.

Place the apples, sweet potatoes, and cherries or raisins in the prepared baking dish.

Place the flour and cinnamon in a small bowl. Gradually whisk in ¼ cup of the broth until the flour dissolves. Whisk in the remaining ¾ cup broth. Pour into the baking dish. Cover loosely with foil.

Bake for 1 hour, or until the potatoes are tender when pierced with a fork. Remove the foil and sprinkle with the pecans. Bake, uncovered, for 10 to 12 minutes, or until the pecans are toasted and all the broth is evaporated.

Makes 8 servings

Per serving
Calories 264 *Sodium 38 mg.*
Total fat 5 g. *Dietary fiber 5 g.*
Saturated fat 2 g. *Protein 4 g.*
Cholesterol 5 mg. *Carbohydrates 55 g.*

APPLES

Apple skin contains large amounts of quercetin, an antioxidant compound that scientific studies suggest may help lower the risk of heart disease and cancer. So unless peeling is necessary for appearance sake, leave the peels on to reap the health benefits. Be sure to scrub the apples before using.

Garlic Mashers

Hands-on time: 10 minutes
Total time: 40 minutes

3 pounds potatoes, peeled and cut into 1" cubes

Roasted Garlic (at right)

³/4-1 cup buttermilk

³/4 teaspoon salt

Set a vegetable steamer in a large saucepan. Fill with water to just below the steamer. Place the potatoes on the steamer. Cover and bring to a boil over high heat. Reduce the heat to medium-high. Cook for 25 to 30 minutes, or until the potatoes are tender when pierced with a fork.

Remove the potatoes to a large bowl. Mash with a potato masher. Stir in the garlic, ¾ cup of the buttermilk, and the salt. Stir until smooth. Add up to ¼ cup more buttermilk to moisten, if needed.

Makes 6 servings

Per serving
Calories 214	*Sodium 332 mg.*
Total fat 1 g.	*Dietary fiber 4 g.*
Saturated fat 0 g.	*Protein 5 g.*
Cholesterol 1 mg.	*Carbohydrates 48 g.*

A New Twist

ROASTED GARLIC

To make roasted garlic, preheat the oven to 400°F. Cut a thin slice from the top of 1 head of garlic to expose the cloves. Set the head, cut side up, on a large piece of foil. Seal the top and sides of the foil tightly. Place in the oven and roast for 35 to 40 minutes, or until the cloves are very soft, lightly browned, and tender. Remove and set aside until cool enough to handle. Squeeze the garlic cloves into a small bowl. With the back of a spoon, mash the garlic with a pinch of salt to make a smooth paste. Makes about 2 to 3 tablespoons.

Spicy Tuscan Fries

Hands-on time: 5 minutes
Total time: 35 minutes

2   tablespoons (¹⁄₂ ounce) grated
    Parmesan cheese

1   teaspoon dried basil

¹⁄₂ teaspoon salt

¹⁄₄ teaspoon ground red pepper

¹⁄₄ teaspoon ground black pepper

4   russet potatoes, peeled and cut in
    ¹⁄₄"-thick sticks

Preheat the oven to 425°F. Arrange 2 oven racks in the upper third and middle third of the oven. Coat 2 baking sheets with nonstick spray.

In a bowl, combine the Parmesan, basil, salt, red pepper, and black pepper.

Arrange the potatoes on the prepared baking sheets in a single layer. Coat with nonstick spray. Sprinkle the seasoning mixture evenly over the potatoes. Toss to coat. Rearrange the potatoes into a single layer with space between the sticks. Coat lightly with nonstick spray.

Bake for 20 minutes. Remove from the oven and turn the potatoes. Coat lightly with nonstick spray. Bake for 10 minutes longer, or until golden and tender when pierced with a fork.

Makes 4 servings

Per serving

Calories 163	*Sodium 365 mg.*
Total fat 1 g.	*Dietary fiber 3 g.*
Saturated fat 1 g.	*Protein 5 g.*
Cholesterol 3 mg.	*Carbohydrates 34 g.*

A New Twist

WELL-SEASONED

Spice up your potatoes with one of these alternative seasonings.

Caribbean seasoning: Combine 1 tablespoon minced dried onion, 2 teaspoons dried thyme, 1 teaspoon garlic powder, 1 teaspoon ground black pepper, ½ teaspoon salt, ½ teaspoon ground allspice, ¼ teaspoon ground nutmeg, and ¼ teaspoon ground red pepper.

Indian seasoning: Combine 2 teaspoons ground coriander, 1 teaspoon ground cumin, 1 teaspoon salt, ¼ teaspoon ground red pepper, ¼ teaspoon ground black pepper, ¼ teaspoon ground turmeric, ⅛ teaspoon ground cinnamon, and ⅛ teaspoon ground cloves.

Curried Potatoes with Cauliflower

Hands-on time: 10 minutes
Total time: 15 minutes

- 1 tablespoon vegetable oil
- 1 small onion, chopped
- 3 cloves garlic, chopped
- 1 1/2 teaspoons grated fresh ginger
- 1 tablespoon curry powder
- 2 russet potatoes, cooked and coarsely mashed
- 1 package (10 ounces) frozen chopped cauliflower, thawed
- 1 cup frozen peas, thawed
- 1/2 teaspoon salt
- 1/8 teaspoon ground red pepper
- 1 tablespoon lemon juice

Warm the oil in a medium nonstick skillet set over medium heat. Add the onion, garlic, ginger, and curry powder. Cook, stirring often, for 6 to 8 minutes, or until the onion is soft. Add the potatoes, cauliflower, peas, salt, and pepper. Cook, stirring gently, until well-combined. Sprinkle with the lemon juice. Stir to mix. Cook for 3 to 5 minutes, or until heated through.

Makes 6 servings

Per serving
Calories 109
Total fat 3 g.
Saturated fat 0 g.
Cholesterol 0 mg.
Sodium 205 mg.
Dietary fiber 4 g.
Protein 4 g.
Carbohydrates 19 g.

Rosemary-Lemon Roasted Potatoes

Photograph on page 283
Hands-on time: 10 minutes
Total time: 1 hour

- 3 pounds red potatoes, cut in lengthwise wedges
- 1 tablespoon olive oil
- 1 tablespoon chopped fresh rosemary
- 2 teaspoons grated lemon peel
- 1 clove garlic, minced
- 1/4 teaspoon salt
- 1/4 teaspoon ground black pepper

Preheat the oven to 400°F.

In a large roasting pan, combine the potatoes, oil, rosemary, lemon peel, garlic, salt, and pepper. Lightly toss to evenly coat. Bake for 45 to 50 minutes, turning halfway through the cooking time, or until golden and tender.

Makes 6 servings

Per serving
Calories 236
Total fat 3 g.
Saturated fat 0 g.
Cholesterol 0 mg.
Sodium 109 mg.
Dietary fiber 4 g.
Protein 5 g.
Carbohydrates 51 g.

Turn a Potato into a Meal

On a stay-at-home weekend afternoon, it's easy to bake several russet potatoes to have on hand for quick weeknight dinners or microwaveable lunches. With these stuffings to choose from, you may want to have one potato, two potatoes, three potatoes, or more a week! Just microwave the cooked potato to reheat, split lengthwise, and load on the stuffings.

Barbecued Turkey Potato. Shred leftover roasted turkey and heat with your favorite barbecue sauce. Spoon over the split potato and top with sautéed chopped red onions and red bell peppers.

Breakfast Potato. Fill the potato with scrambled eggs, diced Canadian bacon, cooked spinach, and a sprinkling of Parmesan cheese.

Broccoli and Cheese Potato. Cook low-fat Cheddar cheese sauce (found in the snack aisle of the supermarket) with thawed frozen broccoli until heated through. Spoon onto the potato with strips of grilled chicken.

Chili Baked Potato. Spoon on homemade or low-fat canned chili and top with fat-free sour cream and chopped scallions.

Loaded Baked Potato. Top with fat-free sour cream, low-fat shredded Cheddar cheese, diced scallions, and 1 piece of cooked crumbled turkey bacon.

Philly Steak and Cheese Potato. Sauté onions, garlic, and mushrooms until golden. Add lean sirloin that has been cut into strips. Cook until just pink. Finish off with a touch of seasoning salt. Sprinkle with shredded low-fat Monterey Jack cheese. Broil 4" from the heat until the cheese bubbles.

Pizza Potato. Transfer all of your favorite low-fat pizza toppings to the baked potato.

Potato Primavera. Grill or sauté some sliced bell peppers, onions, eggplant, zucchini, or mushrooms until softened. Season with rosemary or basil. Spoon over the potato and sprinkle with grated Romano cheese.

Southwest Spud. Spoon heated black beans over the potato and top with salsa, fat-free sour cream, fresh cilantro leaves, shredded low-fat Monterey Jack cheese, and fresh or jarred chopped green chile peppers.

Whipped Sweet Potatoes

Hands-on time: 10 minutes
Total time: 1 hour and 10 minutes

4   pounds sweet potatoes
1   navel orange
2   teaspoons butter or margarine
1   teaspoon ground cinnamon
¹⁄₄ teaspoon salt

Preheat the oven to 425°F. Place the sweet potatoes in the oven and bake for 1 hour, or until tender when pierced with a fork. Remove and set aside to cool slightly.

Meanwhile, grate the colored peel from the orange. Set aside. Squeeze the juice from the orange and set aside.

Melt the butter or margarine in a small skillet over medium heat. Add the orange peel. Sauté for 1 minute, stirring often. Add the orange juice, cinnamon, and salt. Cook, stirring, for 1 minute, or until warm. Remove from the heat.

Cut the sweet potatoes in half. Scoop the flesh into a large bowl. With an electric mixer on medium speed, beat until smooth. Add the orange-juice mixture. Reduce the mixer speed to low and beat just until blended.

Makes 8 servings

Per serving
Calories 248   *Sodium 106 mg.*
Total fat 1 g.   *Dietary fiber 6 g.*
Saturated fat 1 g.   *Protein 4 g.*
Cholesterol 3 mg.   *Carbohydrates 56 g.*

SWEET POTATOES

Try to include more healthful sweet potatoes in your meals. Just one 4-ounce sweet potato far exceeds the Daily Value for vitamin A and provides nearly half of the daily value for vitamin C.

Mashed Potatoes
with Parsnips and Apples

Hands-on time: 10 minutes
Total time: 40 minutes

1 1/2 pounds russet potatoes, peeled and
   cut into 1" pieces

1   pound parsnips, peeled and sliced
    into 1/4"-thick coins

2   apples, peeled and cut into
    1/2" pieces

2   cups fat-free reduced-sodium
    chicken broth

2   cloves garlic, peeled

1   teaspoon dried thyme

1/4 teaspoon salt

In a large pot, combine the potatoes, parsnips, apples, broth, garlic, thyme, and salt. Cover and bring to a boil over high heat. Reduce the heat to medium-high. Cook, stirring, for 25 to 30 minutes, or until the potatoes are fork-tender.

Drain the cooking broth into a bowl and reserve. Mash the potato mixture with a potato masher. Add enough of the reserved cooking broth to make a moist puree. Stir until smooth.

Makes 4 servings

Per serving
Calories 298   *Sodium 105 mg.*
Total fat 1 g.   *Dietary fiber 10 g.*
Saturated fat 0 g.   *Protein 8 g.*
Cholesterol 0 mg.   *Carbohydrates 67 g.*

POTATOES

Potatoes were once regarded as providing not much more than calories but are now recognized as a nutrient-dense food. A 7-ounce baked potato is an excellent source of the antioxidant vitamin C and the mineral potassium.

Vegetables All Ways

Hit the salad bar for lunch. Shop at the farmers' market for dinner. And be sure to order the vegetable stir-fry next time you're eating at the Chinese restaurant. When you choose vegetables, you eat the very best. Research has shown that a diet rich in fruits and vegetables is important for good health.

The wealth of nutrients packed into vegetables is indisputable. Almost all vegetables are naturally low in calories, fat, and sodium. Many are high in vitamin A, vitamin C, and fiber. And phytochemcials, including antioxidants (see page 190), are substances in vegetables that are under intensive scientific scrutiny for their protective effect on cells.

Dig In to Veggies

The U.S. Department of Agriculture Food Guide Pyramid recommends that we add three to five vegetable servings to our daily intake. A serving is 1 cup of raw leafy vegetables or ½ cup of cut-up cooked, frozen, or canned vegetables.

The nutritional value of frozen and canned vegetables is comparable to fresh, so always stock some frozen and canned (choose reduced-sodium options) vegetables for convenience. Canned vegetables are sometimes a better-tasting option when fresh vegetables, such as tomatoes, are not in peak season.

It really is easy to add vegetables to your day. Try some of the following ideas.

- Prepare a salad, or carry out from the salad bar, to accompany your next meal at home.
- Keep baby carrots on hand for quick snacks.
- Add tomato slices, lettuce, or shredded carrots to your next sandwich.
- Make a big pot of chunky vegetable soup.
- At your next party, serve assorted raw vegetables—broccoli, cauliflower, bell peppers, carrots, and celery—with a fat-free dressing.
- Replace your next soda with reduced-sodium vegetable juice cocktail.
- Add extra fresh, frozen, or canned vegetables to your next soup or salad.

Recipes

New Green Bean Casserole

Photograph on page 129
Hands-on time: 15 minutes
Total time: 55 minutes

¹⁄₂ cup buttermilk

¹⁄₂ cup plain dry bread crumbs

1 onion, cut crosswise into ¹⁄₄"-thick slices and separated into rings

¹⁄₂ pound mushrooms, sliced

1 small onion, chopped

¹⁄₂ teaspoon dried thyme

¹⁄₄ teaspoon salt

¹⁄₄ cup unbleached or all-purpose flour

3 cups 1% milk

1 bag (16 ounces) frozen French-cut green beans, thawed and drained

Preheat the oven to 500°F. Coat a medium baking dish with nonstick spray. Coat a baking sheet with nonstick spray.

Place the buttermilk in a shallow bowl. Place the bread crumbs in another shallow bowl. Dip the onion rings into the buttermilk, then dredge in the bread crumbs and place on the baking sheet. Coat lightly with nonstick spray. Bake for 20 minutes, or until tender and golden brown.

Meanwhile, coat a medium saucepan with nonstick spray. Set over medium heat. Add the mushrooms, chopped onion, thyme, and salt. Coat with nonstick spray. Cook, stirring occasionally, for 4 to 5 minutes, or until the mushrooms give off liquid. Sprinkle with the flour. Cook, stirring, for 1 minute. Add the milk. Cook, stirring constantly, for 3 to 4 minutes, or until thickened. Add the green beans. Stir to mix.

Reduce the oven temperature to 400°F. Pour the bean mixture into the prepared baking dish. Scatter the onion rings over the top. Bake for 25 to 30 minutes, or until hot and bubbly.

Makes 8 servings

Per serving

Calories 122	Sodium 197 mg.
Total fat 2 g.	Dietary fiber 3 g.
Saturated fat 1 g.	Protein 7 g.
Cholesterol 4 mg.	Carbohydrates 21 g.

Cooking Note

Fresh green beans can be used instead of frozen. Trim the ends of the beans and cut diagonally into 2" pieces. Cook in a large pot of boiling water for 2 to 3 minutes, or until crisp-tender. Drain and rinse thoroughly with cold water.

Asian-Style Asparagus

Hands-on time: 10 minutes
Total time: 10 minutes

1 tablespoon soy sauce

2 teaspoons rice wine vinegar

$1\frac{1}{2}$ teaspoons toasted sesame oil

$\frac{1}{2}$ teaspoon chopped fresh ginger

1 clove garlic, minced

$\frac{1}{8}$ teaspoon crushed red-pepper flakes

$1\frac{1}{4}$ pounds thin asparagus spears, ends trimmed

In a small bowl, combine the soy sauce, vinegar, oil, ginger, garlic, and red-pepper flakes. Stir well to blend. Set aside.

Coat a large skillet with nonstick spray. Place over medium-high heat. Add the asparagus. Cover and cook, shaking the pan frequently to turn the asparagus, for 4 to 5 minutes, or until crisp-tender and lightly charred. Add the reserved soy mixture. Cook, shaking the pan, for 1 minute, or until the liquid is reduced to a glaze.

Makes 4 servings

Per serving
Calories 54
Total fat 2 g.
Saturated fat 0 g.
Cholesterol 0 mg.
Sodium 153 mg.
Dietary fiber 3 g.
Protein 4 g.
Carbohydrates 7 g.

Roasted Glazed Beets

Hands-on time: 5 minutes
Total time: 1 hour

$1\frac{1}{2}$ pounds beets, peeled and sliced $\frac{1}{4}$" thick

$\frac{1}{3}$ cup raspberry jam

2 tablespoons red wine vinegar

$\frac{1}{2}$ cup cranberry-raspberry juice

1 tablespoon chopped fresh thyme or 1 teaspoon dried

Preheat the oven to 400°F. Coat a medium baking dish with nonstick spray. In the baking dish, combine the beets, jam, vinegar, juice, and thyme. Stir to blend well. Cover with foil. Bake for 45 minutes. Remove the foil and bake for 10 to 15 minutes longer, or until the beets are soft and tender and the juice is syrupy.

Makes 6 servings

Per serving
Calories 108
Total fat 0 g.
Saturated fat 0 g.
Cholesterol 0 mg.
Sodium 96 mg.
Dietary fiber 3 g.
Protein 2 g.
Carbohydrates 26 g.

ROASTED BEET SALAD

Play it Again!

Use leftover Roasted Glazed Beets to make a wonderful salad. Cut about 2 cups of the beets into thick matchsticks. Place in a bowl with ½ red onion that has been halved and thinly sliced, 6 tablespoons fat-free sour cream, and the juice and grated peel of 1 orange. Toss to mix. Season with salt to taste. Makes 4 servings.

Almond Carrots

Hands-on time: 5 minutes
Total time: 15 minutes

1 pound carrots, sliced into ¹/₄" rounds

1 tablespoon butter or margarine

1 small onion, chopped

1 teaspoon grated fresh ginger

¹/₄ cup orange juice

3 tablespoons almond liqueur or
    ¹/₂ teaspoon almond extract

¹/₈ teaspoon salt

1 tablespoon toasted slivered
    almonds, chopped

Set a steamer rack in a medium saucepan filled with 1" of boiling water. Place the carrots on the rack. Cover and cook over high heat for 10 minutes, or until tender.

Meanwhile, in a medium skillet set over medium-high heat, melt the butter or margarine. Add the onion and ginger. Cook for 2 minutes, or until soft. Add the orange juice, almond liqueur or almond extract, and salt. Cook until reduced by half. Add the carrots and toss to coat. Sprinkle with the almonds.

Makes 4 servings

Per serving
Calories 138   *Sodium 167 mg.*
Total fat 4 g.   *Dietary fiber 4 g.*
Saturated fat 1 g.   *Protein 2 g.*
Cholesterol 3 mg.   *Carbohydrates 20 g.*

VEGE-WISE

Don't be fooled into thinking that vegetarian food products are always low in fat. Although a vegetarian eating plan can be very healthy, many prepared foods labeled as vegetarian may contain large amounts of fat when they are made with ingredients such as oils, full-fat cheese, and soy. Always read the Nutrition Facts label and be aware of how foods are prepared.

Antioxidants

Research suggests that the antioxidant vitamins C, E, and beta-carotene (which the body converts to vitamin A) may play a significant role in the body's defenses against heart disease.

The primary job of antioxidants is to whisk away free radicals, unstable oxygen by-products that are produced by normal bodily functions as well as exposure to cigarette smoke, sunlight, and pollution. Free radicals are dangerous because they are chemically unstable. They carry an unmatched electron, unlike stable molecules, which carry a matched pair of electrons. To try to become stable again, free radicals steal electrons from neighboring molecules, which in turn creates more free radicals. The cell damage that takes place can pave the way for the development of serious health conditions such as cancer or heart disease. Antioxidants neutralize these potentially harmful free radicals by binding to them and restoring their balance.

The best way to get these antioxidant vitamins is in foods, since nutrients that come from foods provide more benefits when they are consumed in combination with each other.

Note: Consult your physician about a vitamin E supplement if you cannot fit the calories into your eating plan. Also consult your physician if you are considering taking in more than 200 IU of vitamin E per day.

- Beta-carotene
  Daily Value: none established
  Recommended intake: 5 to 12 milligrams
  Good sources: pumpkin, sweet potatoes, carrots, cantaloupe

- Vitamin C
  Daily Value: 60 milligrams
  Good Sources: cantaloupe, red bell peppers, kiwifruit, citrus fruits, broccoli

- Vitamin E
  Daily Value: 30 IU or 20 milligrams
  Good sources: sunflower seeds, sunflower oil, almonds, wheat germ

Cheesy Baked Cauliflower

Hands-on time: 10 minutes
Total time: 30 minutes

2 teaspoons vegetable oil

1 small onion, chopped

2 cloves garlic, minced

2 tablespoons unbleached or all-purpose flour

1/4 teaspoon salt

1/8 teaspoon ground nutmeg

1 1/2 cups 1% milk

1/2 cup (2 ounces) shredded low-fat Monterey Jack cheese

1/4 cup (1 ounce) grated Parmesan cheese

1 pound frozen cauliflower pieces, thawed

1 pound frozen sliced carrots, thawed

1/3 cup crushed low-fat round snack crackers

Preheat the oven to 350°F. Coat a medium baking dish with nonstick spray.

Warm the oil in a medium saucepan set over medium heat. Add the onion and garlic. Cook, stirring often, for 5 minutes, or until soft. Sprinkle with the flour, salt, and nutmeg. Cook, stirring constantly, for 1 minute. Stir in the milk. Cook, stirring often, for 5 minutes, or until thickened. Remove from the heat. Stir in the Monterey Jack and Parmesan until melted. Add the cauliflower and carrots. Stir to coat. Spoon into the prepared baking dish. Sprinkle with the crackers.

Bake for 15 to 20 minutes, or until heated through and bubbly.

Makes 6 servings

Per serving
Calories 247   *Sodium 572 mg.*
Total fat 7 g.   *Dietary fiber 5 g.*
Saturated fat 3 g.   *Protein 12 g.*
Cholesterol 12 mg.   *Carbohydrates 36 g.*

Cooking Note

You can also use cooked fresh cauliflower (the florets from 1 head) and cooked sliced fresh carrots (1 pound) for this dish.

CREAMY CHEESY CAULIFLOWER SOUP

In a food processor, combine 3 cups of the leftover Cheesy Baked Cauliflower, 1 cup 1% milk, and 1 cup fat-free reduced-sodium chicken broth. Pulse to puree. Pour into a medium saucepan. Cook over medium heat until hot. Season to taste with salt and ground black pepper. Garnish with chopped fresh parsley, if desired. Makes 4 servings.

Corn and Zucchini Cakes

Hands-on time: 15 minutes
Total time: 25 minutes

1/4 cup unbleached or all-purpose flour

1/4 cup cornmeal

1/2 teaspoon baking powder

1/2 teaspoon salt

2 cups fresh or frozen corn kernels, thawed

1/3 cup water

1 small zucchini, cut into 1/4" pieces

1 small onion, chopped

2 tablespoons chopped fresh basil or 1 teaspoon dried

1/4 cup fat-free milk

2 eggs

In a large bowl, combine the flour, cornmeal, baking powder, and salt. Stir to mix. Set aside.

Place the corn and water in a medium skillet set over medium-high heat. Cook for 2 to 3 minutes, or until the corn is tender and the water has evaporated. Remove about 1 cup to a food processor or blender. Add the remaining corn to the bowl with the flour.

Coat the skillet with nonstick spray. Set over medium heat. Add the zucchini, onion, and parsley or basil. Cook for 3 to 4 minutes, or until soft. Remove to the bowl with the flour mixture.

Meanwhile, add the milk and eggs to the food processor or blender. Process to make a coarse puree. Add to the reserved flour mixture and zucchini mixture. Stir to combine.

Coat a large skillet with nonstick spray. Set over medium heat. Spoon about 2 tablespoons

of the batter per cake into the pan to form 3"-wide cakes. Cook for 3 minutes, or until golden brown and crisp on the bottom. Flip the cakes and cook for 3 minutes, or until golden brown and heated through. Repeat with the remaining batter to make a total of 12 cakes.

Makes 4 servings

Per serving
Calories 223	*Sodium 398 mg.*
Total fat 7 g.	*Dietary fiber 4 g.*
Saturated fat 1 g.	*Protein 9 g.*
Cholesterol 107 mg.	*Carbohydrates 35 g.*

A New Twist

CHUNKY TOMATO SAUCE

This light tomato sauce makes a nice special addition to Corn and Zucchini Cakes and is best when made with garden tomatoes. Warm 1 tablespoon extra-virgin olive oil in a medium skillet over medium heat. Add 1 pound peeled, seeded, and chopped tomatoes and 1 minced clove of garlic. Cook, stirring occasionally, for 5 to 7 minutes, or until heated through. Stir in 1/4 cup chopped fresh basil leaves. Season with salt and ground black pepper to taste. Stir to mix. Makes 4 servings.

Eggplant Parmesan

Hands-on time: 20 minutes
Total time: 1 hour

2 eggplants, peeled and cut crosswise
   into $^1/4$"-thick slices

1 cup (8 ounces) liquid egg substitute

$1^1/2$ cups plain dry bread crumbs

$1^1/2$ tablespoons dried Italian seasoning

1 jar (26 ounces) pasta sauce

2 cups (8 ounces) shredded low-fat
   mozzarella cheese

$^1/3$ cup ($1^1/2$ ounces) grated Parmesan
   cheese

Preheat the oven to 400°F. Coat a 13" × 9" baking dish with nonstick spray. Coat 2 baking sheets with nonstick spray.

Arrange the eggplant in a single layer on the prepared baking sheets. Bake for 15 minutes, or until soft.

Meanwhile, pour the egg substitute into a shallow bowl. In another shallow bowl, combine the bread crumbs and Italian seasoning. Stir to blend. One at a time, dip the eggplant slices into the egg substitute and then into the bread crumbs to coat both sides. Return to the baking sheets. Coat with nonstick spray.

Preheat the broiler. Broil the eggplant 4" from the heat for 2 minutes, or until golden. Turn the slices. Coat with nonstick spray. Broil for 2 minutes longer, or until golden.

Preheat the oven to 350°F.

Spread one-third of the pasta sauce in the prepared baking dish. Top with half of the eggplant slices in a single layer. Sprinkle with half of the mozzarella and half of the Parmesan.

Spread with another one-third of the sauce. Top with the remaining eggplant slices. Spread with the remaining sauce. Sprinkle with the remaining mozzarella and Parmesan. Bake for 30 minutes, or until bubbly and the cheese has melted.

Makes 8 servings

Per serving
Calories 293	*Sodium 884 mg.*
Total fat 8 g.	*Dietary fiber 6 g.*
Saturated fat 4 g.	*Protein 20 g.*
Cholesterol 19 mg.	*Carbohydrates 35 g.*

Stuffed Eggplant Pinwheels

Cut 1 eggplant into ¼"-thick lengthwise slices. Arrange in a single layer on a baking sheet coated with nonstick spray. Bake in a 375°F oven for 15 minutes, or until soft. Make your favorite ricotta filling, perhaps with some cooked chopped spinach mixed in. Spoon 2 rounded tablespoons of the filling onto each eggplant slice and roll up. Place in a baking dish coated with nonstick spray. Top with pasta sauce and a little low-fat shredded mozzarella cheese. Bake in a 375°F oven for 15 minutes, or until heated through.

Spaghetti Squash Casserole

Photograph on page 128
Hands-on time: 15 minutes
Total time: 1 hour and 5 minutes

1 spaghetti squash, halved lengthwise and seeds removed

1 tablespoon vegetable oil

1 small onion, chopped

2 cloves garlic, chopped

1 teaspoon dried basil

2 plum tomatoes, chopped

1 cup (8 ounces) 1% cottage cheese

1/2 cup (2 ounces) shredded low-fat mozzarella cheese

1/4 cup chopped parsley

1/4 teaspoon salt

1/4 cup (1 ounce) grated Parmesan cheese

3 tablespoons seasoned dry bread crumbs

Preheat the oven to 400°F. Coat a 13" × 9" baking dish and a baking sheet with nonstick spray. Place the squash, cut side down, on the sheet. Bake for 30 minutes, or until tender when pierced with a sharp knife. With a fork, scrape the squash strands into a large bowl.

Meanwhile, warm the oil in a medium skillet set over medium heat. Add the onion, garlic, and basil. Cook for 4 to 5 minutes, or until the onion is soft. Add the tomatoes. Cook for 3 to 4 minutes, or until the mixture is dry.

To the bowl with the squash, add the cottage cheese, mozzarella, parsley, salt, and the onion mixture. Stir to mix. Pour into the prepared baking dish. Sprinkle with the Parmesan and bread crumbs.

Bake for 30 minutes, or until bubbly and heated through.

Makes 6 servings

Per serving
Calories 202   *Sodium 547 mg.*
Total fat 6 g.   *Dietary fiber 5 g.*
Saturated fat 2 g.   *Protein 13 g.*
Cholesterol 12 mg.   *Carbohydrates 25 g.*

Cooking Note
Spaghetti squash can also be cooked in the microwave oven. Pierce the squash in several places with a knife. Place on a microwaveable plate and cover loosely with a piece of plastic wrap. Microwave on high power for 20 minutes, turning twice, or until tender when pierced with a knife. Remove and allow to stand for 5 minutes to cool. Carefully cut the squash in halve lengthwise. Scoop out and discard the seeds and pulp. With a fork, scrape the squash strands into a large bowl.

A New Twist

SPAGHETTI SQUASH FLORENTINE CASSEROLE

Add 2 ounces prosciutto, trimmed of fat and chopped, and 1 box (10 ounces) frozen chopped spinach that has been thawed, drained, and squeezed dry.

Stuffed Acorn Squash

Photograph on page 131
Hands-on time: 15 minutes
Total time: 45 minutes

Makes 6 servings

Per serving
Calories 309   Sodium 284 mg.
Total fat 3 g.   Dietary fiber 8 g.
Saturated fat 1 g.   Protein 6 g.
Cholesterol 0 mg.   Carbohydrates 68 g.

3 acorn squash, cut in half lengthwise, seeds removed

2 teaspoons vegetable oil

1 small onion, chopped

1 rib celery, chopped

1 clove garlic, chopped

3 ounces mushrooms, sliced

¹/₄ cup chopped fresh parsley and/or thyme or sage or 2 teaspoons dried

1 cup coarse fresh bread crumbs

²/₃ cup dried cranberries

1 teaspoon grated lemon peel

¹/₄ teaspoon salt

²/₃ cup quick-cooking barley, cooked

¹/₄–¹/₂ cup vegetable broth or apple juice

Preheat the oven to 400°F. Place the squash, cut side up, on a baking sheet. Coat the cut sides lightly with nonstick spray. Bake for 30 minutes, or until fork-tender.

Meanwhile, warm the oil in a medium nonstick skillet set over medium heat. Add the onion, celery, and garlic. Cook for 2 minutes. Add the mushrooms and parsley and/or thyme or sage. Cook for 4 minutes, or until the mushrooms are soft. Remove from the heat. Add the bread crumbs, cranberries, lemon peel, salt, and barley. Stir to mix. Add up to ½ cup broth or juice to moisten and bind the stuffing.

Reduce the oven temperature to 350°F. Spoon the stuffing into the squash halves. Bake for 10 to 12 minutes, or until heated through.

Good for You

INGREDIENT OPTIONS

Ingredients for savory recipes should be considered options, not dictates. If you don't care for an ingredient in the list, feel free to make substitutions. Any number of grains can take the place of barley in Stuffed Acorn Squash, for example. Try quinoa, millet, cracked wheat berries, or even chunks of whole-grain bread. Instead of cranberries, use dried cherries, dried apricots, diced apples, diced pears, or another fresh or dried fruit of your choice. By tailoring recipes to suit your tastes, a heart-healthy eating plan is sure to succeed.

All about Onions and Garlic

Great flavor runs in the allium family. Onions, garlic, scallions, leeks, shallots, and chives are alliums that cooks around the world turn to as aromatic bases for a variety of dishes. But scientists are discovering a host of health benefits in these foods, as well. Members of the allium family contain dozens of compounds that provide protection from heart disease, high cholesterol, high blood pressure, and cancer.

Proper storage is important to make sure that the onions and garlic you buy give you the best flavor and health benefits.

Garlic bulbs are best stored in an open container in a cool, dry place. Be sure to store away from other foods. Whole bulbs should last up to 2 months. Once a bulb has been broken, try to use the cloves within 3 weeks.

Green onions, such as scallions, leeks, and chives, should be refrigerated in a plastic bag in the vegetable crisper of the refrigerator and used within a week.

Dry onions, such as white and red onions and shallots, are mature onions covered with a papery skin. They can be stored longer and have a stronger taste. Store dry onions in a cool, dry place, preferably in a container that al-lows air to circulate around the vegetables. Dry onions can be stored successfully for 2 to 3 months, depending on their condition when purchased and the level of humidity in the storage area.

Garlic is typically minced and used as a flavoring in sauces. But do try roasting garlic, which turns the cloves into a mild creamy spread that makes a delicious fat-free flavorful bread topping.

Onions are very versatile, and different methods of cooking bring out different sides of their flavor personalities. Some common methods of preparation are raw, caramelized, sautéed, braised, grilled, roasted, or stewed.

Don't let fear of crying prevent you from using more onions. When an onion is cut, it emits a sulfuric compound that aggravates many people's eyes. To alleviate this, some cooks recommend refrigerating an onion for about 15 minutes prior to cutting. Another tip is to light a match as soon as you have made the first cut. The theory is that a compound in the match neutralizes the sulfur from the onion. Many cooking experts also advise keeping the root end in tact when cutting an onion to minimize some of the powerful fumes.

Roasted Carrots and Parsnips

Photograph on page 286
Hands-on time: 10 minutes
Total time: 55 minutes

1 pound carrots, cut in 1" chunks

1 pound parsnips, cut in 1" chunks

4 small red onions, cut into wedges

6 cloves garlic

$^1\!/_2$ tablespoon olive oil

$^1\!/_2$ teaspoon salt

$^1\!/_2$ teaspoon grated lemon peel

Preheat the oven to 375°F. Coat a medium baking dish with nonstick spray. Add the carrots, parsnips, onions, garlic, oil, salt, and lemon peel. Toss to coat evenly. Bake for 40 to 45 minutes, stirring halfway through the cooking time, or until golden and tender.

Makes 6 servings

Per serving
Calories 117
Total fat 1 g.
Saturated fat 0 g.
Cholesterol 0 mg.

Sodium 256 mg.
Dietary fiber 6 g.
Protein 3 g.
Carbohydrates 27 g.

Try it — HOME COOKING

"This would be a great dish for vegetarians. I found that it made the house smell unusually good. Quartered red-skin potatoes would be a nice addition," says Marcy Ravdin, part-time administrative assistant and mother of one.

Root Vegetable Mash

Photograph on page 225
Hands-on time: 10 minutes
Total time: 25 minutes

3 pounds sweet potatoes, peeled and cut into small chunks

1 pound celery root, peeled and cut into small chunks

2 cloves garlic

$^1\!/_3$ cup 1% milk, warmed

1$^1\!/_2$ tablespoons olive oil

$^1\!/_2$ teaspoon salt

In a large saucepan, combine the sweet potatoes, celery root, and garlic. Add water to cover. Cover and bring to a boil over high heat. Reduce the heat to medium-high. Cook for 20 minutes, or until the celery root is very tender when pierced with a fork. Drain and return to the pan. With a potato masher, mash into a coarse puree. Add the milk, oil, and salt. Mash to blend.

Makes 8 servings

Per serving
Calories 191
Total fat 3 g.
Saturated fat 0.5 g.
Cholesterol 0 mg.

Sodium 239 mg.
Dietary fiber 6 g.
Protein 4 g.
Carbohydrates 39 g.

Mediterranean Vegetables with Beans

Hands-on time: 10 minutes
Total time: 20 minutes

4 medium-large zucchini and/or yellow squash, sliced diagonally $1/4$" thick

4 carrots, peeled and sliced diagonally $1/4$" thick

1 red onion, cut in half and into wedges

1 red bell pepper, seeded and cut into $1/2$"-wide strips

2 tablespoons fat-free reduced-sodium chicken broth

1 tablespoon red wine vinegar

$1^{1}/2$ teaspoons olive oil

$1^{1}/2$ teaspoons Dijon mustard

1 clove garlic, minced

1 teaspoon sugar

1 teaspoon dried basil

$1/4$ teaspoon salt

1 can (15 ounces) cannellini beans, rinsed and drained

Coat a grill rack or broiler pan with nonstick spray. Preheat the grill or broiler.

Place the zucchini and/or yellow squash, carrots, onion, and bell pepper on the prepared rack or pan. Coat with nonstick spray. Grill or broil, turning occasionally, for 8 to 10 minutes, or until tender.

Meanwhile, in a large bowl, combine the broth, vinegar, oil, mustard, garlic, sugar, basil, and salt. Whisk to blend. Add the beans.

Remove the zucchini and/or yellow squash, carrots, onion, and bell pepper to the bowl with the beans. Toss to coat.

Makes 6 servings

Per serving
Calories 161   *Sodium 160 mg.*
Total fat 2 g.   *Dietary fiber 8 g.*
Saturated fat 0 g.   *Protein 9 g.*
Cholesterol 0 mg.   *Carbohydrates 30 g.*

A New Twist

MEDITERRANEAN VEGETABLE-BEAN PASTA SALAD

Grill or broil half the amount of the zucchini, carrots, onion, and red bell pepper. Cook 8 ounces penne or other tube-shaped pasta according to package directions. Drain and rinse with cold water. Transfer to the large bowl with the other ingredients. Add 1/3 cup (1½ ounces) grated Parmesan cheese. Toss to blend well. Makes 6 servings.

Roasted Vegetable Strudels

Hands-on time: 20 minutes
Total time: 1 hour

2 medium-large zucchini and/or
   yellow squash, cut into $1/2$" cubes

1 large red onion, coarsely chopped

1 large red bell pepper, cut into
   $1/2$" cubes

1 eggplant, cut into $1/2$" cubes

2 ounces fat-free cream cheese

$1/2$ cup (2 ounces) goat cheese

$1/3$ cup chopped fresh basil

$1/4$ teaspoon salt

12 sheets (17" × 11") frozen phyllo
   dough, thawed

Preheat the oven to 400°F. Coat 2 baking sheets with nonstick spray.

Spread the zucchini and/or yellow squash, onion, bell pepper, and eggplant out on the prepared baking sheets in an even layer. Coat with nonstick spray. Bake, turning occasionally, for 25 minutes, or until soft.

Meanwhile, in a large bowl, combine the cream cheese and goat cheese. Stir in the roasted vegetables, basil, and salt.

Rinse 1 baking sheet and wipe dry. Coat with nonstick spray. Set aside.

Place 1 sheet of phyllo dough on a work surface, long side facing you. Coat lightly with nonstick spray. Top with 3 more sheets, coating each sheet lightly with nonstick spray. Starting at the center of the top edge, cut the stack in half. You will now have 2 smaller rectangles with the shorter sides facing you.

Divide the roasted vegetable mixture into 6 equal portions. Spoon one-sixth of the vegetables in the center of one stack, leaving a 1" inch border along all sides. Starting at the bottom, roll the dough over the vegetables once, jelly-roll style, then fold in the sides of the dough. Continue to roll away from you to form a tight cylinder. Place on the prepared baking sheet. Spoon another one-sixth of the vegetables in the center of the second stack. Roll into a cylinder and place on the baking sheet.

Repeat with the remaining 8 sheets of phyllo and vegetables to form 4 more strudels. Lightly coat the strudels with nonstick spray. Bake for 10 to 12 minutes, or until golden brown and heated through.

Makes 6 servings

Per serving
Calories 342   *Sodium 566 mg.*
Total fat 9 g.   *Dietary fiber 6 g.*
Saturated fat 3 g.   *Protein 12 g.*
Cholesterol 8 mg.   *Carbohydrates 54 g.*

A New Twist

ROASTED RED PEPPER PUREE

Try this colorful sauce with the Roasted Vegetable Strudels. Place 2 roasted red peppers in a blender or food processor. Puree until smooth. Add ¼ cup fat-free reduced-sodium chicken broth or water, 1 tablespoon olive oil, and ⅛ teaspoon each salt and ground black pepper. Pulse to mix. Drizzle over the strudels before serving. Makes 6 servings.

Autumn Vegetable Casserole

Hands-on time: 20 minutes
Total time: 1 hour and 10 minutes

Juice and grated peel of 1 orange

2 teaspoons cornstarch

2 pounds sweet potatoes, peeled and cut into $^1/2$" cubes

2 carrots, peeled and sliced into $^1/2$"-thick rounds

$^3/4$ cup pitted prunes, halved

1 can (8 ounces) unsweetened pineapple chunks

2 tablespoons chopped crystallized ginger

1 teaspoon ground cinnamon

$^1/4$ cup toasted chopped pecans

Preheat the oven to 375°F. Coat a 13" × 9" baking dish with nonstick spray.

In a large bowl, combine the orange juice with the cornstarch. Stir to dissolve. Add the orange peel, sweet potatoes, carrots, prunes, pineapple chunks (with juice), ginger, and cinnamon. Stir well to blend. Pour into the prepared baking dish. Cover with foil.

Bake for 45 minutes. Remove the foil. Sprinkle with the pecans. Bake for 15 minutes longer, or until the vegetables are fork-tender and the sauce is syrupy.

Makes 8 servings

Per serving

Calories 238	*Sodium 21 mg.*
Total fat 3 g.	*Dietary fiber 7 g.*
Saturated fat 0 g.	*Protein 3 g.*
Cholesterol 0 mg.	*Carbohydrates 54 g.*

Cooking Note

For a quicker version, substitute ½ cup prepared orange juice for the fresh squeezed and eliminate the peel.

SPICES

Spices are aromatic or pungent seasonings that come from the bark, buds, fruits, roots, seeds, or stems of plants or trees. Cinnamon, black pepper, and ginger are but three vibrant spices that add a lot of flavor excitement to dishes with no added fat.

It can be the best of dines. It can be the worst of dines. The popular salad bar offers Americans probably their most frequent dining-out opportunity to load up on healthful vegetables and fruits. But it also serves up fat-laden dressings and condiments that can sink the noblest healthful eating intentions.

Composing a salad for flavor and health—whether at home or at a restaurant—is easy once you know the basics. "Salads are beautifully flexible. They're *the* health food for the new millenium," says Kathy Fleegler, certified culinary professional and cooking teacher at the University of Pennsylvania in Philadelphia. "Make them simple or complex, hot or cold, raw or cooked. They are nature's way of putting antioxidants on a plate instead of in a pill," she says. "Healthy and bursting with flavor, you can transform vegetables into a exciting meal. The choice is yours."

Fortunately, nature has color-coded the most healthful salad vegetables to make it easy for us. All we have to do is choose greens and vegetables with the deepest color. The deeper the color, the greater the nutrients. Spinach, broccoli, carrots, curly endive, escarole, arugula, radicchio, watercress, romaine, green-leaf lettuce, red-leaf lettuce, bell peppers, tomatoes, green cabbage, and red cabbage are all better choices than iceberg lettuce, which pales nutritionally in comparison.

Have a variety of greens washed and in your refrigerator so that you can put together a snack salad or dinner salad in just minutes. You can buy prewashed packaged mixed greens. Or, you can wash and dry greens and store in paper towel–lined plastic storage bags.

Salads can be as simple as leaf lettuce lightly dressed in extra-virgin olive oil and wine vinegar or as elaborate as a taco salad with red-leaf lettuce, corn, beans, low-fat cheese, and baked tortilla chips.

With the addition of a lean protein, main-dish options expand. Canned tuna packed in water, grilled chicken or turkey breast, cubed tofu, and cooked shrimp are a few tasty possibilities. Drizzle salads with purchased or homemade low-fat dressings (see "All Dressed Up" on page 206) and top with highly flavored naturally low-fat condiments such as minced fresh herbs, chopped raw onions or grilled onions, raisins, and low-fat croutons. Just a teaspoon of intensely flavored grated cheeses, such as Parmesan or Romano, can make an immense flavor difference.

Recipes

Fiesta Pasta Salad

Photograph on page 133
Hands-on time: 10 minutes
Total time: 15 minutes

1 can (5½ ounces) vegetable juice cocktail

2 tablespoons lime juice

½–1 teaspoon hot-pepper sauce

2 cloves garlic, minced

½ teaspoon sugar

¼ teaspoon ground cumin

¼ teaspoon salt

8 ounces rotelle pasta, cooked and drained

3 ounces sliced smoked turkey ham, cut into 1" strips

1 can (15 ounces) dark red kidney beans, rinsed and drained

8 ounces frozen corn kernels, thawed

1 cup (4 ounces) shredded low-fat Cheddar cheese

3 plum tomatoes, chopped

3 scallions, sliced

2 ounces sliced pitted black olives

In a large bowl, combine the vegetable juice, lime juice, ½ teaspoon hot-pepper sauce, garlic, sugar, cumin, and salt. Whisk to mix. Add the pasta, ham, beans, corn, Cheddar, tomatoes, scallions, and olives. Toss to mix. Taste and add up to ½ teaspoon more hot-pepper sauce, if desired.

Makes 8 servings

Per serving

Calories 237	Sodium 376 mg.
Total fat 3 g.	Dietary fiber 7 g.
Saturated fat 1 g.	Protein 14 g.
Cholesterol 8 mg.	Carbohydrates 40 g.

PLANT POWER

Phytochemicals are compounds produced by plants, including fruits, vegetables, legumes, and whole grains, to protect themselves against viruses, bacteria, and insect predators. Scientific research has found that these same compounds fight heart disease, cancer, and other diseases in humans. Eating a variety of fresh fruits and vegetables is currently the wisest option to take in as many of these compounds as possible.

Asian Slaw

Photograph on page 281
Hands-on time: 15 minutes
Total time: 15 minutes

1/4 cup rice wine vinegar or white wine vinegar

2 tablespoons soy sauce

1 teaspoon grated fresh ginger

1 teaspoon toasted sesame oil

1/2 head Chinese or Savoy cabbage, shredded

2 carrots, shredded

3 scallions, sliced

1/2 red bell pepper, cut into slivers

2 tablespoons chopped fresh cilantro

2 teaspoons sesame seeds, toasted

In a large bowl, combine the vinegar, soy sauce, ginger, and oil. Add the cabbage, carrots, scallions, bell pepper, and cilantro. Toss to coat. Sprinkle each serving with sesame seeds.

Makes 4 servings

Per serving
Calories 85   *Sodium 634 mg.*
Total fat 2 g.   *Dietary fiber 5 g.*
Saturated fat 0 g.   *Protein 4 g.*
Cholesterol 0 mg.   *Carbohydrates 16 g.*

CARROTS

Carrots are the leading source of the antioxidant beta-carotene and a good source of soluble fiber, both of which are beneficial for a healthy heart. Fortunately, carrots are such an easy, appealing snack that's it's easy to get all you need. Keep cleaned carrot sticks or bags of precut baby carrots on hand for munching. Grated carrots can be easily added to soups and salads for a nutrient boost.

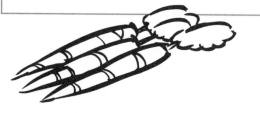

Yankee Doodle Macaroni Salad

Photograph on page 215
Hands-on time: 15 minutes
Total time: 1 hour and 15 minutes

- 1/2 cup fat-free sour cream
- 1/4 cup low-fat mayonnaise
- 1 1/2 tablespoons red wine vinegar or cider vinegar
- 1/2 teaspoon salt
- 8 ounces macaroni, cooked and drained
- 4 ribs celery, sliced
- 3 scallions, sliced
- 1/2 cup frozen peas, thawed
- 1 jar (4 ounces) diced pimientos, drained
- 2 hard-cooked eggs, coarsely chopped
- 2 tablespoons chopped parsley

In a large bowl, combine the sour cream, mayonnaise, vinegar, and salt. Add the macaroni, celery, scallions, peas, pimientos, eggs, and parsley. Toss to coat. Cover and refrigerate for at least 1 hour.

Makes 8 servings

Per serving
Calories 154   *Sodium 294 mg.*
Total fat 1 g.   *Dietary fiber 2 g.*
Saturated fat 0 g.   *Protein 7 g.*
Cholesterol 27mg.   *Carbohydrates 28 g.*

Good for You

Maybe Not Mayonnaise

Mayonnaise-based salads can contain as much fat and sodium as french fries or potato chips. Steer clear of creamy potato salad, macaroni salad, and coleslaw from delicatessens or salad bars. Make your own healthier versions at home using low-fat mayonnaise or yogurt. Or, dress them with low-fat vinaigrettes.

All Dressed Up

Many health-conscious individuals turn to commercial low-fat or fat-free dressings to pare the fat from their salads. Unfortunately, many fat-free dressings are very acidic and lack flavor. So, the next time you put together a salad, give it a toss with one of these easy-to-make reduced-fat dressings. Each one makes about 1 cup. They can all be refrigerated, in a sealed container, for up to 1 week.

Asian Dressing. Whisk ⅓ cup orange juice, ⅓ cup soy sauce, ¼ cup honey, and 1 teaspoon grated fresh ginger. Add 1 teaspoon sesame seeds or ⅛ teaspoon toasted sesame oil, if desired.

Balsamic Vinaigrette. Whisk ⅔ cup balsamic vinegar, ⅓ cup extra-virgin olive oil, 1 teaspoon Dijon mustard, 1 teaspoon honey, and a pinch each of salt and ground black pepper.

Cool-and-Spicy Cucumber Dressing. Peel and shred enough cucumber to make ½ cup. Squeeze out all excess moisture. Combine with 1 cup fat-free plain yogurt or fat-free sour cream, 1 teaspoon Dijon mustard, 1 minced clove garlic, and a pinch each of salt and ground black pepper.

Tarragon Ranch Dressing. Combine 1 cup buttermilk, 1 tablespoon lemon juice, 2 minced cloves garlic, 1 tablespoon chopped fresh tarragon or 2 teaspoons dried tarragon, and a pinch each of salt, ground black pepper, and sugar.

Sunny Waldorf Salad

Hands-on time: 10 minutes
Total time: 10 minutes

³/4 cup low-fat plain yogurt

¹/2 cup orange juice

1¹/2 tablespoons honey

¹/2 teaspoon ground cinnamon

3 apples, cut into ¹/2" chunks

1 large orange, separated into segments

1 rib celery, chopped

¹/2 cup golden raisins

3 tablespoons coarsely chopped cashews

In a large bowl, combine the yogurt, orange juice, honey, and cinnamon. Add the apples, orange segments, celery, raisins, and cashews. Stir to mix.

Makes 6 servings

Per serving
Calories 162
Total fat 3 g.
Saturated fat 1 g.
Cholesterol 2 mg.
Sodium 57 mg.
Dietary fiber 4 g.
Protein 3 g.
Carbohydrates 34 g.

Good for You

TEXTURIZE

When creating a salad, try to balance textures and flavors by combining crunchy with soft, raw with cooked, and robust flavors rounded out by milder seasonings. To an assortment of greens, add crunchy bean sprouts, water chestnuts, sunflower seeds, fresh and roasted vegetables, fresh and dried fruits, and fresh herbs.

Spinach-Orange Salad with Sesame

Hands-on time: 10 minutes
Total time: 15 minutes

1	teaspoon sugar
1/2	teaspoon cornstarch
1/3	cup orange juice
1 1/2	tablespoons rice wine vinegar
1	teaspoon grated fresh ginger or 1/4 teaspoon ground
1	clove garlic, chopped
1 1/2	teaspoons toasted sesame oil
10	ounces baby spinach leaves
2	navel oranges, separated into segments
1	small red onion, thinly sliced
1	kiwifruit, sliced

Place the sugar and cornstarch in a small saucepan. Gradually add the orange juice and vinegar, whisking to dissolve the dry ingredients. Add the ginger and garlic. Cook, stirring, over medium-high heat for 2 to 3 minutes, or just until the mixture boils. Remove and whisk in the oil. Allow to cool.

In a large bowl, combine the spinach, orange segments, onion, and kiwifruit. Add the dressing. Toss to coat evenly.

Makes 4 servings

Per serving

Calories 113	Sodium 60 mg.
Total fat 2 g.	Dietary fiber 6 g.
Saturated fat 0 g.	Protein 4 g.
Cholesterol 0 mg.	Carbohydrates 23 g.

CLASSIC STAR

KIWIFRUIT

Kiwifruit is a vitamin C gold mine that also contains potassium, magnesium, and fiber. Add slices or wedges to salads or fruit desserts or eat them out-of-hand for a satisfying snack anytime. For the best-tasting kiwifruit, choose ones that yield slightly when pressed.

Bean Counter Salad

Hands-on time: 10 minutes
Total time: 15 minutes

10 ounces green beans, cut into 1¹/₂" pieces

2 tablespoons apple cider vinegar

¹/₄ cup apple juice

1 small onion, chopped

2 teaspoons vegetable oil

2 teaspoons honey

1 teaspoon Dijon mustard

¹/₂ teaspoon Italian seasoning

¹/₈ teaspoons salt

1 can (15 ounces) red kidney beans, rinsed and drained

1 tomato, chopped

Set a steamer rack in a medium saucepan filled with 1" of boiling water. Place the green beans on the rack. Cover and cook over high heat for 5 to 6 minutes, or until tender. Drain and rinse under cold running water.

Meanwhile, in a large bowl, combine the vinegar, apple juice, onion, oil, honey, mustard, Italian seasoning, and salt. Whisk to blend. Add the green beans, kidney beans, and tomato. Toss to coat.

Makes 6 servings

Per serving
Calories 130	*Sodium 75 mg.*
Total fat 2 g.	*Dietary fiber 8 g.*
Saturated fat 0 g.	*Protein 6 g.*
Cholesterol 0 mg.	*Carbohydrates 23 g.*

Good for You

WATER WORKS

Fluids are extremely important year-round, but they're critical throughout the summer months when the heat can dehydrate you. Don't wait until you are thirsty—sip beverages throughout the day to ensure that you stay hydrated. Strive for 8 cups of caffeine-free beverages and even more if you are physically active. Water is the best choice, but other fluids can add variety. Fruit juices with seltzer water added are refreshing. Smoothies made with yogurt, fresh or frozen fruit, and fruit juices are nutritious and energy-boosting.

Mexican Cobb Salad

Hands-on time: 15 minutes
Total time: 15 minutes

- 1 large head romaine lettuce, chopped
- 1 package (10 ounces) frozen corn kernels, thawed
- 1 can (15 ounces) black beans, rinsed and drained
- 1 large tomato, chopped
- 2 ribs celery, chopped
- 1 green bell pepper, chopped
- 1 red onion, chopped
- 1 1/2 cups (6 ounces) shredded fat-free Monterey Jack cheese
- 8 slices turkey bacon, cooked and crumbled
- 1 ripe avocado, cut into chunks
- 1 1/2 cups buttermilk
- 2 tablespoons lime juice
- 1/2 teaspoon hot-pepper sauce

Arrange the lettuce on a large platter. Arrange the corn, beans, tomato, celery, bell pepper, onion, Monterey Jack, and bacon crosswise in strips over the lettuce.

In a food processor or blender, combine the avocado, buttermilk, lime juice, and hot-pepper sauce. Process until smooth. Drizzle over the salad.

Makes 8 servings

Per serving
Calories 221	Sodium 618 mg.
Total fat 7 g.	Dietary fiber 7 g.
Saturated fat 2 g.	Protein 16 g.
Cholesterol 16 mg.	Carbohydrates 27 g.

A New Twist

CILANTRO VINAIGRETTE

If you prefer a vinaigrette to a creamy dressing, this one goes great with Mexican Cobb Salad. In a medium bowl, whisk ¾ cup apple cider vinegar, ½ cup chopped fresh cilantro, 6 tablespoons apple juice, 2 tablespoons extra-virgin olive oil, 3 seeded and minced pickled jalapeño chile peppers, 2 minced cloves garlic, 2 teaspoons Dijon mustard, and 2 teaspoons honey. Season with salt and ground black pepper to taste.

BLT Bread Salad

Hands-on time: 10 minutes
Total time: 20 minutes

6 plum tomatoes, chopped

2 cloves garlic, minced

1/3 cup chopped fresh basil or 1 1/2 teaspoons dried

3 tablespoons balsamic vinegar

1/2 teaspoon salt

12 slices turkey bacon, cooked and crumbled

1/2 small red onion, halved and thinly sliced

8 ounces French bread, cubed (about 6 cups)

1/2 pound romaine lettuce leaves, shredded

In a large bowl, combine the tomatoes, garlic, basil, vinegar, and salt. Mash the tomatoes and garlic with a fork until coarsely pureed. Add the bacon, onion, and bread. Toss to coat. Let stand for 10 minutes so that the bread absorbs some of the juices. Toss in the lettuce.

Makes 6 servings

Per serving

Calories 180	*Sodium 682 mg.*
Total fat 5 g.	*Dietary fiber 3 g.*
Saturated fat 1 g.	*Protein 8 g.*
Cholesterol 16 mg.	*Carbohydrates 27 g.*

Good for You

EASY ON ALCOHOL

Although research shows a potential correlation between the reduced risk of heart disease and light to moderate alcohol consumption, it is not recommended for anyone to begin drinking alcohol for the sake of heart health. While light to moderate alcohol intake may decrease heart disease rates, overconsumption of alcohol decreases longevity. Moderate intake is defined as two drinks or fewer a day for men and one drink or fewer for women. One drink equals 12 ounces of beer, 5 ounces or wine, or 1½ ounces of hard liquor.

Strive for Five

The Five-a-Day program to increase fruit and vegetable consumption was launched by the Produce for Better Health Foundation and the National Cancer Institute, with the support of every major health promotion and disease prevention program in the country. The goal is to decrease individuals' risk of developing heart disease and certain cancers.

Eating more fruits and vegetables is easy with a little forethought and planning. Availability is the key. If you buy them, you just may eat them. If you shop for groceries once a week, purchase some fresh vegetables and fruits to enjoy early in the week as well as an assortment of canned and frozen produce to carry you through to the next shopping day. Here are just a few of the many tasty ways you can up your intake of fruits and vegetables.

- Try topping your next breakfast with some fruit. Whether it's a banana on a bowl of cereal, berries over freezer waffles, or sliced strawberries over fat-free plain yogurt, this fruit serving, along with a 6-ounce glass of pure fruit juice, will rack up 2 servings before your day even begins.
- Keep a bowl of fresh fruit visible at all times. So instead of going for a high-calorie dessert, the fruit will be available and appealing.
- Plan for fruit or vegetable snacks on the go or at the office. Many fruits and vegetables come already packaged by nature. Bananas, apples, oranges, and peaches are all neat, sweet, and easy to pack. Baby carrots, broccoli, and cauliflower florets are portable when packed in resealable plastic bags.
- Fruit smoothies (see Shakes, Smoothies, and Other Drinks on page 341) provide all the satisfaction of a creamy, rich ice cream shake with none of the fat.
- Many restaurant entrées come with something fried on the side. Ask for a baked potato, a green salad, or fresh fruit instead. Most of the time, this healthful exchange will be yours for the asking.
- Combination dishes such as casseroles, pastas, soups, and stir-fries are like welcome mats for more vegetables. Simply decrease the meat or poultry in the recipe by half and replace that amount with cut-up fresh or frozen vegetables. With ready-to-eat vegetables crowding the produce counter shelves, there's just no excuse not to eat your produce.

Main-Dish Seafood Salad

Hands-on time: 10 minutes
Total time: 30 minutes

- $^1/_2$ cup rice wine vinegar or white wine vinegar
- $^1/_4$ cup water
- $1^1/_2$ tablespoons sugar
- 1 tablespoon grated fresh ginger
- 2 teaspoons soy sauce
- 2 teaspoons vegetable oil
- $1^1/_2$ teaspoons toasted sesame oil
- 1 pound large shrimp, peeled and deveined, and/or sea scallops
- $^1/_4$ teaspoon salt
- 1 pound mixed greens
- 1 red bell pepper, cut into strips
- 1 cup snow peas
- 4 scallions, thinly sliced on the diagonal

In a small saucepan, combine the vinegar, water, sugar, and ginger. Bring to a boil over medium-high heat. Reduce the heat to medium. Cook for 20 minutes, or until reduced to ¼ cup. Strain into a large bowl. Whisk in the soy sauce, vegetable oil, and sesame oil. Let cool slightly.

Meanwhile, coat a grill rack or broiler pan with nonstick spray. Preheat the grill or broiler.

Thread the shrimp and/or scallops onto metal skewers. Season with the salt. Place on the prepared rack or pan. Grill or broil for 2 to 3 minutes per side, or until lightly browned and opaque.

Evenly divide the greens, bell pepper, snow peas, and scallions among 4 plates. Drizzle with the vinaigrette. Top with the shrimp and/or scallops, removing from the skewers, if desired.

Makes 4 servings

Per serving

Calories 217	*Sodium 478 mg.*
Total fat 6 g.	*Dietary fiber 3 g.*
Saturated fat 1 g.	*Protein 16 g.*
Cholesterol 90 mg.	*Carbohydrates 26 g.*

Pan-Seared Salmon Salad

Hands-on time: 15 minutes
Total time: 25 minutes

- 3 tablespoons chopped dry-pack sun-dried tomatoes
- 3 tablespoons balsamic vinegar
- 2 teaspoons extra-virgin olive oil
- 1½ teaspoons dried basil
- 1 teaspoon Dijon mustard
- ⅛ teaspoon salt
- 1 roasted red pepper, cut into small strips
- 1 pound mixed salad greens
- 4 ounces button or shiitake mushrooms, sliced
- 1 small onion, minced
- 4 salmon fillets (3 ounces each), skin removed
- 1 teaspoon Italian seasoning

Place the sun-dried tomatoes in a small bowl. Cover with boiling water. Allow to soak for 10 minutes, or until soft. Drain and discard the liquid.

In a large bowl, whisk the vinegar, oil, basil, mustard, and salt until smooth. Place the pepper, sun-dried tomatoes, and greens in the bowl but do not toss. Set aside.

Lightly coat a medium nonstick skillet with nonstick spray. Add the mushrooms and onion. Coat lightly with nonstick spray. Cook over medium-high heat for 5 to 7 minutes, or until soft. Remove to a plate to cool.

Wipe the skillet with a paper towel. Coat with nonstick spray. Set over high heat. Lightly coat the salmon with nonstick spray. Sprinkle with the Italian seasoning. Add the salmon to the skillet. Cook for 3 minutes on each side, or until the fish flakes easily. Check by cutting into 1 fillet.

Add the mushrooms and onion to the reserved bowl. Toss to mix. Spoon the salad onto 4 plates. Top each with a salmon fillet.

Makes 4 servings

Per serving
Calories 197	*Sodium 257 mg.*
Total fat 9 g.	*Dietary fiber 3 g.*
Saturated fat 1 g.	*Protein 20 g.*
Cholesterol 47 mg.	*Carbohydrates 11 g.*

Salmon Salad Wrap

Pan-Seared Salmon Salad can double as a sandwich. Warm 4 large whole-wheat flour tortillas in a microwave oven for 30 seconds, or until pliable. Arrange the salad ingredients over the tortillas. Crumble the salmon into chunks and place over the greens. Roll up and serve. Makes 4 wrap sandwiches.

❤ Pasta e Fagiole (page 245) ❤

~Quinoa and Vegetable Casserole (page 257)~

❧ Quick Chicken Gumbo (page 237) ❧

~New England Clam Chowder (page 239)~   219

❧Mediterranean Chickpea Salad (page 267)❧

♥ Vegetable Paella (page 255) ♥

❤Risotto with Shrimp, Peas, and Fennel (page 260)❤

❤ Mushroom-Barley Soup (page 241) ❤

❤ Creamy Black Bean Enchiladas (page 266) ❤

❤ Root Vegetable Mash (page 197) and Cornmeal-Crusted Catfish (page 273) ❤   225

❧ Orange Roughy Veracruz (page 298) ❧

~Teriyaki Tuna with Pineapple (page 303)~

~Baked Cod with Mustard Crumbs (page 277)~

~Baked Scallops Newburg (page 300)~

❤Five-Alarm Shrimp (page 302)❤

Apricot Chicken and Rice Salad

Hands-on time: 10 minutes
Total time: 10 minutes

- ³/₄ cup apricot nectar
- 3 tablespoons red wine vinegar
- 1¹/₂ teaspoons dried basil
- ¹/₄ teaspoon salt
- 1¹/₂ cups long-grain rice, cooked and cooled
- ³/₄ pound boneless, skinless chicken breasts, cooked and thinly sliced
- 1 roasted red pepper, coarsely chopped
- ³/₄ cup dried apricots, sliced
- 4 scallions, sliced
- ¹/₄ cup chopped pecans, toasted

In a large bowl, whisk the apricot nectar, vinegar, basil, and salt. Add the rice, chicken, pepper, apricots, and scallions. Toss to coat. Sprinkle with the pecans.

Makes 6 servings

Per serving
Calories 393
Total fat 6 g.
Saturated fat 1 g.
Cholesterol 48 mg.
Sodium 152 mg.
Dietary fiber 4 g.
Protein 23 g.
Carbohydrates 63 g.

APRICOT NECTAR MARINADE

This apricot nectar vinaigrette performs well both as a marinade and as a glaze for 1 pound of chicken or pork. To use as a marinade, double the amount of vinegar. Pour the marinade over the chicken or pork in a shallow dish. Cover and refrigerate, turning occasionally, for 2 to 4 hours. While the chicken or pork is grilling or broiling, pour the marinade into a small saucepan. Cook over medium heat for at least 5 minutes. Continue cooking for 3 minutes, or until it becomes syrupy. Brush over the chicken or pork during the final moments of cooking or drizzle over the meat after slicing.

Chinese Chicken Salad

Photograph on page 134
Hands-on time: 10 minutes
Total time: 15 minutes

8 wonton wrappers, cut into
   $1/4$"-wide strips

$1/4$ cup rice wine vinegar or white
   wine vinegar

2 tablespoons hoisin sauce

2 tablespoons water

1 tablespoon grated fresh ginger

1 clove garlic, minced

$1/4$ teaspoon crushed red-pepper flakes

1 pound mixed greens

1 cup bean sprouts

$1/2$ pound cooked boneless, skinless
   chicken breasts, shredded

2 carrots, shredded

2 scallions, thinly sliced

Preheat the oven to 400°F. Coat a baking sheet with nonstick spray. Separate the wonton strips and place on the baking sheet. Coat lightly with nonstick spray. Bake for 3 to 5 minutes, or until golden brown and crisp. Remove and set aside.

In a large bowl, whisk the vinegar, hoisin sauce, water, ginger, garlic, and red-pepper flakes until blended. Add the greens, sprouts, chicken, carrots, scallions, and reserved wonton strips. Toss gently to mix.

Makes 4 servings

Per serving
Calories 228   Sodium 985 mg.
Total fat 5 g.   Dietary fiber 3 g.
Saturated fat 1 g.   Protein 22 g.
Cholesterol 50 mg.   Carbohydrates 24 g.

CUSTOM LABELING

The "% Daily Value" for fat listed on food product labels should be considered a reference point for computing your personal needs. The figure on the label reflects 30 percent of calories from fat and 10 percent of the calories from saturated fat based on a 2,000-calorie-a-day eating plan. If you consume more or less than 2,000 calories or your goal is to consume less than 30 percent of your calories from fat, you will need to adjust the % Daily Value for your eating plan.

Autumn Turkey Salad

Photograph on page 132
Hands-on time: 15 minutes
Total time: 15 minutes

1/4 cup low-fat mayonnaise

1/2 cup fat-free sour cream

2 teaspoons chopped fresh thyme or
1 teaspoon dried

2 teaspoons lemon juice

1/2 teaspoon grated lemon peel

1 pound cooked skinless turkey
breasts, cut into 1/2" cubes

2 ribs celery, chopped

1 apple, cut into 1/2" cubes

1/3 cup dried apricots, sliced

1/4 cup toasted coarsely chopped
walnuts

In a large bowl, whisk the mayonnaise, sour cream, thyme, lemon juice, and lemon peel until smooth. Add the turkey, celery, apple, and raisins. Toss gently to coat.

Sprinkle with the walnuts.

Makes 4 servings

Per serving
Calories 281	*Sodium 225 mg.*
Total fat 5 g.	*Dietary fiber 3 g.*
Saturated fat 1 g.	*Protein 37 g.*
Cholesterol 95 mg.	*Carbohydrates 21 g.*

A New Twist

HAWAIIAN TURKEY SALAD IN PINEAPPLE BOATS

Cut a pineapple in quarters lengthwise, leaving the leaves intact. Remove the core and discard. Using a small knife, hollow out the pineapple, leaving a 1/2" rim. Cut the pineapple into 1/2" cubes. Replace the apricots with the pineapple chunks. Replace the walnuts with almonds. Replace the thyme with 1 teaspoon curry powder. Add 1/2 cup bean sprouts and 1/4 cup mango chutney. To serve, spoon the salad into the pineapple quarters.

Country Coleslaw

Hands-on time: 15 minutes
Total time: 3 hours

1/2 cup apple cider vinegar

1/3 cup apple juice

1/3 cup sugar

1   tablespoon vegetable oil

1   teaspoon celery seeds

1   head cabbage, thinly sliced (about 6 cups)

3   carrots, grated

1   bunch scallions, sliced

1   apple, grated

In a small saucepan, combine the vinegar, apple juice, sugar, oil, and celery seeds. Cook, stirring, over medium-high heat for 2 to 3 minutes, or until the sugar dissolves. Remove to cool.

Meanwhile, in a large bowl, combine the cabbage, carrots, scallions, and apple. Add the cooled dressing. Toss to coat. Cover and chill, tossing occasionally, for 2 to 3 hours, or until well-chilled.

Makes 8 servings

Per serving
Calories 98   *Sodium 26 mg.*
Total fat 2 g.   *Dietary fiber 3 g.*
Saturated fat 0 g.   *Protein 2 g.*
Cholesterol 0 mg.   *Carbohydrates 19 g.*

Good for You

HUG THE WALLS

Be sensible when you do your grocery shopping. Shop the perimeter of the supermarket for the most nutritious foods. It is here that you will find fresh and frozen fruits and vegetables as well as whole-grain breads, which are all high in vitamins, minerals, and fiber. Also on the outside edge are meats and seafood (sources of iron and protein) and low-fat dairy products, which provide calcium. Be much choosier in the center aisles, where you'll find most of the highly processed foods that are high in sugar, fat, and sodium.

The Soup Pot

oup is a great way to get a variety of nutritious vegetables and grains in just one bowl," says dietitian Melanie Polk, R.D., director of nutrition education for the American Institute for Cancer Research in Washington, D.C.

"For example, fresh vegetables in season or a combination of frozen vegetables can be added to soups even if the recipe doesn't call for them. Beans of all varieties can be added to provide fiber and low-fat protein. Vegetables can be easily pureed to mimic the consistency of cream soup without the fat. Soups can also be made with a variety of fruits, which are especially cool and refreshing in the summer," Polk says.

Souper Tips

Think about layering the flavors when preparing a soup. Start by sautéing aromatic vegetables such as onions, garlic, carrots, and celery in a small amount of oil to bring out their natural sweetness and flavor.

The next important component is the liquid base. Homemade stock, canned fat-free reduced-sodium broth, and water are options. But remember, if your tap water doesn't taste great, it won't make a great-tasting soup. You might want to try filtered or distilled water, which can make a big difference in the final flavor.

If you use dried herbs, add them at the beginning of the cooking time because they continue to release their properties over a long period of time. Fresh herbs release their essence over a shorter period of time and should be added only during the last 20 minutes of cooking to add a refreshing note to your soup.

Many cooks are comfortable departing from the recipe to embellish soups with flavor boosters. Here are a few that you might want to try. Stir them into the pot and taste to see if you'd like to add more.

- 1 teaspoon to 1 tablespoon tomato paste
- 1 teaspoon Worcestershire sauce
- 1 teaspoon to 1 tablespoon soy sauce
- ¼ to ½ teaspoon ground pepper or ground nutmeg (particularly good in cream soups)
- 1 to 2 tablespoons lemon juice or lime juice
- 1 teaspoon to 1 tablespoon Pesto (page 137) or grated Parmesan cheese blended into soup just before serving

Recipes

Quick Chicken Gumbo

Photograph on page 218
Hands-on time: 15 minutes
Total time: 35 minutes

1/3 cup long-grain white or brown rice

2 teaspoons olive oil

1 small onion, chopped

1 small green bell pepper, chopped

2 ribs celery, chopped

2 cloves garlic, chopped

1 tablespoon gumbo filé powder (optional); see note

1 teaspoon paprika

1 teaspoon dried thyme

1/4 teaspoon salt

2 cans (14 1/2 ounces each) fat-free reduced-sodium chicken broth

2 cups (1/2 pound) shredded cooked boneless, skinless chicken breasts

1 can (8 ounces) tomato sauce

Cook the rice according to the package directions.

Warm the oil in a Dutch oven set over medium heat. Add the onion, bell pepper, celery, garlic, filé powder, paprika, thyme, and salt. Cook, stirring often, for 5 to 7 minutes, or until the vegetables are soft.

Add the broth, chicken, tomato sauce, and 1 cup water. Stir to mix. Cook, stirring occasionally, for 15 minutes to blend the flavors. To serve, spoon the gumbo into shallow bowls. Top with a dollop of rice.

Makes 8 servings

Per serving

Calories 138	Sodium 387 mg.
Total fat 3 g.	Dietary fiber 2 g.
Saturated fat 1 g.	Protein 16 g.
Cholesterol 30 mg.	Carbohydrates 12 g.

Cooking Note

Made from the bark of the sassafras tree, filé powder is the traditional thickener for Creole gumbos. Look for filé powder in the spice section of your supermarket.

Chicken and Potato Soup

Hands-on time: 10 minutes
Total time: 35 minutes

2   teaspoons vegetable oil

1   onion, chopped

2   ribs celery, chopped

1   tablespoon chopped fresh rosemary
or 1 teaspoon dried

3   cans (14¹/2 ounces each) fat-free
reduced-sodium chicken broth

1   pound potatoes, cut into ¹/2" cubes

¹/4   teaspoon salt

1¹/2   cups (6 ounces) shredded cooked
boneless, skinless chicken breasts

8   ounces baby spinach leaves, stems
removed

Warm the oil in a Dutch oven set over medium heat. Add the onion, celery, and rosemary. Cook, stirring occasionally, for 5 to 7 minutes, or until the celery is soft. Add the broth, potatoes, and salt. Cook for 20 minutes, or until the potatoes are tender. Add the chicken and spinach. Cook for 3 minutes, or until the spinach is wilted and the chicken is heated through.

Makes 6 servings

Per serving
Calories 186   *Sodium 339 mg.*
Total fat 3 g.   *Dietary fiber 3 g.*
Saturated fat 1 g.   *Protein 20 g.*
Cholesterol 30 mg.   *Carbohydrates 19 g.*

A New Twist

CREAMY CHICKEN AND POTATO SOUP

For a thicker soup, increase the amount of potatoes by ½ pound. Transfer one-third of the cooked potatoes to a blender or food processor. Add ½ cup 1% milk. Process until pureed. Return to the pot. Cook for 1 to 2 minutes, or until heated through. Makes 8 servings.

New England Clam Chowder

Photograph on page 219
Hands-on time: 25 minutes
Total time: 50 minutes

Makes 8 servings

Per serving
Calories 237
Total fat 5 g.
Saturated fat 2 g.
Cholesterol 17 mg.
Sodium 359 mg.
Dietary fiber 4 g.
Protein 12 g.
Carbohydrates 32 g.

- 2 cans (6^1/2 ounces each) minced clams
- 2 strips bacon, chopped
- 1 large onion, chopped
- 3 ribs celery, chopped
- 2 cans (14^1/2 ounces each) fat-free reduced-sodium chicken broth
- 1 teaspoon dried thyme
- 1 bay leaf
- 1 pound potatoes, cut into ^{1}/2" chunks
- ^{1}/4 cup unbleached or all-purpose flour
- 1^1/2–2 cups 2% milk
- 1^1/2 cups frozen corn kernels
- ^{1}/4 cup chopped fresh parsley

Drain the clams and reserve the juice. Set aside.

In a Dutch oven, cook the bacon, stirring often, over medium heat for 3 minutes. Add the onion and celery. Cook for 5 minutes, or until the onion is soft. Add the broth, thyme, bay leaf, and reserved clam juice. Bring to a boil and stir well. Add the potatoes.

Cook for 20 to 25 minutes, or until the potatoes are tender. Meanwhile, place the flour in a small bowl. Gradually add 1½ cups milk, whisking until smooth. Add to the pot along with the corn, parsley, and reserved clams. Cook, stirring frequently, for 10 minutes, or until thickened. Add up to ½ cup more milk for a thinner chowder, if desired. Remove and discard the bay leaf.

Cheddar and Broccoli Soup

Hands-on time: 15 minutes
Total time: 30 minutes

2 heads broccoli

1 can (14$\frac{1}{2}$ ounces) fat-free reduced-sodium chicken broth

1 cup water

$\frac{1}{4}$ cup unbleached or all-purpose flour

1 onion, chopped

1 clove garlic, chopped

$\frac{1}{2}$ teaspoon dried thyme

$\frac{1}{2}$ teaspoon salt

$\frac{1}{8}$ teaspoon ground red pepper

2 cups 1% milk

1 cup (4 ounces) shredded low-fat extra-sharp Cheddar cheese

Cut the florets from the broccoli heads. You should have 6 cups florets. Reserve the stems for another use.

In a stockpot, combine the broccoli, broth, and water. Cover and bring to a boil over medium-high heat. Cook for 4 to 6 minutes, or until tender. Remove from the heat. With a slotted spoon, remove half of the broccoli to a bowl. Set aside. Place the remaining broccoli and broth in a blender or food processor, working in batches if necessary. Process until pureed. Sprinkle with the flour. Process to combine. Set aside.

Coat the pot with nonstick spray. Add the onion, garlic, thyme, salt, and pepper. Coat with nonstick spray. Cook, stirring occasionally, over medium heat for 5 to 7 minutes, or until the onion is soft. Add the reserved broccoli puree and the milk. Cook, stirring often, for 5 to 7 minutes, or until thickened. Add the

Cheddar. Stir until melted. Stir in the reserved broccoli florets. Cook for 2 minutes, or until heated through.

Makes 6 servings

Per serving
Calories 151	Sodium 488 mg.
Total fat 5 g.	Dietary fiber 3 g.
Saturated fat 3 g.	Protein 15 g.
Cholesterol 17 mg.	Carbohydrates 14 g.

SHEPHERD'S PIE CASSEROLE

In a small saucepan, cook about 2 cups leftover Cheddar and Broccoli Soup until thickened. Crumble about 1 pound leftover meat loaf or any cooked ground meat filling into a medium baking dish coated with nonstick spray. Cover with the reduced soup. Top with 1 pound mashed potatoes. Bake in a 350°F oven for 15 minutes, or until heated through. Makes 4 servings.

Mushroom-Barley Soup

Photograph on page 223
Hands-on time: 10 minutes
Total time: 40 minutes

1 ounce dried mushrooms

3 cups water

1 large onion, chopped

2 carrots, chopped

1 rib celery, chopped

12 ounces cremini or button mushrooms, stems removed, sliced

1¹⁄₂ teaspoons dried oregano

2 cans (14¹⁄₂ ounces each) fat-free reduced-sodium chicken broth

¹⁄₂ cup barley

¹⁄₄ teaspoon salt

In a small saucepan, bring the dried mushrooms and water to a boil. Remove and let stand for 15 minutes.

Meanwhile, coat a Dutch oven with nonstick spray. Add the onion, carrots, and celery. Coat lightly with nonstick spray. Set over medium heat. Cook, stirring occasionally, for 3 minutes. Add the sliced mushrooms and oregano. Cook, stirring occasionally, for 6 to 8 minutes, or until all the vegetables are soft. Add the broth, barley, and salt. Cook for 10 minutes.

Line a fine mesh sieve with a coffee filter or paper towel. Strain the dried mushroom water into the pot. Remove and discard the filter or paper towel. Rinse the dried mushrooms under running water to remove any grit. Chop and add to the pot.

Cook for 10 to 15 minutes, or until the barley is tender.

Makes 6 servings

Per serving

Calories 148	*Sodium 294 mg.*
Total fat 1 g.	*Dietary fiber 6 g.*
Saturated fat 0 g.	*Protein 10 g.*
Cholesterol 0 mg.	*Carbohydrates 24 g.*

Good for You

PLANT THE HEALTH SEED

Try a "plants only" meal several times a week to decrease the amount of saturated fat in your diet. Meals based on plant foods such as vegetables, grains, and legumes provide lots of fiber and nutrients while eliminating saturated fat and cholesterol that come with eating meats, poultry, cheese, and eggs.

Minestrone

Hands-on time: 15 minutes
Total time: 45 minutes

1 tablespoon olive oil

1 onion, chopped

2 large cloves garlic, chopped

2 carrots, chopped

2 ribs celery, chopped

2 teaspoons Italian seasoning

1 can (48 ounces) fat-free reduced-sodium chicken broth or vegetable broth

1 can (15 ounces) diced tomatoes

3/4 pound green beans, cut into 1" lengths

1 large zucchini, cut into 1/4" cubes

1/4 Savoy or green cabbage, thinly sliced

1/2 cup ditalini or other small pasta

1/4 teaspoon salt

1 can (19 ounces) cannellini or red kidney beans, rinsed and drained

Warm the oil in a Dutch oven set over medium heat. Add the onion and garlic. Cook, stirring often, for 3 minutes, or until the onion starts to soften. Add the carrots, celery, and Italian seasoning. Cook for 3 minutes, or until the carrots are crisp-tender. Add the broth. Increase the heat to high and bring to a boil. Reduce the heat to medium-low. Cook for 10 minutes, or until the carrots are almost tender. Add the tomatoes (with juice), green beans, zucchini, cabbage, pasta, salt and beans. Simmer for 10 to 12 minutes, or until the pasta is cooked and all the vegetables are soft.

Makes 8 servings

Per serving

Calories 202	*Sodium 372 mg.*
Total fat 4 g.	*Dietary fiber 9 g.*
Saturated fat 2 g.	*Protein 15 g.*
Cholesterol 5 mg.	*Carbohydrates 27 g.*

A New Twist

MORE ON MINESTRONE

Grate 1/2 cup (2 ounces) Parmesan cheese to sprinkle over this hearty Italian vegetable soup. For a special enhancement, you can stir a tablespoon of homemade Pesto (page 137) or purchased pesto into each serving of soup.

Black Bean Soup

Hands-on time: 15 minutes
Total time: 40 minutes

1 tablespoon olive oil

1 large onion, chopped

3 carrots, chopped

2 ribs celery, chopped

3 cloves garlic, minced

2 slices Canadian bacon, cut into bite-size pieces

1 jalapeño chile pepper, seeded and chopped (wear plastic gloves when handling)

1 tablespoon ground cumin

1 can (48 ounces) fat-free reduced-sodium chicken broth

1 cup water

2 cans (15 ounces each) black beans, rinsed and drained

1/2 teaspoon salt

Warm the oil in a Dutch oven set over medium heat. Add the onion, carrots, celery, and garlic. Cook, stirring occasionally, for 4 minutes, or until the onion starts to soften. Add the bacon, chile pepper, and cumin. Cook for 3 minutes, or until the bacon is lightly browned.

Add the broth and water to the pot. Increase the heat to high. Bring to a boil. Reduce the heat to medium-low. Cook for 15 minutes, or until the vegetables are tender. Add the beans. Cook for 5 minutes, or until heated through.

Ladle 3 cups of the soup into a food processor or blender. Puree until smooth. Return to the pot. Add the reserved bacon and salt. Cook for 5 minutes, or until heated through.

Makes 8 servings

Per serving
Calories 229
Total fat 2 g.
Saturated fat 0 g.
Cholesterol 4 mg.
Sodium 426 mg.
Dietary fiber 12 g.
Protein 18 g.
Carbohydrates 34 g.

Cooking Note

If desired, stir 1/4 cup sherry into the Black Bean Soup along with the beans. The soup can be garnished with chopped onion, chopped fresh cilantro leaves, or a dollop of fat-free sour cream.

BLACK BEAN DIP

Play it Again!

In a medium saucepan, cook 3 cups of the soup until very thick and reduced to about 1 1/2 cups. With a potato masher, coarsely mash into a chunky paste. Spread over the bottom of a pie pan coated with nonstick spray. Cover with 1 1/2 cups Guacamole (page 78). Spread with 1 jar (15 1/2 ounces) salsa, drained. Top with 1 cup fat-free sour cream mixed with 1/2 teaspoon ground cumin. Sprinkle with 3/4 cup shredded low-fat Cheddar cheese and 1/3 cup chopped scallions. Serve chilled or bake in a 400°F oven for 12 minutes, or until heated through. Serve with baked tortilla chips.

Tomato Tortellini Soup

Hands-on time: 10 minutes
Total time: 25 minutes

1 onion, chopped

2 cloves garlic, chopped

1 can (28 ounces) chopped tomatoes

1 can (14$\frac{1}{2}$ ounces) fat-free reduced-sodium chicken broth

1 cup water

$\frac{1}{2}$ cup chopped fresh basil or 2 teaspoons dried

1 cup 2% milk

4 ounces low-fat fresh or frozen cheese tortellini, cooked and drained

$\frac{1}{2}$ teaspoon salt

Coat a medium saucepan with nonstick spray. Add the onion and garlic. Coat with nonstick spray. Cook, stirring often, over medium heat for 5 to 7 minutes, or until softened. Add the tomatoes (with juice). Cook for 2 minutes.

Remove from the heat and place in a food processor or blender. Process until pureed. Return to the saucepan. Add the broth, water, and basil. Stir to mix. Cook over medium heat for 5 minutes. Add the milk, tortellini, and salt. Cook for 1 to 2 minutes, or until heated through.

Makes 6 servings

Per serving
Calories 132
Total fat 2 g.
Saturated fat 1 g.
Cholesterol 10 mg.
Sodium 375 mg.
Dietary fiber 3 g.
Protein 9 g.
Carbohydrates 19 g.

Good for You

MEAL TIME

When you are trying to regulate your calorie intake, it is important to balance meals throughout the day. Skipping a meal, like breakfast or lunch, makes it easier to overindulge later in the day. Research shows that it's easiest to maintain a healthy weight when you eat several small meals throughout the day.

Pasta e Fagiole

Photograph on page 216
Hands-on time: 10 minutes
Total time: 25 minutes

- 2 teaspoons olive oil
- 1 small onion, chopped
- 2 cloves garlic, chopped
- 2 cans (14$\frac{1}{2}$ ounces each) fat-free reduced-sodium chicken broth
- 1 can (15 ounces) diced tomatoes
- 1 can (15 ounces) cannellini or white beans, rinsed and drained
- $\frac{1}{2}$ cup ditalini or other small pasta
- $\frac{1}{2}$ pound Swiss chard leaves or spinach leaves, coarsely chopped
- $\frac{1}{4}$ teaspoon salt

Warm the oil in a Dutch oven set over medium heat. Add the onion and garlic. Cook, stirring occasionally, for 3 to 5 minutes, or until the onion is soft.

Add the broth, tomatoes (with juice), beans, and pasta. Cook, stirring occasionally, for 15 minutes, or until the pasta is cooked. Add the Swiss chard or spinach and salt. Cook, stirring occasionally, for 2 to 3 minutes, or until the chard or spinach is wilted.

Makes 6 servings

Per serving
Calories 157	*Sodium 410 mg.*
Total fat 2 g.	*Dietary fiber 6 g.*
Saturated fat 0 g.	*Protein 10 g.*
Cholesterol 0 mg.	*Carbohydrates 23 g.*

Cooking Note

For added flavor, sprinkle grated Parmesan cheese and ground black pepper on the pasta e fagiole just before serving.

BAKED PASTA E FAGIOLE

Play it Again!

Extend leftover pasta e fagiole into another meal by making a pasta casserole. In a large skillet, cook ½ pound cooked lean ground beef until no longer pink. Drain and return to the skillet. Add 3 cups of the pasta e fagiole. Cook until thickened. Add ¾ cup cubed low-fat mozzarella cheese. Pour the mixture into a medium baking dish coated with nonstick spray. Sprinkle with 2 tablespoons grated Parmesan cheese. Bake in a 350°F oven for 15 to 20 minutes, or until heated through. Makes 2 servings.

Wild Rice Soup

Hands-on time: 15 minutes
Total time: 1 hour and 30 minutes

$^1/_2$ cup wild rice

2 teaspoons olive oil

2 carrots, finely chopped

2 ribs celery, finely chopped

1 leek, white part only, halved
    lengthwise, rinsed well, and sliced

$^1/_4$ pound mushrooms, thinly sliced

1 teaspoon dried thyme

$^1/_4$ cup unbleached or all-purpose flour

1 can (14$^1/_2$ ounces) fat-free reduced-
    sodium chicken broth

2 cups 1% milk

$^1/_4$ teaspoon salt

Cook the rice according to the package directions.

Meanwhile, warm the oil in a Dutch oven set over medium heat. Add the carrots, celery, leek, mushrooms, and thyme. Cook, stirring occasionally, for 8 to 10 minutes, or until tender. Stir in the flour. Gradually add the broth and milk, stirring constantly. Cook, stirring often, for 15 minutes, or until thickened. Add the rice and salt. Stir to mix.

Makes 6 servings

Per serving
Calories 158	*Sodium 220 mg.*
Total fat 3 g.	*Dietary fiber 3 g.*
Saturated fat 1 g.	*Protein 8 g.*
Cholesterol 4 mg.	*Carbohydrates 26 g.*

WILD RICE

This form of rice is not a grain but actually a grass seed. It's rich and nutty in flavor and provides the nutritional bonus of low-fat protein as well as an outstanding supply of niacin, folic acid, and magnesium.

Cauliflower Puree with Red Pepper Blush

Hands-on time: 10 minutes
Total time: 30 minutes

Makes 8 servings

Per serving
Calories 114
Total fat 4 g.
Saturated fat 1 g.
Cholesterol 8 mg.
Sodium 271 mg.
Dietary fiber 3 g.
Protein 8 g.
Carbohydrates 15 g.

- 2 teaspoons vegetable oil
- 1 large onion, chopped
- 1 large head cauliflower, cored and broken into florets
- 1 can (14$\frac{1}{2}$ ounces) fat-free reduced-sodium chicken broth
- 3$\frac{1}{2}$ cups 2% milk
- $\frac{1}{2}$ teaspoon salt
- $\frac{1}{8}$ teaspoon ground nutmeg
- $\frac{1}{8}$ teaspoon ground red pepper
- 2 roasted red peppers
- $\frac{1}{4}$ cup water

Warm the oil in a Dutch oven over medium heat. Add the onion. Cook for 5 to 7 minutes, or until soft. Add the cauliflower and broth. Cover and cook for 10 minutes, or until the cauliflower is very tender. Transfer to a blender or food processor, working in batches if necessary. Process until pureed.

Return the mixture to the pot. Add the milk, salt, nutmeg, and red pepper. Cook over medium-low heat for 10 minutes.

Rinse the blender or food processor. Place the roasted peppers in the blender or food processor with the water. Puree until smooth.

To serve, ladle the soup into bowls. Swirl 1½ tablespoons of the roasted pepper puree into each bowl.

Soup's on Hold

Most soups freeze so well that it just makes good sense to make double batches. For the same amount of time, you get a bonus batch for the freezer. Since bacteria develops most rapidly in the temperature zone of 45° to 140°F, it's critical to cool a hot soup quickly. Pour the soup into a large shallow bowl and place it on a low shelf toward the back of the refrigerator, which is the coldest spot. Refrigerate, uncovered, for several hours or overnight until very cold.

To store the soup in the freezer, line plastic freezer containers with plastic freezer bags, pressing the bags tightly against the sides of the containers. Ladle the cooled soup into the bags, leaving 1" of headspace for expansion. Place the bags in the freezer for several hours, or until frozen solid. Remove the bag of frozen soup, seal tightly, and label with the name, amount, and date. Most soups freeze well for up to 6 months.

Keep in mind that cream soups made with milk may separate when they are thawed. To be able to freeze cream soups, prepare the soup according to the recipe without adding the milk. Stir in the milk after you thaw and reheat the soup.

Curried Butternut Squash Soup

Hands-on time: 15 minutes
Total time: 40 minutes

1 butternut squash, halved and seeded
2 teaspoons vegetable oil
1 large onion, chopped
1 rib celery, finely chopped
2 cloves garlic, minced
2 teaspoons curry powder
1 tablespoon grated fresh ginger
$1/3$ cup white wine or apple juice
2 cans (14$1/2$ ounces each) fat-free reduced-sodium chicken broth or vegetable broth
$1/4$ teaspoon salt
$1/2$ cup low-fat plain yogurt, at room temperature

Place the squash, cut side down, on a microwaveable tray. Microwave on high power, rotating once, for 8 to 10 minutes, or until tender. Remove and let stand for 5 minutes. Scoop out the flesh and place in a large bowl.

Meanwhile, warm the oil in a Dutch oven over medium heat. Add the onion, celery, and garlic. Cook, stirring often, for 10 minutes, or until the vegetables are soft. Add the curry powder and ginger. Cook for 3 minutes. Add the wine or apple juice. Bring to a boil. Add the broth, the reserved squash, and salt. Reduce the heat to medium. Cook for 10 minutes.

In batches, transfer the soup to a blender or food processor. Puree until smooth. Return to the pot. Stir in the yogurt.

Makes 8 servings

Per serving
Calories 106
Total fat 2 g.
Saturated fat 0 g.
Cholesterol 0 mg.
Sodium 178 mg.
Dietary fiber 5 g.
Protein 6 g.
Carbohydrates 19 g.

CLASSIC STAR

BUTTERNUT SQUASH

Butternut squash can be regarded as the queen of beta-carotene. Just 1 cup of cooked squash supplies well over 100 percent of the Daily Value of this important nutrient.

Thai Shrimp Bisque

Hands-on time: 15 minutes
Total Time: 40 minutes

- 2 teaspoons butter or margarine
- 1 small onion, finely chopped
- 1 carrot, finely chopped
- 1 rib celery, finely chopped
- 1 clove garlic, minced
- 3/4 pound large shrimp, peeled, deveined, and cut into thirds
- 2 cans (14 1/2 ounces each) fat-free reduced-sodium chicken broth
- 2 cups water
- 1 can (15 ounces) diced tomatoes, drained
- 1/3 cup long-grain white rice
- 1 1/2 teaspoons paprika
- 1/4 teaspoon salt
- 1 cup reduced-fat coconut milk
- 2 teaspoons grated fresh ginger
- 1-2 tablespoons lime juice

Melt the butter or margarine in a Dutch oven over medium heat. Add the onion, carrot, celery, and garlic. Cook, stirring often, over medium heat for 5 minutes. Add the shrimp. Cook, stirring, for 2 to 3 minutes, or until the shrimp are opaque. Remove the shrimp. Set aside.

Add the broth, water, tomatoes, rice, paprika, and salt. Bring to a boil. Reduce the heat to medium-low. Partially cover and cook for 20 minutes, or until the rice is tender. Return half of the shrimp to the pot.

Transfer the soup to a food processor or blender, working in batches if necessary. Process until pureed. Set a fine strainer over the pot. Pass the soup through the strainer, pressing with the back of a spoon. Discard the pulp. Add the reserved shrimp, coconut milk, and ginger. Cook over low heat for 4 to 5 minutes, or until heated though. Season with the lime juice to taste.

Makes 6 servings

Per serving

Calories 194	Sodium 443 mg.
Total fat 4 g.	Dietary fiber 2 g.
Saturated fat 2 g.	Protein 15 g.
Cholesterol 84 mg.	Carbohydrates 18 g.

Chilled Mango-Lime Soup

Hands-on time: 10 minutes
Total time: 1 hour and 10 minutes

- 2 ripe mangoes, cut into chunks (see note)
- $1/2$ cup (4 ounces) low-fat plain yogurt
- $1/2$ cup orange juice
- $1/2$ cup ginger ale
- $1/4$ cup lime juice
- 1 tablespoon honey

In a blender or food processor, combine the mangoes, yogurt, orange juice, ginger ale, lime juice, and honey. Process until pureed. Add some ice water if a thinner soup is desired. Cover and refrigerate for 1 hour.

Makes 4 servings

Per serving

Calories 131	*Sodium 26 mg.*
Total fat 1 g.	*Dietary fiber 2 g.*
Saturated fat 0 g.	*Protein 2 g.*
Cholesterol 2 mg.	*Carbohydrates 31 g.*

Cooking Notes

• *To pit and cube a mango, cut 2 thick slices from the sides of the fruit, cutting as close as possible to the pit. Peel the skin around the pit and cut away the fruit surrounding the pit. Place the mango slices, skin side down, on a work surface. With a paring knife, score the flesh into squares, cutting just to the skin but not through it. One at a time, pick up each slice and push the skin side down so that it forms a convex curve. Cut the squares away from the skin.*

• *The mangoes can be replaced with 4 ripe peaches, if desired.*

• *Fresh mint sprigs and lime slices make a pretty garnish for Chilled Mango-Lime Soup.*

BREAKFAST SMOOTHIE — Play it Again!

Leftover Chilled Mango-Lime Soup makes a wonderful breakfast beverage. In a blender or food processor, combine ¾ cup soup, ¾ cup fat-free frozen vanilla yogurt, and 4 frozen strawberries. Process until pureed. Add 1 tablespoon protein powder, if desired. Makes 1 serving.

Grains and Beans

A myriad of grains and beans are grown worldwide, which is a testament to their health-giving nutrients. "With so many individuals turning to a plant-based diet, the combination of beans and grains provides complete protein without the fat and also the bonus of vitamins and minerals such as folate," says licensed dietitian Kristine Napier, R.D., author of *Power Nutrition for Your Chronic Illness*.

In addition, these complex-carbohydrate foods are sources of disease-preventing dietary fiber (see "Finding Fiber" on page 261). A wonderful yet often overlooked benefit of grains and beans is that they are filling and therefore a wonderful aid for weight control.

Grain foods such as multigrain breads, pasta, rice, and cereals form the base of the U.S. Department of Agriculture Food Guide Pyramid. It recommends 6 to 11 servings a day, a greater number than any other food group. Whole-grain foods, in particular, are dense in B vitamins.

Legumes are plants that develop seed pods that split down both sides to reveal nutrient-rich edible seeds. Beans, lentils, peas, and soybeans are all legumes. Rich in folic acid, potassium, magnesium, and zinc, beans—with the exception of soybeans—are also very low in fat. Legumes are also a good source of saponins, a phytochemical believed to help prevent both heart disease and cancer.

Ease grains into your meals and snacks. Stock your freezer with whole-grain breads and bagels, which have more fiber than their white-flour counterparts. Whole-grain cereals are another effortless passport. For cooked grain main and side dishes, turn to brown rice, barley, quinoa, bulgur, cornmeal, millet, and pasta. Look for quick-cooking versions of these grains.

Legumes are sold canned, dried, and some, such as butter beans, green soybeans, and lima beans, are frozen. They can be added to salads, soups, and stews. Pureed legumes make excellent dips, sandwich or tortilla spreads, and soup thickeners.

Canned beans are really convenient because they are already cooked and simply need reheating. Thoroughly rinse and drain canned beans before using them to reduce the added sodium. You can use them in any recipe calling for dried beans, but add them during the final minutes of cooking just to heat through. Keep in mind that if a recipe calls for 1 cup of dried beans, that equals 2 to 3 cups of cooked beans.

Recipes

Vegetable Paella

Photograph on page 221
Hands-on time: 15 minutes
Total time: 40 minutes

1 tablespoon olive oil

1 onion, chopped

3 cloves garlic, chopped

1 cup basmati or long-grain white rice

1 yellow squash, cut into $^1/_2$" cubes

1 red bell pepper, cut into $^1/_2$" pieces

1 can (15 ounces) diced tomatoes

1 can (14$^1/_2$ ounces) reduced-sodium vegetable broth

1 cup water

1 bay leaf

$^1/_4$ teaspoon salt

1 can (15 ounces) cannellini or great Northern beans, rinsed and drained

1 cup frozen peas, thawed

Warm the oil in a Dutch oven over medium heat. Add the onion and garlic. Cook, stirring, for 3 minutes, or until lightly browned. Add the rice, squash, and bell pepper. Cook for 5 minutes, stirring occasionally, or until the pepper starts to soften. Add the tomatoes (with juice), broth, water, bay leaf, and salt. Reduce the heat to medium-low.

Cover and simmer for 20 minutes, or until the rice is tender. Add the beans and peas. Cook, stirring gently, for 3 to 5 minutes, or until heated through. Remove and discard the bay leaf.

Makes 6 servings

Per serving

Calories 247	Sodium 319 mg.
Total fat 3 g.	Dietary fiber 8 g.
Saturated fat 0 g.	Protein 9 g.
Cholesterol 0 mg.	Carbohydrates 45 g.

CLASSIC STAR

BEAN FIBER

Just a single serving of hearty Vegetable Paella provides you with 8 grams of dietary fiber, which is one-third of your daily goal. The National Cancer Institute recommends that we get between 20 and 35 milligrams of fiber a day.

Barley, Corn, and Shrimp Salad

Hands-on time: 15 minutes
Total time: 35 minutes

- $3/4$ cup quick-cooking barley
- 1 cup buttermilk
- $1/4$ cup lime juice
- 2 teaspoons honey
- $1/2$ teaspoon ground cumin
- $1/4$ teaspoon salt
- 2 cups fresh or frozen corn kernels, thawed
- 1 pound medium shrimp, peeled and deveined
- 1 tomato, chopped
- 1 rib celery, chopped
- 3 scallions, sliced
- 2 tablespoons chopped fresh cilantro or basil

Cook the barley according to the package directions. Drain and rinse under cold water.

Meanwhile, in a large bowl, combine the buttermilk, lime juice, honey, cumin, and salt.

Coat a medium skillet with nonstick spray. Add the corn and coat with nonstick spray. Cook, stirring occasionally, over high heat for 3 to 5 minutes, or until flecked with brown. Add the shrimp. Cook, stirring occasionally, for 3 to 5 minutes, or until the shrimp is opaque. Remove to the bowl with the buttermilk mixture. Add the tomato, celery, scallions, cilantro or basil, and the reserved barley. Toss to coat.

Makes 4 servings

Per serving

Calories 367	Sodium 400 mg.
Total fat 4 g.	Dietary fiber 9 g.
Saturated fat 1 g.	Protein 32 g.
Cholesterol 175 mg.	Carbohydrates 55 g.

SEASIDE ENCHILADAS

Play it Again!

Barley, Corn, and Shrimp Salad makes an interesting filling for enchiladas. For each enchilada, in a small bowl, combine 1/2 cup salad and 2 to 3 tablespoons green taco sauce. Place 1 flour tortilla (8" diameter) on a work surface. Fill with the salad mixture. Sprinkle with 1 tablespoon shredded low-fat Monterey Jack cheese. Roll into a cylinder. Place in a baking dish or on a baking sheet that has been coated with nonstick spray. Drizzle with 1 to 2 tablespoons green taco sauce. Bake in a 350°F oven for 12 to 15 minutes, or until heated through.

Quinoa and Vegetable Casserole

Photograph on page 217
Hands-on time: 20 minutes
Total time: 45 minutes

- 4 yellow or red bell peppers
- 2 portobello mushroom caps
- 2 tomatoes, cut into thick slices
- 1 small red onion, cut into 4 thick slices
- 1 can (14½ ounces) fat-free reduced-sodium chicken broth or vegetable broth
- 1 cup quinoa, rinsed and drained
- ½ cup (2 ounces) chopped or crumbled fontina or goat cheese
- 3 tablespoons chopped fresh basil or 2 teaspoons dried
- ⅛ teaspoon salt

Coat a broiler pan with nonstick spray. Preheat the broiler.

Arrange the bell peppers, mushrooms, tomatoes, and onion on the prepared broiler pan. Coat with nonstick spray. Broil, turning occasionally, for 10 to 15 minutes, or until the onion and mushrooms are softened. Remove the mushrooms, tomatoes, and onion to a plate. Broil the peppers for 5 to 10 minutes longer, or until lightly blackened. Transfer the peppers to a paper bag and allow to steam for 5 minutes. Slice the mushroom caps into ¼"-thick strips.

Peel the peppers. Remove and discard the stems and seeds. Cut the peppers into wide strips. Set aside.

Meanwhile, in a medium saucepan set over high heat, bring the broth to a boil. Add the quinoa. Stir well. Reduce the heat to low. Cover and simmer for 15 minutes, or until the broth is absorbed. Remove from the heat. Add the fontina or goat cheese, basil, and salt. Stir to mix.

Preheat the oven to 375°F. Coat a 9" × 9" baking dish with nonstick spray.

Arrange half of the peppers on the bottom of the prepared baking dish. Top with half of the quinoa. Layer the onion, mushrooms, and tomatoes over the quinoa. Top with the remaining quinoa and the remaining peppers.

Bake for 15 minutes, or until heated through.

Makes 4 servings

Per serving
Calories 307
Total fat 8 g.
Saturated fat 3 g.
Cholesterol 16 mg.
Sodium 343 mg.
Dietary fiber 7 g.
Protein 15 g.
Carbohydrates 47 g.

A New Twist

ROASTED POBLANO PEPPER SAUCE

For a special entrée, serve Quinoa and Vegetable Casserole with this sauce. Preheat the broiler. On a broiler pan coated with nonstick spray, broil 4 poblano chile peppers, turning occasionally, for 10 to 15 minutes, or until lightly blackened. Transfer to a paper bag and allow to steam for 5 minutes. Peel the peppers (wear plastic gloves when handling). Remove and discard the stems and seeds. Place in a food processor or blender. Process until smooth. Add 1 to 2 tablespoons chicken broth, ½ teaspoon ground cumin, and a pinch each of salt and ground black pepper.

Stuffed Pasta Shells

Hands-on time: 15 minutes
Total time: 45 minutes

- 1 jar (48 ounces) pasta sauce
- 1 small onion, chopped
- 2 cloves garlic, chopped
- 1¹⁄₂ cups (12 ounces) fat-free ricotta cheese
- 1 egg white
- 1 cup canned cannellini beans, rinsed and drained
- ³⁄₄ cup (3 ounces) shredded low-fat mozzarella cheese
- ¹⁄₈ teaspoon ground nutmeg
- 12 jumbo pasta shells (4 ounces), cooked, drained, and cooled
- ¹⁄₄ cup (1 ounce) grated Parmesan cheese

Preheat the oven to 350°F. Coat a 13" × 9" baking dish with nonstick spray. Pour 2 cups of the sauce into the prepared baking dish. Set aside.

Coat a small nonstick skillet with nonstick spray. Add the onion and garlic. Coat with nonstick spray. Cook, stirring often, over medium heat for 5 to 7 minutes, or until soft.

In a large bowl, combine the ricotta, egg white, beans, mozzarella, nutmeg, and the onion mixture. Stir gently to mix. Spoon into the pasta shells. Arrange the stuffed pasta shells in the baking dish over the sauce. Spoon the remaining sauce over the shells. Sprinkle with the Parmesan.

Bake for 30 minutes, or until heated through.

Makes 4 servings

Per serving

Calories 462	Sodium 499 mg.
Total fat 7 g.	Dietary fiber 10 g.
Saturated fat 4 g.	Protein 33 g.
Cholesterol 44 mg.	Carbohydrates 65 g.

A New Twist

Pasta Sauce

Jarred pasta sauces are convenient, but when time permits, a homemade sauce can be a treat. Here's a quick recipe. Warm 1 tablespoon olive oil in a large saucepan set over medium heat. Add 1 small chopped onion and 4 cloves minced garlic. Cook for 5 to 7 minutes, or until the onion is soft. Add 1 can (28 ounces) tomato sauce and 1 can (15½ ounces) whole tomatoes (with juice). Crush the tomatoes with a spoon. Season with 1 tablespoon dried oregano, 2 teaspoons dried basil, 2 teaspoons sugar, and ground black pepper to taste. Simmer for 15 minutes, or until thickened. Makes about 6 cups.

Polenta with Mushroom Sauce

Hands-on time: 20 minutes
Total time: 25 minutes

1 small onion, minced

2 cloves garlic, minced

1 pound portobello or cremini mushrooms, stems removed and thinly sliced

2 teaspoons chopped fresh rosemary or $^3/4$ teaspoon dried

1 tablespoon cornstarch

3 cups fat-free reduced-sodium chicken broth

1 tablespoon balsamic vinegar

2 teaspoons Dijon mustard

$^1/4$ teaspoon salt

$^1/2$ cup cornmeal

$^1/3$ cup (1$^1/2$ ounces) grated Parmesan cheese

Coat a medium nonstick skillet with nonstick spray. Add the onion and garlic. Coat with nonstick spray. Cook, stirring occasionally, over medium heat for 2 to 3 minutes, or until fragrant. Add the mushrooms and rosemary. Cover and cook, stirring occasionally, for 4 minutes, or until the mushrooms have released some liquid. Uncover and cook for 4 minutes, or until the mushrooms start to brown.

Meanwhile, place the cornstarch in a small bowl. Gradually whisk in 1 cup of the broth until blended. Add to the skillet along with the vinegar. Cook, stirring constantly, for 3 to 4 minutes, or until thickened. Add the mustard and salt. Stir to mix. Reduce the heat to low.

Place the cornmeal in a large saucepan. Gradually add the remaining 2 cups broth, stirring constantly, until smooth. Cook, stirring constantly, over medium-high heat for 4 to 5 minutes, or until the mixture boils. Reduce the heat to low. Cook, stirring occasionally, for 3 to 4 minutes, or until thick and creamy. Remove from the heat. Stir in the Parmesan. Serve the polenta topped with the mushroom sauce.

Makes 4 servings

Per serving
Calories 202	Sodium 444 mg.
Total fat 4 g.	Dietary fiber 2 g.
Saturated fat 2 g.	Protein 12 g.
Cholesterol 7 mg.	Carbohydrates 27 g.

POLENTA TOASTS

You can double the polenta recipe to make planned leftovers. Spread the leftover polenta in an even layer in a baking dish coated with nonstick spray. Cover and refrigerate for at least 3 hours or up to 24 hours. Cut the polenta into 2½" to 3" squares, then into triangles. Place on a baking sheet coated with nonstick spray. Bake in a 400°F oven for 10 minutes per side, or until golden. Serve as an appetizer topped with chopped roasted bell peppers or eggplant or as a starchy accompaniment to soups and stews.

Risotto with Shrimp, Peas, and Fennel

Photograph on page 222
Hands-on time: 20 minutes
Total time: 35 minutes

- 2 cans (14$\frac{1}{2}$ ounces) fat-free reduced-sodium chicken broth
- $\frac{1}{2}$ cup dry white wine or nonalcoholic white wine
- $\frac{1}{4}$ teaspoon salt
- 2 teaspoons olive oil
- 1 large leek, white part only, sliced
- 1 bulb fennel, trimmed, cored, quartered, and thinly sliced
- 1 cup Arborio rice
- $\frac{3}{4}$ pound medium shrimp, peeled and deveined
- 1$\frac{1}{2}$ cups fresh or frozen peas
- $\frac{1}{2}$ cup (2 ounces) grated Parmesan cheese

In a medium saucepan, combine the broth, wine, salt, and 1 cup water. Bring to a boil over high heat. Reduce the heat to low.

Meanwhile, warm the oil in a Dutch oven set over medium heat. Add the leek and fennel. Cook for 3 to 4 minutes, or until the fennel starts to soften. Add the rice. Cook, stirring, for 1 minute to coat the grains.

Add about 1 cup of the broth mixture. Cook, stirring constantly, for 5 minutes, or until all the broth is absorbed. Cook, stirring frequently and adding $\frac{1}{2}$ cup of the broth mixture at a time, for 20 minutes, or until the rice is almost tender.

Add the shrimp and peas. Cook, stirring constantly, for 5 minutes, or until the shrimp is opaque and the rice is tender. Remove from the heat. Top with the Parmesan.

Makes 4 servings

Per serving
Calories 412
Total fat 7 g.
Saturated fat 3 g.
Cholesterol 131 mg.
Sodium 692 mg.
Dietary fiber 4 g.
Protein 28 g.
Carbohydrates 52 g.

Cooking Note
Arborio rice, a short-grained high-starch rice appropriate for risotto, is sold in many supermarkets and in Italian food stores.

Finding Fiber

The American Heart Association and the National Cancer Institute recommend that Americans eat more dietary fiber for better health—between 25 and 35 grams a day is optimal.

Fiber only comes from plant foods, including fruits, vegetables, and grains. It is the structural part of a plant that actually passes through the human body undigested.

Two types of fiber, soluble and insoluble, promote health in different ways. Soluble fiber, found in foods such as beans, oats, barley, and apples, can help lower cholesterol by forming a gel in the intestine that traps cholesterol and escorts it out of the body.

Insoluble fiber, which is found in wheat bran and most cereals, can help prevent certain types of cancers by moving potentially harmful substances through the intestine more quickly.

Because most fiber-rich foods contain a combination of soluble and insoluble fiber, it is wise to eat a variety of plant foods daily. Choose whole-grain foods such as whole-wheat breads, brown rice, bulgur, and barley to get the highest amount of fiber. Leaving the peel on vegetables and fruits can also boost fiber.

When you start to increase your fiber intake, drink more water and other fluids, which will help your body manage the extra fiber comfortably. Acquaint yourself with high-fiber foods and find ways to work them into your day's meals and snacks. A ½-cup serving of butter, navy, or kidney beans—an easy addition to a salad—contributes nearly 7 grams of dietary fiber. And for real convenience, some ready-to-eat breakfast cereals are also excellent sources of fiber. Some all-bran cereals, for example, contain nearly 14 grams of fiber in just ½ cup.

Another benefit to eating high-fiber foods is that they automatically help you cut back on calories and lower your fat intake because they are naturally low in fat and calories and offer plenty of appetite satisfaction.

Barley Risotto with Mushrooms

Hands-on time: 20 minutes
Total time: 35 minutes

1 ounce dried mushrooms

2 cups boiling water

2 cups fat-free reduced-sodium beef broth

2 teaspoons olive oil

1/4 pound button mushrooms, sliced

1 small onion, chopped

3 cloves garlic, chopped

1 cup barley

2 teaspoons dried sage

1/4 teaspoon salt

1/2 cup (2 ounces) grated Parmesan cheese

In a medium bowl, combine the dried mushrooms and water. Let stand for 15 minutes.

Line a fine sieve with a coffee filter or paper towels. Set over a medium saucepan. Pour the mushroom liquid through the sieve. Chop the mushrooms and set aside. Add the broth to the saucepan. Place over medium-low heat.

Meanwhile, warm the oil in a Dutch oven set over medium heat. Add the button mushrooms, onion, garlic, and reserved dried mushrooms. Cook, stirring occasionally, for 3 to 4 minutes, or until the mushrooms start to soften. Add the barley, sage, and salt. Cook, stirring, for 2 minutes.

Add about 1 cup of the broth mixture. Cook, stirring constantly, for 5 minutes, or until the broth is absorbed. Cook, stirring frequently and adding 1/2 cup of the broth mixture at a time, for 20 to 25 minutes, or until the barley is tender. Top with the Parmesan.

Makes 6 servings

Per serving
Calories 221
Total fat 5 g.
Saturated fat 2 g.
Cholesterol 7 mg.
Sodium 310 mg.
Dietary fiber 7 g.
Protein 10 g.
Carbohydrates 35 g.

BARLEY

Barley is a complex carbohydrate that is rich in fiber. This cereal grain is usually sold pearled, meaning that the husk is removed and the kernel is polished. Look for pearled barley in the rice and pasta section of your supermarket. Other barley products you may want to try include quick-cooking barley, barley flour, and barley flakes.

Island Rice

Hands-on time: 10 minutes
Total time: 30 minutes

   1 cup long-grain white rice
 1/4 teaspoon salt
   4 scallions, sliced
   1 small jalapeño chile pepper, seeded and finely chopped (wear plastic gloves when handling)
   1 teaspoon grated fresh ginger
 1/3 cup unsweetened reduced-fat coconut milk
      Juice and grated peel of 1 lime

Cook the rice according to the package directions.

Meanwhile, coat a small nonstick skillet with nonstick spray. Set over medium heat. Add the scallions, chile pepper, and ginger. Cook for 2 minutes, or until crisp-tender. Add the coconut milk, lime juice, and lime peel. Toss to blend. Stir into the rice.

Makes 4 servings

Per serving
Calories 200   *Sodium 158 mg.*
Total fat 2 g.   *Dietary fiber 1 g.*
Saturated fat 1 g. *Protein 4 g.*
Cholesterol 0 mg.   *Carbohydrates 41 g.*

CHILE PEPPERS

Chile peppers not only provide plenty of excitement for your palate but they may also help lower low-density lipoprotein (LDL) cholesterol, the "bad" cholesterol associated with stroke, high blood pressure, and heart disease.

Southern Cornbread Dressing

Hands-on time: 15 minutes
Total time: 45 minutes

1 small onion, chopped

2 ribs celery, chopped

1/4 pound mushrooms, stems removed and sliced

5 cups crumbled low-fat cornbread (see note)

2 cups cubed white bread

1 1/2 teaspoons dried sage

1/8 teaspoon salt

1 1/2 cups fat-free reduced-sodium chicken broth

Preheat the oven to 375°F. Coat a medium baking dish with nonstick spray.

Coat a medium skillet with nonstick spray. Add the onion, celery, and mushrooms. Coat with nonstick spray. Cook, stirring occasionally, over medium heat for 5 to 7 minutes, or until soft. Transfer to a large bowl. Set aside to cool.

To the bowl, add the cornbread, white bread, sage, and salt. Toss to mix. Add the broth, tossing to coat evenly. Spoon into the prepared baking dish. Bake for 30 minutes, or until golden.

Makes 6 servings

Per serving
Calories 215   *Sodium 711 mg.*
Total fat 5 g.   *Dietary fiber 3 g.*
Saturated fat 1 g. *Protein 8 g.*
Cholesterol 36 mg. *Carbohydrates 33 g.*

Cooking Note

Use your favorite recipe for low-fat cornbread or prepare 1 package (6 1/2 ounces) low-fat cornbread mix for this recipe.

A New Twist

DRESSING UP

Southern Cornbread Dressing is a versatile, tasty accompaniment for chicken breasts baked on the bone, grilled pork chops, or a vegetable-based meal of Molasses Baked Beans (page 269) and Country Coleslaw (page 234).

Couscous with Pistachios and Currants

Hands-on time: 10 minutes
Total time: 15 minutes

1	teaspoon olive oil
2	ounces mushrooms, sliced
1	small red bell pepper, chopped
¹/₂	teaspoon ground cinnamon
1	can (14¹/₂ ounces) fat-free reduced-sodium chicken broth
10	ounces couscous
¹/₃	cup currants or raisins
¹/₄	cup coarsely chopped pistachios
¹/₄–¹/₂	cup orange juice

Warm the oil in a large nonstick skillet over medium heat. Add the mushrooms, bell pepper, and cinnamon. Cook, stirring, for 4 minutes, or until soft. Add the broth. Bring to a boil. Add the couscous and currants or raisins. Stir to mix. Remove from the heat. Cover and let stand for 5 minutes.

Place the couscous mixture in a large bowl. Add the pistachios and ¼ cup orange juice. Toss to mix. Add the remaining ¼ cup orange juice to moisten, if needed.

Makes 6 servings

Per serving
Calories 263	*Sodium 63 mg.*
Total fat 4 g.	*Dietary fiber 4 g.*
Saturated fat 1 g.	*Protein 10 g.*
Cholesterol 0 mg.	*Carbohydrates 47 g.*

A New Twist

COUSCOUS-STUFFED TOMATOES

For a terrific summer main dish, hollow out 6 large tomatoes. Fill the tomatoes with the Couscous with Pistachios and Currants. Garnish with chopped fresh cilantro or mint leaves.

Creamy Black Bean Enchiladas

Photograph on page 224
Hands-on time: 20 minutes
Total time: 45 minutes

Makes 6 servings

Per enchilada
Calories 353   Sodium 586 mg.
Total fat 7 g.   Dietary fiber 9 g.
Saturated fat 4 g.   Protein 18 g.
Cholesterol 21 mg.   Carbohydrates 54 g.

2/3 cup white rice

3/4 cup (6 ounces) fat-free sour cream

3 ounces reduced-fat cream cheese, softened

3 scallions, finely chopped

1 jar (4 ounces) chopped green chile peppers, drained

1/2 teaspoon ground cumin

1 can (15 ounces) black beans, rinsed and drained

6 corn or flour tortillas (6" diameter)

1 cup (4 ounces) shredded low-fat Monterey Jack or Cheddar cheese

1/2 cup mild red taco sauce

Preheat the oven to 375°F. Coat a 13" × 9" baking dish with nonstick spray.

Cook the rice according to the package directions.

Meanwhile, in a medium bowl, combine the sour cream, cream cheese, scallions, chile peppers, and cumin. Stir until well-blended. Add the beans and rice. Stir gently to mix.

Place the tortillas on a work surface. Spoon some of the bean filling down the center of each tortilla. Sprinkle with Monterey Jack or Cheddar. Roll into cylinders. Place, seam side down, in the prepared baking dish. Drizzle with the taco sauce.

Bake for 12 to 15 minutes, or until heated through.

Mediterranean Chickpea Salad

Photograph on page 220
Hands-on time: 15 minutes
Total time: 25 minutes

1 can (15 ounces) chickpeas, rinsed and drained

1/2 small red onion, quartered and thinly sliced

1/2 cucumber, peeled, seeded, and chopped

1 roasted red pepper, chopped

3 plum tomatoes, chopped

2 tablespoons chopped parsley

2 cloves garlic, chopped

3 tablespoons lemon juice

2 teaspoons extra-virgin olive oil

1/4 teaspoon salt

In a large bowl, combine the chickpeas, onion, cucumber, pepper, tomatoes, parsley, garlic, lemon juice, olive oil, and salt. Toss to mix. Allow to stand at room temperature for 10 minutes for flavors to blend.

Makes 8 servings

Per serving
Calories 77
Total fat 3 g.
Saturated fat 0 g.
Cholesterol 0 mg.
Sodium 155 mg.
Dietary fiber 4 g.
Protein 3 g.
Carbohydrates 12 g.

A New Twist

MEDITERRANEAN CHICKPEA SALAD WITH FETA

A bit of feta cheese adds a pleasantly tangy, creamy note to this salad. Crumble 6 tablespoons (1½ ounces) feta cheese over the salad. It will increase the fat only slightly, to about 4 grams per serving.

Cooking Dried Beans and Lentils

Dried legumes can be bought in bulk or in prepacked plastic bags. Purchase them from a store with a high turnover rate. Old legumes are tough and may sometimes never soften properly. At home, legumes should be stored in tightly sealed glass containers in a cool, dry place.

To prepare dried beans, pick out and discard any stones or broken beans. Rinse under cold water to remove dust. Place the beans in a large pot and cover with plenty of cold water. Allow to soak, changing the water several times, for at least 4 hours or as long as 12 hours. Soaking allows them to gradually rehydrate and expand, thus reducing the cooking time. It also helps break down the indigestible sugars that can cause flatulence.

To cook dried beans, drain the soaking water and return the beans to the pot. Add enough cold water to cover the beans by at least two inches. Bring to a boil over high heat, then immediately reduce the heat to medium-low so that the beans just simmer. Cooking times vary depending upon the type and age of the bean. Start testing for doneness after an hour. A cooked bean should hold its shape but be completely tender inside. If the water evaporates below the beans during cooking, be sure to add enough hot water to recover the beans.

To add flavor, add chunks of onion, celery, or carrots or cloves of garlic. Fresh parsley stems, dried thyme, bay leaf, dried sage, dried savory, and whole cloves are herbs and spices that complement beans. Remove these aromatics and discard before using the beans. Do not add salt or acidic foods such as tomatoes and vinegars to beans until they are cooked, or they won't soften properly. You can freeze cooked dried beans in a tightly covered plastic container for up to six months.

Lentils and split peas cook in less time than dried beans, generally about 30 to 45 minutes. They do not require any soaking. Due to their softer nature, they can quickly break down and lose their shape. Monitor lentils as they cook if you want them to maintain their shape, for instance, for a salad recipe. If you want them cooked to puree as the base for a dip, simply cook them until they are completely softened.

Lentils come in several colors. The most common brown lentils have a soft texture. Green lentils take a little longer to cook but hold their shape nicely for salads and side dishes. Red and yellow lentils break down in cooking and are best in soups, stews, or dips.

Molasses Baked Beans

Hands-on time: 15 minutes
Total time: 45 minutes

3 cans (15 ounces each) pinto beans
1 strip bacon, chopped
1 small onion, chopped
½ cup ketchup
½ cup molasses
1 tablespoon coarse ground mustard
2 teaspoons Worcestershire sauce

Preheat the oven to 350°F. Lightly coat a 2-quart baking dish with nonstick spray.

Drain the beans, reserving ½ cup of the liquid. Rinse and drain the beans.

In a medium skillet, cook the bacon, stirring frequently, over medium heat for 3 to 4 minutes, or until crisp. Remove with a slotted spoon to a paper towel to drain. Add the onion to the skillet. Cook, stirring occasionally, for 5 to 7 minutes, or until tender.

Meanwhile, in the prepared baking dish, combine the beans, reserved bean liquid, ketchup, molasses, mustard, and Worcestershire sauce. Add the bacon and onion.

Bake, stirring occasionally, for 30 minutes, or until bubbly.

Makes 6 servings

Per serving
Calories 381	*Sodium 607 mg.*
Total fat 3 g.	*Dietary fiber 15 g.*
Saturated fat 1 g.	*Protein 17 g.*
Cholesterol 3 mg.	*Carbohydrates 72 g.*

Good for You

Bean Careful

Keep a careful eye on the type of canned beans that you buy. When foods are processed with added ingredients, the nutritional value can be affected. Plain canned beans are extremely low in fat, but canned baked beans with added frankfurters, for example, can get as much as 42 percent of calories from fat.

Ginger Tabbouleh

Hands-on time: 10 minutes
Total time: 30 minutes

$^3/_4$ cup finely ground bulgur

$^1/_4$ cup + 2 tablespoons rice wine or white wine vinegar

1 tablespoon soy sauce

1 teaspoon grated fresh ginger

1 clove garlic, minced

1 teaspoon toasted sesame oil
    Pinch of sugar

3 scallions, finely chopped

$^1/_2$ cup chopped fresh parsley and/or cilantro

$^1/_2$ pound thin asparagus, cut into $^1/_2$" pieces, steamed and cooled

1 carrot, shredded

Place the bulgur in a medium bowl. Cover with cold water. Allow to soak for 20 to 25 minutes, or until soft. Drain.

Meanwhile, in a medium bowl, combine the vinegar, soy sauce, ginger, garlic, oil, and sugar. Whisk until blended. Add the scallions, parsley and/or cilantro, asparagus, carrot, and bulgur. Toss to mix.

Makes 4 servings

Per serving
Calories 137	*Sodium 369 mg.*
Total fat 2 g.	*Dietary fiber 6 g.*
Saturated fat 0 g.	*Protein 5 g.*
Cholesterol 0 mg.	*Carbohydrates 29 g.*

ASPARAGUS

Asparagus, a low-calorie springtime vegetable, is an outstanding source of folic acid, which some heart researchers believe may be as important as controlling cholesterol in the prevention of heart disease.

Fish and Shellfish

A large body of evidence supports the beneficial effects of eating seafood regularly. In fact, populations who eat seafood on a regular basis run lower risks of heart disease. "Seafood is a great protein source full of numerous vitamins and minerals," says Julie Avery, R.D., a licensed dietitian with the Cleveland Clinic Foundation in Ohio.

Health officials say that eating seafood at least twice a week—about 6 ounces total—can be beneficial to your health. Seafood is rich in high-quality protein, vitamins, and minerals. Depending on the variety, seafood can deliver B vitamins, iron, zinc, magnesium, and potassium.

Research has shown that highly polyunsaturated omega-3 fatty acids, found in greatest concentrations in dark-fleshed fish such as salmon, are highly beneficial in lowering cholesterol, preventing heart disease, and relieving premenstrual syndrome, arthritis, and even asthma.

Seafood in a Flash

Don't let lack of experience keep you from adding seafood to your meals. As you begin to serve seafood, you'll not only reap health benefits but you'll find that meals get on the table faster as well.

Seafood generally cooks in minutes because it lacks the connective tissue that meat and poultry have. Quick cooking times make seafood nature's easiest and most delicious fast food.

Grilling, broiling, poaching, baking, and steaming are just a few of the cooking methods that you can use with seafood. Accompaniments can range from a simple lemon wedge to a complex fresh Mexican salsa.

Shop for convenience forms of seafood to always have a variety of this healthful ingredient on hand. Individually flash-frozen fish fillets, shrimp, and scallops cook in minutes. Canned tuna, salmon, and clams are cupboard staples ideal for sandwiches, salads, pastas, and casseroles.

Seafood departments in many supermarkets offer convenient ready-steamed fish or shellfish. Take advantage of these to serve at home topped with low-fat seasonings or sauces. Or, cut the cooked seafood into chunks and add to casseroles, salads, or pasta dishes.

Recipes

Cornmeal-Crusted Catfish

Photograph on page 225
Hands-on time: 15 minutes
Total time: 30 minutes

$^1/_2$ cup buttermilk

  1 tablespoon lime juice

$^1/_3$ cup cornmeal

$^1/_3$ cup unbleached or all-purpose flour

  4 scallions, minced

$^1/_4$ teaspoon salt

$^1/_4$ teaspoon ground cumin

  4 catfish fillets (5 ounces each)

Line a large plate with waxed paper.

In a medium shallow bowl, combine the buttermilk and lime juice. In another shallow bowl, combine the cornmeal, flour, scallions, salt, and cumin. Stir to mix. Dip the fillets into the buttermilk mixture, then into the cornmeal mixture, pressing gently to adhere. Place on the prepared plate. Refrigerate for 15 minutes.

Place a large nonstick skillet over medium-high heat. Coat the tops of the fillets with nonstick spray. Place the fillets, coated side down, in the pan. Cook for 4 to 5 minutes, or until golden brown on the bottom. Remove the pan from the heat. Coat the tops of the fillets with nonstick spray. Turn and cook over medium-high heat for 4 to 5 minutes, or until the fish flakes easily.

Makes 4 servings

Per serving
Calories 339	*Sodium 264 mg.*
Total fat 14 g.	*Dietary fiber 0 g.*
Saturated fat 3 g.	*Protein 31 g.*
Cholesterol 84 mg.	*Carbohydrates 20 g.*

A New Twist

SALSA CRUDA

This fresh salsa is a zesty accompaniment to crispy pan-fried fish. In a small bowl, combine 4 chopped plum tomatoes, ¼ cup chopped red onion, 2 minced cloves garlic, 2 tablespoons lime juice, 2 tablespoons chopped fresh cilantro, 1 seeded and minced jalapeño chile pepper (wear plastic gloves when handling), 1 teaspoon sugar, and a pinch each of salt and pepper. Allow the salsa to sit at room temperature for 15 to 20 minutes for the flavors to develop.

Steamed Sea Bass in Black Bean Sauce

Hands-on time: 10 minutes
Total time: 20 minutes

- 1 pound sea bass
- 3 cloves garlic, minced
- 1 tablespoon minced fresh ginger or ¹⁄₂ teaspoon ground
- 1 tablespoon soy sauce
- 2 teaspoons Asian garlic black bean sauce (optional); see note
- 1¹⁄₂ teaspoons toasted sesame oil
- ¹⁄₂ teaspoon sugar
- 2 scallions, sliced

Set a steamer rack in a large skillet filled with 2" of boiling water. Set the fish on a heat-proof plate that will fit into the pan.

In a small bowl, combine the garlic, ginger, soy sauce, black bean sauce (if desired), oil, sugar, and scallions. Stir until well-blended. Pour over the fish. Turn the fish to coat both sides.

Place the plate with the fish on the steamer rack. Cover tightly. Cook over medium heat for 10 minutes per inch of thickness, or until the fish flakes easily. Serve the fish topped with the black bean sauce.

Makes 4 servings

Per serving
Calories 140 *Sodium 239 mg.*
Total fat 4 g. *Dietary fiber 0 g.*
Saturated fat 1 g. *Protein 21 g.*
Cholesterol 47 mg. *Carbohydrates 2 g.*

Cooking Note

Garlic black bean sauce is a pungent sauce made from fermented black soybeans. It can be found in the Asian section of many supermarkets and in most Asian markets.

A New Twist

Toasted Sesame Oil

Look for dark-colored toasted sesame oil in the Asian ingredients section of your supermarket. Keep a small bottle on hand in a cool cupboard to add an enticing nutty essence to salad dressings, stir-fries, and marinades. Just a little bit of this highly flavored oil—which is pressed from sesame seeds that have been toasted—adds a lot of flavor.

Mediterranean Flounder

Hands-on time: 10 minutes
Total time: 25 minutes

4 flounder, scrod, or cod fillets (5 ounces each)

1 teaspoon dried oregano

1/4 teaspoon salt

1/2 cucumber, halved, peeled, seeded, and sliced

3 plum tomatoes, sliced

1/3 cup (1 1/2 ounces) crumbled feta cheese

2 tablespoons chopped pitted Kalamata olives

6 tablespoons fat-free reduced-sodium chicken broth or water

Preheat the oven to 350°F. Arrange 4 sheets of foil (12" × 12" each) on a work surface.

Place 1 fillet in the center of each piece of foil. Season with oregano and salt. Bring the sides of the foil pieces up slightly to cup each fillet.

Top each fillet with equal amounts of cucumber, tomatoes, feta, and olives. Add 1½ tablespoons of the broth or water to each packet. Bring the edges of each piece of foil together and crimp to seal. Place the packets on a baking sheet.

Bake for 15 minutes, or until the fish flakes easily. Check for doneness by opening 1 packet very carefully (steam will be released). To serve, transfer the contents of each packet to a plate.

Makes 4 servings

Per serving
Calories 200
Total fat 5 g.
Saturated fat 2 g.
Cholesterol 77 mg.
Sodium 423 mg.
Dietary fiber 2 g.
Protein 29 g.
Carbohydrates 6 g.

Red Snapper with Fruit Sauce

Hands-on time: 10 minutes
Total time: 25 minutes

4 red snapper fillets (5 ounces each)
$1/2$ cup + 2 tablespoons orange juice
2 nectarines, cut into small pieces
1 banana, cut into small pieces
$1/2$ small red onion, minced
1 serrano or jalapeño chile pepper, seeded and minced (wear plastic gloves when handling)
2 tablespoons chopped fresh cilantro
1 tablespoon packed light brown sugar
$1/8$ teaspoon salt

Coat a grill rack or broiler pan with nonstick spray. Preheat the grill or broiler.

Place the fillets in a shallow dish. Pour ½ cup of the orange juice over the fillets, turning them to coat. Cover and refrigerate for 15 minutes.

Meanwhile, in a medium bowl, combine the nectarines, banana, onion, chile pepper, cilantro, the remaining 2 tablespoons orange juice, brown sugar, and salt. Toss gently to mix.

Remove the snapper from the orange juice. Discard the juice. Place on the prepared rack or pan. Grill or broil for 4 to 5 minutes per side, or until the fish flakes easily. Serve topped with the nectarine mixture.

Makes 4 servings

Per serving
Calories 244	*Sodium 167 mg.*
Total fat 3 g.	*Dietary fiber 0 g.*
Saturated fat 1 g.	*Protein 31 g.*
Cholesterol 52 mg.	*Carbohydrates 24 g.*

THE HEALTHY TRAVELER

When planning a trip, think of ways to maintain your healthy eating habits away from home. Pack your own snacks, like bagels, dried fruit, and bottled water, to nourish yourself when meals are delayed. If traveling by air, request a vegetarian or low-fat meal when you make your reservation.

Baked Cod
with Mustard Crumbs

Photograph on page 228
Hands-on time: 15 minutes
Total time: 35 minutes

Makes 4 servings

Per serving
Calories 271
Total fat 6 g.
Saturated fat 1 g.
Cholesterol 67 mg.

Sodium 579 mg.
Dietary fiber 1 g.
Protein 31 g.
Carbohydrates 20 g.

1 small onion, chopped

3 plum tomatoes, chopped

$\frac{1}{3}$ cup dry white wine or fat-free reduced-sodium chicken broth

4 cod, flounder, or scrod fillets (5 ounces each)

$\frac{1}{4}$ teaspoon salt

$\frac{3}{4}$ cup fresh bread crumbs

2 tablespoons chopped parsley

1 tablespoon butter or margarine, melted

2 teaspoons Dijon mustard

Preheat the oven to 400°F.

Coat a large ovenproof skillet with nonstick spray. Add the onion. Coat with nonstick spray. Cook, stirring occasionally, over medium heat for 3 to 4 minutes, or until soft. Add the tomatoes. Cook, stirring occasionally, for 2 to 3 minutes, or until soft. Increase the heat to medium-high. Add the wine or broth. Cook for 2 minutes, or until reduced by half. Remove from the heat. Arrange the fillets in a single layer over the mixture. Sprinkle with the salt.

Meanwhile, in a small bowl, combine the bread crumbs, parsley, butter or margarine, and mustard. Sprinkle evenly over the fillets. Press gently to adhere.

Bake for 15 to 20 minutes, or until the fish flakes easily.

Swordfish Pitas with Herb Chutney

Hands-on time: 15 minutes
Total time: 35 minutes

2 tablespoons lemon juice

2 teaspoons dried oregano

1 clove garlic, minced

1 pound swordfish, cut into 1" cubes

4 plum tomatoes, halved lengthwise and seeded

1 red onion, cut into ¼"-thick slices

4 pitas, cut in half crosswise
   Herb Chutney (at right)

In a shallow bowl, combine the lemon juice, oregano, and garlic. Add the swordfish. Toss to coat. Cover and refrigerate for 15 minutes.

Coat a grill rack or broiler pan with nonstick spray. Preheat the grill or broiler.

Thread the swordfish onto 4 skewers (6" long). Place the skewers, tomatoes (cut side up), and onion on the prepared rack or pan. Grill or broil, turning the skewers occasionally, for 7 to 10 minutes, or until the fish is opaque, the tomatoes are lightly charred, and the onion is soft. Remove to a plate. Cover loosely with foil to keep warm.

Place the pitas in a single layer on the grill rack or on a baking sheet. Grill or broil for 1 to 2 minutes per side, or until heated through. Stuff each pita half with swordfish, tomato, and onion. Top with chutney.

Makes 4 servings

Per serving
Calories 315
Total fat 5 g.
Saturated fat 1 g.
Cholesterol 31 mg.
Sodium 497 mg.
Dietary fiber 3 g.
Protein 24 g.
Carbohydrates 44 g.

A New Twist

Herb Chutney

Peel and seed 1 small cucumber. Coarsely shred and then squeeze it dry. Place in a small bowl. Add ½ cup fat-free plain yogurt, ¼ cup chopped fresh cilantro, 1 tablespoon lemon juice, 1 minced clove garlic, and ⅛ teaspoon each of salt and ground black pepper. Stir to mix.

❤ Rosemary Roast Chicken (page 318) ❤

❤ California Chicken (page 319) ❤

~Chinese Barbecued Pork Chops (page 315) and Asian Slaw (page 204)~ 281

❤Stir-Fried Beef and Broccoli (page 308)❤

284

❤ Beef Stroganoff (page 307) ❤

~Honey-Roasted Turkey Breast (page 322)~

♥ Chocolate Soufflé Cake (page 337) ♥

❤ Chocolate Chippers (page 327) ❤

❤ Peach Tart (page 333) ❤

❤Apple-Cheese Strudel (page 332)❤

~Plum-Blueberry Cobbler (page 334)~

❧Chocolate-Cherry Bread Pudding (page 331)❧

◆Fresh Berry Shortcake (page 339)◆

❧ Berry Berry Smoothie (page 343) and Peachy Smoothie (page 344) ❧

Creamy Dill Salmon in Phyllo

Hands-on time: 20 minutes
Total time: 40 minutes

1/3 cup (3 ounces) fat-free sour cream

1 tablespoon chopped fresh dill or
   1 teaspoon dried

1 teaspoon Dijon mustard

1/4 teaspoon salt

1 large leek, sliced

8 sheets (17" × 11") frozen phyllo
   dough, thawed

4 salmon fillets (4 ounces each), skin
   removed

Preheat the oven to 375°F. Coat a baking sheet with nonstick spray.

In a small bowl, combine the sour cream, dill, mustard, and salt. Stir to blend. Set aside.

Coat a medium skillet with nonstick spray. Add the leek and coat with nonstick spray. Cook, stirring occasionally, over medium heat for 4 to 5 minutes, or until soft. Remove from the heat and set aside.

Place 1 sheet of phyllo on a work surface, long side facing you. Coat lightly with nonstick spray. Top with 3 more phyllo sheets, coating each with nonstick spray. Starting at the top center, cut the stack in half down through the middle. You will have 2 rectangles with the shorter sides facing you.

Place a fillet in the center of each phyllo stack. Top with one-quarter of the sour-cream mixture and one-quarter of the leek mixture. Fold the bottom of the dough over the fillet, then fold in the sides of the dough. Continue to roll away from you to form a tight package. Place, seam side down, on the prepared baking sheet.

Repeat with the remaining ingredients to form 2 more phyllo bundles. Coat the tops and sides of the bundles with nonstick spray. Bake for 18 to 20 minutes, or until golden brown and the salmon is opaque.

Makes 4 servings

Per serving
Calories 344   *Sodium 466 mg.*
Total fat 13 g.   *Dietary fiber 2 g.*
Saturated fat 3 g.   *Protein 28 g.*
Cholesterol 66 mg.   *Carbohydrates 28 g.*

Try it — EASY ELEGANCE

"I served Creamy Dill Salmon in Phyllo for a family dinner party," says travel agent Lisa Luft Waxman. "It was very easy to prepare but made a beautiful presentation. It was so delicious, nobody believed that it was low in fat and calories."

Sole with Stir-Fried Vegetables

Hands-on time: 15 minutes
Total time: 25 minutes

Makes 4 servings

Per serving
Calories 203   Sodium 522 mg.
Total fat 4 g.   Dietary fiber 0 g.
Saturated fat 1 g.   Protein 30 g.
Cholesterol 68 mg.   Carbohydrates 10 g.

- 3 tablespoons soy sauce
- 3 tablespoons dry sherry or fat-free reduced-sodium chicken broth
- 2 cloves garlic, minced
- 2 teaspoons grated fresh ginger or $\frac{1}{2}$ teaspoon ground
- 2 teaspoons cornstarch
- 1 $\frac{1}{2}$ teaspoons sugar
- 2 teaspoons vegetable oil
- 4 ounces snow peas
- $\frac{1}{4}$ pound shiitake or button mushrooms, sliced
- 1 small red bell pepper, cut into strips
- 1 cup mung bean sprouts
- 1 teaspoon toasted sesame oil
- 4 sole fillets (5 ounces each)

In a small bowl, combine the soy sauce, sherry or broth, garlic, ginger, cornstarch, and sugar. Stir to blend well. Set aside.

In a large skillet or wok, heat the vegetable oil over high heat. Add the snow peas, mushrooms, and bell pepper. Cook, tossing, for 3 to 4 minutes, or until the pepper starts to soften. Add the bean sprouts and sesame oil. Toss to combine. Reduce the heat to medium. Add the reserved sauce. Cook, stirring, for 2 to 3 minutes, or until thickened. Place the fillets in a single layer over the vegetables. Cover tightly.

Cook for 10 to 12 minutes, or until the fish flakes easily.

Fishing for Supper

Even if you've never cooked fish in your life, you can have these tasty main dishes on your supper table in 30 minutes or less.

Asian Fish. Buy steamed fish fillets or cooked shrimp at the seafood counter at your supermarket. Drizzle with a mixture of chicken broth, soy sauce, grated fresh ginger, and sliced scallions. Serve with steamed or grilled vegetables or a tossed salad of mixed greens.

Italian-Style Baked Fish. Place 4 fish fillets in a baking dish coated with non-stick spray. Mix some pasta sauce with a bit of fat-free reduced-sodium chicken broth or water to thin slightly. Pour over the fish. Cover and bake in a 375°F oven for 20 to 25 minutes, or until the fish flakes easily. Serve with cooked pasta or rice.

Sardine Sandwich. Grill 2 slices of rye bread. Spread with mustard. Drain canned sardines and pat dry. Cover 1 slice of bread with sardines. Top with a slice of red onion, a slice of tomato, a lettuce leaf and the remaining slice of bread.

Seafood Soup. Cook equal amounts of sliced onion, carrot, and celery in a little olive oil in a pot until soft. Add 4 fish fillets and ½ pound medium shrimp or sea scallops. Add enough bottled clam juice or chicken broth to cover. Cover and simmer over medium-low heat for 15 to 20 minutes, or until the fish flakes easily and the shrimp or scallops are opaque. Serve in shallow bowls over toasted slices of French bread that have been rubbed with garlic.

Tuna Pasta. Toss drained canned water-packed tuna with hot cooked pasta and frozen peas (add the peas to the pasta pot 1 minute before draining), 1 tablespoon olive oil, and enough chicken broth to moisten. Toss with 2 tablespoons grated Parmesan cheese.

Orange Roughy Veracruz

Photograph on page 226
Hands-on time: 15 minutes
Total time: 35 minutes

- 4 orange roughy or red snapper fillets (4 ounces each)
- 1 tablespoon lime juice
- 1 teaspoon dried oregano
- 2 teaspoons olive oil
- 1 onion, chopped
- 1 clove garlic, minced
- 1 can (15 ounces) Mexican-style diced tomatoes
- 12 pimiento-stuffed olives, coarsely chopped
- 2 tablespoons chopped parsley

Preheat the oven to 350°F. Coat an 8" × 8" baking dish with nonstick spray. Place the fillets in the baking dish. Sprinkle with the lime juice and oregano. Set aside.

Warm the oil in a medium skillet set over medium heat. Add the onion and garlic. Cook, stirring occasionally, for 5 to 6 minutes, or until soft. Add the tomatoes, olives, and parsley. Cook, stirring occasionally, for 5 minutes, or until thickened. Spoon over the fillets. Cover tightly with foil.

Bake for 18 to 20 minutes, or until the fish flakes easily.

Makes 4 servings

Per serving
Calories 163
Total fat 4 g.
Saturated fat 1 g.
Cholesterol 23 mg.
Sodium 503 mg.
Dietary fiber 2 g.
Protein 18 g.
Carbohydrates 12 g.

A New Twist

VERSATILE VERACRUZ

This oven-baked fish dish can be changed according to your taste or the ingredients that you have on hand. If you like hot chile peppers, you can add 1 seeded and minced jalapeño chile pepper (wear plastic gloves when handling) or ½ teaspoon hot-pepper sauce to the tomato mixture. If you don't have olives, you can replace them with 1 tablespoon drained capers. And, instead of parsley, try chopped fresh cilantro leaves.

Shrimp and Crab Cakes

Hands-on time: 15 minutes
Total time: 25 minutes

2 slices white bread

1 egg white

2 tablespoons low-fat mayonnaise

1 teaspoon Worcestershire sauce

1 teaspoon Dijon mustard

1/2 pound large shrimp, peeled, deveined, and finely chopped

1/2 pound lump crabmeat, picked over for shells and flaked

1 rib celery, finely chopped

3 scallions, white part only, chopped

2 tablespoons chopped parsley

Toast the bread and allow to cool. Crumble into fine crumbs. Set aside.

In a large bowl, combine the egg white, mayonnaise, Worcestershire sauce, and mustard. Whisk to blend. Add the shrimp, crabmeat, celery, scallions, parsley, and one-third of the reserved bread crumbs. Toss to mix.

Shape into 8 cakes, about ½" thick. Spread the remaining bread crumbs on a shallow plate. Dip the cakes into the crumbs, pressing lightly to adhere.

Coat a large nonstick skillet with nonstick spray. Place the cakes in the skillet. Cook over medium heat for 2 to 3 minutes, or until lightly browned on the bottom. Remove the pan from the heat and coat the cakes lightly with nonstick spray. Return the pan to the heat. Carefully turn the cakes. Cook for 2 minutes, or until lightly browned on the bottom. Turn the cakes two more times, coating with nonstick spray each time. Cook for 2 minutes longer per side, or until cooked through.

Makes 4 servings

Per serving
Calories 248   *Sodium 678 mg.*
Total fat 5 g.   *Dietary fiber 1 g.*
Saturated fat 1 g.   *Protein 25 g.*
Cholesterol 121 mg.   *Carbohydrates 24 g.*

RÉMOULADE SAUCE

For a special meal, serve Shrimp and Crab Cakes with rémoulade, a classic French mayonnaise-based sauce. In a small bowl, combine ⅓ cup low-fat mayonnaise, ⅓ cup fat-free sour cream, 1 tablespoon chopped parsley, 1 teaspoon chopped fresh tarragon, 2 teaspoons chopped gherkins, 1 teaspoon drained capers, ½ teaspoon Dijon mustard, and 1 minced small clove garlic. Stir to blend well.

Baked Scallops Newburg

Photograph on page 229
Hands-on time: 20 minutes
Total time: 30 minutes

1/4 cup plain dry bread crumbs

2 teaspoons butter or margarine, melted

2 tablespoons unbleached or all-purpose flour

1/4 teaspoon salt

1/8 teaspoon ground red pepper

1 1/2 cups 1% milk

1 egg yolk

1 pound bay scallops, rinsed, drained, and patted dry

1/2 pound mushrooms, sliced

3 scallions, sliced

2 tablespoons chopped fresh tarragon or 2 teaspoons dried

Preheat the oven to 400°F. Place 4 small round baking dishes (8 ounces each) on a baking sheet. Coat the dishes with nonstick spray.

In a small bowl, combine the bread crumbs and butter or margarine. Toss to mix. Set aside.

Place the flour, salt, and red pepper in a medium saucepan. Gradually whisk in the milk until blended. Cook, stirring often, over medium heat for 5 to 7 minutes, or until thickened. Add the egg yolk. Cook, stirring constantly, for 2 minutes, or until the mixture bubbles.

Meanwhile, coat a medium nonstick skillet with nonstick spray. Place over medium heat. Place the scallops in the skillet. Cook, stirring, for 2 to 3 minutes, or until opaque. With a slotted spoon, transfer the scallops to the saucepan.

Dry the skillet with a paper towel. Coat with nonstick spray. Add the mushrooms. Place over medium heat. Cook, stirring occasionally, for 2 to 3 minutes, or until they release liquid. Add the scallions and tarragon. Cook for 1 minute, or until the mushrooms are soft. Add to the saucepan. Stir to combine. Spoon the mixture into the prepared baking dishes. Sprinkle with the reserved bread crumbs.

Bake for 6 to 8 minutes, or until golden and bubbly.

Makes 4 servings

Per serving
Calories 236	*Sodium 462 mg.*
Total fat 6 g.	*Dietary fiber 1 g.*
Saturated fat 2 g.	*Protein 25 g.*
Cholesterol 94 mg.	*Carbohydrates 18 g.*

A New Twist

Plain or Fancy

For a less expensive dish, you can replace the scallops with 1" chunks of catfish or orange roughy. For a more indulgent dish, replace the scallops with 1" chunks of cooked lobster.

Shrimp and Pasta with Red Bell Pepper Sauce

Hands-on time: 20 minutes
Total time: 30 minutes

- 8 ounces orzo or other small pasta
- 4 roasted red peppers
- 2/3 cup fat-free reduced-sodium chicken broth
- 2 teaspoons olive oil
- 3/4 pound small shrimp, peeled and deveined
- 1 small onion, chopped
- 2 cloves garlic, minced
- 1/4 teaspoon ground red pepper
- 1/4 teaspoon salt
- 1 tablespoon unbleached or all-purpose flour
- 3/4 cup 1% milk
- 2 tablespoons chopped parsley

Cook the orzo according to package directions. Drain.

In a food processor or blender, combine the roasted peppers and broth. Process until pureed. Set aside.

Warm the oil in a medium skillet set over medium heat. Add the shrimp. Cook, stirring, for 2 to 3 minutes, or until the shrimp is opaque. Remove to a plate. Set aside.

Coat the skillet with nonstick spray. Add the onion, garlic, ground red pepper, and salt. Cook, stirring, for 2 to 3 minutes, or until soft. Sprinkle with the flour. Stir to mix. Add the milk. Cook, stirring constantly, for 4 to 5 minutes, or until thickened. Add the roasted pepper puree, orzo, parsley, and reserved shrimp. Stir to blend.

Makes 4 servings

Per serving
Calories 388	Sodium 347 mg.
Total fat 5 g.	Dietary fiber 1 g.
Saturated fat 1 g.	Protein 25 g.
Cholesterol 123 mg.	Carbohydrates 57 g.

Five-Alarm Shrimp

Photograph on page 230
Hands-on time: 15 minutes
Total time: 20 minutes

¹/₄ cup cornstarch

¹/₂ teaspoon salt

1 pound jumbo shrimp, peeled and deveined

1 tablespoon vegetable oil

4 scallions, coarsely chopped

1 small red or yellow bell pepper, cut into slivers

2 tablespoons chopped fresh cilantro or parsley

2 cloves garlic, minced

1 serrano chile pepper, seeded and chopped (wear plastic gloves when handling)

1 tablespoon lime juice

1 teaspoon sugar

³/₄ teaspoon crushed black peppercorns

In a shallow bowl, combine the cornstarch and salt. Add the shrimp. Toss to coat.

Warm the oil in a large nonstick skillet over medium-high heat. Remove the shrimp from the cornstarch mixture and place in the pan. Cook for 1½ minutes per side, or until just opaque. Add the scallions, bell pepper, cilantro or parsley, garlic, and chile pepper. Cook, stirring often, for 1 minute. Add the lime juice, 3 tablespoons water, sugar, and peppercorns. Cook, stirring constantly, for 1 minute, or until the shrimp are opaque.

Makes 4 servings

Per serving

Calories 171	Sodium 714 mg.
Total fat 5 g.	Dietary fiber 1 g.
Saturated fat 0 g.	Protein 18 g.
Cholesterol 161 mg.	Carbohydrates 13 g.

Soft Shrimp Tacos

Play it Again!

Five-Alarm Shrimp makes a fantastic filling for soft tacos. Spoon the cooked shrimp mixture down the center of 8 warmed flour or corn tortillas (6" diameter). Sprinkle with low-fat shredded Monterey Jack cheese. Makes 4 servings.

Teriyaki Tuna with Pineapple

Photograph on page 227
Hands-on time: 15 minutes
Total time: 30 minutes

- 1/4 cup soy sauce
- 3 tablespoons dry sherry or fat-free reduced-sodium chicken broth
- 1 tablespoon sugar
- 1 tablespoon grated fresh ginger or 1 teaspoon ground
- 3 cloves garlic, chopped
- 4 tuna steaks (5 ounces each)
- 1 pineapple, halved, cored, peeled, and cut into 8 wedges
- 1 red bell pepper, quartered lengthwise

In a small bowl, combine the soy sauce, sherry or broth, sugar, ginger, and garlic. Stir to blend. Divide the marinade into 2 medium shallow bowls. Place the steaks in one bowl and the pineapple and bell pepper in the other. Turn the tuna, pineapple, and bell pepper to coat both sides. Cover and refrigerate for 15 minutes.

Coat a grill rack or broiler pan with nonstick spray. Preheat the grill or broiler.

Arrange the tuna, pineapple, and bell pepper on the rack or pan. Discard the marinade from the tuna bowl. Grill or broil, basting occasionally with the marinade from the pineapple bowl, for 4 to 5 minutes per side, or until the tuna is just opaque and the pineapple and bell pepper are heated through and glazed.

Makes 4 servings

Per serving
Calories 261	*Sodium 593 mg.*
Total fat 2 g.	*Dietary fiber 3 g.*
Saturated fat 1 g.	*Protein 35 g.*
Cholesterol 64 mg.	*Carbohydrates 24 g.*

M eat and poultry are favorites with most families and have a home in a healthy eating plan. Lean cuts of meat and poultry are good sources of protein, iron, zinc, and B vitamins. "Protein is the most critical nutrient for tissue repair and growth and can be found in every cell in the body," says licensed dietitian Chavanne B. Hanson, R.D., of the University Hospitals of Cleveland Synergy Program in Ohio. Meat and poultry are considered complete protein sources and provide all the amino acids that the body needs to function properly. Knowing how to obtain the most nutrients while taking in the least amount of fat is the key to serving meat and poultry wisely.

The red meat category includes beef, veal, lamb, and pork. The U.S. Department of Agriculture (USDA) has its own system of grading red meats, which is based on the amount of marbling, or visible fat, in the meat. To learn about the leanest grades of meat and the leanest cuts within those grades, see "Lean on Your Butcher" on page 313.

In the poultry category, you will find chicken and turkey. The leanest cuts of poultry are the breast, followed by the drumstick and the thigh. It is important to know that the fat in poultry is clustered directly under the skin and is therefore easy to remove. Leave the skin on whenever possible during cooking to retain the moisture and the flavor but remove it just before serving to get rid of excess fat.

"You no longer need to let meat and poultry take center stage on the plate; you can more healthfully make meat an accompaniment. Serve these foods with a variety of vegetables and grains for a well-balanced meal, as the USDA Food Guide Pyramid recommends," says Hanson. "For most individuals, two daily servings of meat or poultry (about three ounces each) supplies the necessary nutrients from these protein-rich foods."

Try roasting, broiling, grilling, or poaching meat and poultry instead of frying, batter-dipping, or sautéing. Marinades made with fat-free condiments, fat-free salad dressings, fresh herbs, and ground spices can contribute a lot of flavor and moisture with no added fat.

Recipes

Beef Stroganoff

Photograph on page 284
Hands-on time: 15 minutes
Total time: 30 minutes

12 ounces medium no-yolk egg noodles

1 teaspoon vegetable oil

3/4 pound beef tenderloin or top round, trimmed of all visible fat and cut crosswise into thin strips

1/4 teaspoon salt

1 small onion, quartered and thinly sliced

1/2 pound mushrooms, stems removed and caps sliced

1 1/2 tablespoons unbleached or all-purpose flour

1 can (14 1/2 ounces) fat-free reduced-sodium beef broth

1 teaspoon Worcestershire sauce

1/4 cup (2 ounces) fat-free sour cream

2 tablespoons chopped fresh parsley

Prepare the noodles according to package directions. Drain and place in a serving bowl.

Meanwhile, warm the oil in a large nonstick skillet set over medium-high heat. Sprinkle the beef with the salt. Place in the skillet. Cook, turning occasionally, for 2 to 3 minutes, or until browned. Remove to a plate.

Coat the skillet with nonstick spray. Reduce the heat to medium. Add the onion. Cook, stirring occasionally, for 3 minutes. Add the mushrooms. Cook, stirring occasionally, for 2 to 3 minutes, or until they begin to release liquid. Sprinkle with the flour. Cook, stirring constantly, for 1 minute. Add the broth and Worcestershire sauce. Cook, stirring, for 2 to 3 minutes, or until slightly thickened. Remove from the heat. Add the sour cream and parsley. Stir to mix. Return the beef to the skillet. Place over low heat. Cook for 3 minutes, or until heated through.

Serve the stroganoff over the noodles.

Makes 6 servings

Per serving
Calories 430	*Sodium 167 mg.*
Total fat 12 g.	*Dietary fiber 4 g.*
Saturated fat 5 g.	*Protein 26 g.*
Cholesterol 49 mg.	*Carbohydrates 52 g.*

Good for You

DREAMING OF CREAM?

Fat-free or low-fat sour cream may not pass for the real thing when eaten on its own over a baked potato, but in a sauce with other vibrant seasonings, fat-free sour cream contributes the luscious mouth-feel that we associate with real sour cream. If you don't like your first try at fat-free sour cream, shop around, as brands vary in taste, texture, and consistency.

Stir-Fried Beef and Broccoli

Photograph on page 282
Hands-on time: 30 minutes
Total time: 35 minutes

$1/4$ cup fat-free reduced-sodium chicken broth

3 tablespoons dry sherry or fat-free reduced-sodium chicken broth

$1/2$ cup orange juice

1 teaspoon grated orange peel (optional)

2 tablespoons soy sauce

1 tablespoon grated fresh ginger

1 tablespoon sugar

2 teaspoons cornstarch

1 teaspoon toasted sesame oil

$1/2$ teaspoon crushed red-pepper flakes

1 pound beef sirloin, trimmed of all visible fat and cut into $1/4$"-thick strips

$2/3$ cup white rice

2 teaspoons vegetable oil

$1^1/2$ pounds broccoli florets

1 bunch scallions, cut in $1/4$" diagonal slices

3 cloves garlic, chopped

In a medium bowl, combine the broth, sherry or broth, orange juice, orange peel (if desired), soy sauce, ginger, sugar, cornstarch, sesame oil, and red-pepper flakes. Stir to mix. Add the beef, tossing to coat evenly. Allow to marinate for 20 minutes.

Meanwhile, prepare the rice according to package directions.

Heat a large skillet over medium-high heat. Coat with 1 teaspoon of the vegetable oil. Lift the beef from the marinade into the skillet. Reserve the marinade. Cook the beef, stirring constantly, for 2 to 3 minutes, or until browned. Remove to a plate.

Add the remaining 1 teaspoon vegetable oil to the skillet. Add the broccoli, scallions, and garlic. Cook, stirring occasionally, for 2 minutes. Add 2 tablespoons water. Cover the pan and cook for 1 to 2 minutes, or until the broccoli is crisp-tender. Add the reserved marinade. Cook, stirring constantly, for 3 minutes, or until the mixture boils and thickens slightly.

Reduce the heat to medium-low. Return the beef to the pan. Cook, stirring, for 2 minutes, or until the beef is heated through. Serve over the rice.

Makes 4 servings

Per serving
Calories 412
Total fat 10 g.
Saturated fat 3 g.
Cholesterol 71 mg.
Sodium 363 mg.
Dietary fiber 4 g.
Protein 32 g.
Carbohydrates 47 g.

Southwest Round Steak

Hands-on time: 15 minutes
Total time: 55 minutes

1 1/2 pounds beef top round steak
       (1" thick), trimmed of all visible fat

1/4   cup lime juice

1   jar (4 ounces) chopped green chile
     peppers, drained

2   tablespoons chopped fresh cilantro

3   cloves garlic, minced

1 1/2 teaspoons ground cumin

1   teaspoon dried oregano

1   teaspoon sugar

1/4   teaspoon salt

Place the steak on a cutting board. With the tip of a sharp paring knife, puncture the steak both across the grain and with the grain. Turn the steak over and repeat on the other side.

In a blender or food processor, combine the lime juice, chile peppers, cilantro, garlic, cumin, oregano, sugar, and salt. Process to a chunky puree. Pour into an 8" × 8" baking dish. Add the steak. Turn several times to coat evenly. Cover with plastic wrap and refrigerate for at least 30 minutes or up to 4 hours. Turn the steak over several times as it marinates.

Coat a grill rack or broiler pan with nonstick spray. Preheat the grill or broiler. Remove the steak from the dish, scraping off and reserving the marinade. Grill or broil 6" from the heat for 10 to 12 minutes, turning once during cooking, or until a thermometer inserted in the center registers 155°F for medium. Transfer the steak to a clean cutting board and loosely cover with foil. Let stand for 5 minutes.

Pour the reserved marinade into a small saucepan. Bring to a boil over medium heat. Cook, stirring, for 5 minutes. Slice the steak and serve with the marinade.

Makes 4 servings

Per serving
Calories 278   *Sodium 566 mg.*
Total fat 7 g.   *Dietary fiber 1 g.*
Saturated fat 3 g.   *Protein 46 g.*
Cholesterol 119 mg.   *Carbohydrates 5 g.*

IRON

To increase the iron in your diet, cook in cast-iron pots. The longer you cook the food and the more acidic the ingredients, the more iron will be absorbed into your food. Vitamin C also helps your body use the iron in food. When trying to increase your iron intake, always combine iron-rich food with food that is rich in vitamin C such as tomatoes, bell peppers, and oranges.

Braised Beef Brisket

Hands-on time: 15 minutes
Total time: 2 hours and 45 minutes

2 pounds beef brisket, trimmed of all visible fat

¼ teaspoon salt

¼ teaspoon ground black pepper

1 large onion, halved and thinly sliced

1 can (28 ounces) chopped tomatoes

1 cup fat-free reduced-sodium beef broth

5 carrots, sliced

2 ribs celery, sliced

1½ teaspoons dried thyme

Preheat the oven to 350°F.

Season the brisket on both sides with the salt and pepper. Coat with nonstick spray.

Place a Dutch oven over medium-high heat. When the pot is hot, add the brisket. Cook for 2 minutes per side, or until browned. Remove the brisket to a plate.

Lower the heat to medium. Add the onion. Cook for 5 to 6 minutes, or until soft. Return the brisket to the pot. Add the tomatoes, broth, ½ cup water, carrots, celery, and thyme. Cover tightly with a lid or foil. Place in the oven.

Bake for 1½ hours, turning the brisket after 45 minutes. Remove from the oven. Remove the brisket and place on a cutting board. Slice across the grain into ¼"-thick slices. Return the sliced brisket to the pot. Cover.

Bake for 1 hour, or until the brisket and vegetables are fork-tender.

Makes 6 servings

Per serving

Calories 305   Sodium 508 mg.
Total fat 12 g.   Dietary fiber 3 g.
Saturated fat 5 g.   Protein 34 g.
Cholesterol 34 mg.   Carbohydrates 15 g.

BARBECUED BEEF SANDWICHES

Play it Again!

Tender beef brisket makes the best barbecued beef sandwiches, which can be served for lunch or dinner the following day. Shred 1½ cups cooked beef brisket and place in a medium bowl with ½ cup of your favorite barbecue sauce. Stir to mix. Cook in the microwave oven on high power for 2 minutes. Slice 2 Kaiser rolls in half and lightly toast. Cover each of the roll bottoms with ⅓ cup shredded lettuce, half the beef mixture, and ⅓ cup coleslaw. Cover with the roll tops. Makes 2 sandwiches.

Not Your Mother's Meat Loaf

Hands-on time: 15 minutes
Total time: 1 hour and 15 minutes

1/2 small onion, chopped

1 rib celery, chopped

1/3 cup finely chopped red or green bell pepper

1 clove garlic, minced

1 can (15 ounces) chopped tomatoes, drained

1/3 cup chopped fresh parsley

1/3 cup fat-free milk

1 egg

2 teaspoons Worcestershire sauce

2 teaspoons Italian seasoning

1 pound extra-lean ground round beef

1 pound ground turkey breast

1 1/2 cups fresh bread crumbs

Preheat the oven to 350°F. Coat a 9" × 5" loaf pan with nonstick spray.

Coat a medium skillet with nonstick spray. Add the onion, celery, bell pepper, and garlic. Coat with nonstick spray. Set over medium heat. Cook, stirring often, for 4 to 5 minutes, or until soft. Place in a large bowl. Add 1 cup of the tomatoes, the parsley, milk, egg, Worcestershire sauce, Italian seasoning, beef, turkey, and bread crumbs. Stir until well-blended. Pat the mixture into the prepared loaf pan.

Bake for 1 hour, or until a thermometer inserted in the center registers 160°F and the meat is no longer pink. During the last 15 minutes of baking, spread the remaining tomatoes down the center of the meat loaf.

Remove from the oven and drain off any accumulated juices from the pan. Let stand for 5 minutes before slicing.

Makes 8 servings

Per serving
Calories 287
Total fat 8 g.
Saturated fat 3 g.
Cholesterol 94 mg.
Sodium 368 mg.
Dietary fiber 2 g.
Protein 33 g.
Carbohydrates 20 g.

Cooking Note
When making meat loaf, you can double the recipe with little extra effort. Cook a loaf for dinner and wrap the uncooked loaf in plastic wrap and then in foil. You can freeze for up to 1 month. Completely thaw in the refrigerator before cooking.

A New Twist

CREAMY MUSTARD GRAVY

Try this mustard gravy with meat loaf, mashed potatoes, or roasted chicken or pork. Place 2 tablespoons cornstarch or flour in a small saucepan. Gradually add 1 cup fat-free reduced-sodium chicken broth, whisking until smooth. Cook, stirring, over medium heat for 2 to 3 minutes, or until thickened. Add 1 cup 1% milk and 2 to 3 tablespoons Dijon mustard. Stir to blend. Season with a pinch of salt and pepper. Cook for 2 minutes, or until heated through. Makes 8 servings.

Roast Pork with Cherry Sauce

Photograph on page 286
Hands-on time: 5 minutes
Total time: 35 minutes

1 center-cut boneless pork loin roast (1³/4 pounds), trimmed of all visible fat

¹/4 teaspoon salt

1 tablespoon butter or margarine

1 small onion, chopped

1 tablespoon chopped fresh rosemary or 1 teaspoon dried

¹/3 cup ruby port wine or cranberry juice cocktail

1 can (14¹/2 ounces) fat-free reduced-sodium chicken broth

¹/2 cup dried tart cherries

3 tablespoons packed light brown sugar

2 tablespoons balsamic vinegar

1 tablespoon cornstarch

Preheat the oven to 375°F. Season the pork with the salt. Coat lightly with nonstick spray.

Warm an ovenproof skillet over medium-high heat. Place the pork in the skillet. Cook, turning, for 3 to 5 minutes, or until brown on all sides. Place the skillet in the oven.

Roast for 20 to 25 minutes, or until a thermometer inserted in the center registers 155°F and the juices run clear. Transfer the pork to a cutting board and loosely cover with foil.

Warm the skillet over medium heat. Melt the butter or margarine. Add the onion and rosemary. Cook, stirring occasionally, for 3 minutes, or until the onion is soft. Add the wine or cranberry juice. Increase the heat to medium-high. Bring to a boil, scraping up the brown bits on the bottom of the pan. Boil for 2 to 3 minutes, or until reduced by half. Add half of the broth, the cherries, brown sugar, and vinegar. Reduce the heat to low. Cover and simmer for 5 minutes.

Place the cornstarch in a small bowl. Gradually add the remaining broth, whisking until smooth. Add to the skillet, stirring constantly. Cook for 1 minute, or until slightly thickened.

Slice the pork and serve with the cherry sauce.

Makes 6 servings

Per serving
Calories 313	*Sodium 234 mg.*
Total fat 9 g.	*Dietary fiber 1 g.*
Saturated fat 3 g.	*Protein 39 g.*
Cholesterol 105 mg.	*Carbohydrates 20 g.*

Lean on Your Butcher

Selecting the leanest cuts of meat and poultry is easy once you know a few key points. Also, be sure to talk to your butcher and ask if your supermarket stocks specially bred leaner meats. Many brands carry the American Heart Association (AHA) Heart Check Certification Mark, which means that the product meets AHA food criteria for saturated fat and cholesterol for healthy people over the age of two.

For red meats, first check the grade, which indicates the amount of marbling (or fat) found throughout the meat. *Select* grade is the leanest choice because it contains the least marbling. *Choice* is the second-leanest grade. *Prime* grade has the most marbling and is therefore the highest in fat.

The cut of meat, which refers to the part on the animal where the meat comes from, also affects the fat content. On red meats, such as beef, veal, lamb, and pork, choose cuts with the words *loin* or *round* in the name. Good choices are top round, eye of round, tenderloin, tip round, and top sirloin. For the leanest ground beef, choose one of these cuts and have it trimmed before the butcher grinds it.

Most veal cuts tend to be lean. Just be sure that it is trimmed of all visible fat. To get the leanest ground veal, it's advisable to select a lean cut and ask the butcher to trim and grind it.

Most of the fat on lamb is on the outside of the meat and is easy to trim. Lean lamb cuts include the leg and loin.

Lean pork cuts are the loin cuts, such as tenderloin, loin chops, and loin roast.

For poultry, such as chicken, turkey, or duck, skinless breast or breast tenders offer the least fat. You can leave the skin on during cooking to maintain moisture, then remove and discard it before eating. Most of the fat in poultry clings to the underside of the skin and is easily removed and discarded. When choosing ground poultry, go with 100 percent skinless breast meat for the leanest choice.

Pork Tenderloin with Peach Chutney

Hands-on time: 15 minutes
Total time: 30 minutes

- 1¹⁄₂ pounds pork tenderloin, trimmed of all visible fat
- ¹⁄₄ teaspoon salt
- ¹⁄₂ teaspoon poultry seasoning
- ¹⁄₂ small red onion, finely chopped
- ¹⁄₂ cup cider vinegar
- ¹⁄₂ cup packed light brown sugar
- ¹⁄₂ cup dried currants
- 1 tablespoon grated fresh ginger or 1 teaspoon ground
- ¹⁄₂ teaspoon ground cinnamon
- ¹⁄₈ teaspoon ground red pepper
- 16 ounces frozen unsweetened sliced peaches, thawed

Preheat the oven to 375°F.

Season all sides of the pork with the salt and poultry seasoning. Coat an ovenproof skillet with nonstick spray. Place the pork in the pan. Cook, turning, over medium-high heat for 3 to 5 minutes, or until all sides are browned.

Place the skillet in the oven. Roast for 20 minutes, or until a thermometer inserted in the center reaches 155°F and the juices run clear. Remove and allow to rest on a cutting board for 5 minutes.

Meanwhile, coat a small saucepan with nonstick spray. Add the onion and coat with nonstick spray. Cook, stirring, over medium heat for 3 to 4 minutes, or until softened. Add the vinegar, brown sugar, currants, ginger, cin-namon, and red pepper. Cook, stirring, for 3 to 5 minutes or until it becomes syrupy. Add the peaches. Cook for 3 minutes, or until the peaches are heated through.

Slice the pork and serve with the chutney.

Makes 4 servings

Per serving
Calories 450   *Sodium 238 mg.*
Total fat 7 g.   *Dietary fiber 4 g.*
Saturated fat 2 g. *Protein 42 g.*
Cholesterol 112 mg. *Carbohydrates 56 g.*

PORK TENDERLOIN AND PEACH CHUTNEY SANDWICHES

For each sandwich, thinly slice the pork tenderloin and arrange on a split sesame seed bun. Top with 2 tablespoons of the chutney and 2 lettuce leaves.

Chinese Barbecued Pork Chops

Photograph on page 281
Hands-on time: 5 minutes
Total time: 15 minutes

- ¹/₃ cup ketchup
- ¹/₄ cup hoisin sauce
- 3 tablespoons rice wine vinegar or white wine vinegar
- 2 tablespoons dry sherry or fat-free reduced-sodium chicken broth
- 3 cloves garlic, chopped
- 1 tablespoon grated fresh ginger
- 4 boneless center-cut pork chops, (4 ounces each), trimmed of all visible fat

In a small saucepan, combine the ketchup, hoisin sauce, vinegar, sherry or broth, garlic, and ginger. Bring to a gentle boil over medium-high heat. Cook, stirring often, for 3 to 5 minutes, or until reduced to a syrupy consistency. Set aside.

Coat a grill rack or broiler pan with nonstick spray. Preheat the grill or broiler. Grill or broil the chops for 8 minutes, turning once. Cook, brushing with the reserved sauce and turning occasionally, for 3 to 4 minutes longer, or until a thermometer inserted in the center of a chop registers 160°F and the juices run clear.

Makes 4 servings

Per serving
Calories 356	*Sodium 682 mg.*
Total fat 12 g.	*Dietary fiber 0 g.*
Saturated fat 5 g.	*Protein 33 g.*
Cholesterol 81 mg.	*Carbohydrates 31 g.*

A New Twist

RASPBERRY BARBECUE SAUCE

For a variation, replace the Chinese sauce with this Raspberry Barbecue Sauce: In a small saucepan, combine 1 cup of your favorite barbecue sauce, ½ cup melted raspberry jam, ¼ cup red wine vinegar, 1 cup fresh or frozen raspberries, and 1 chopped small onion. Cook over medium heat for 5 to 10 minutes, or until slightly thickened.

Grilled Pork Chops

Photograph on page 283
Hands-on time: 5 minutes
Total time: 45 minutes

- 2 tablespoons fat-free reduced-sodium chicken broth
- 3 tablespoons balsamic vinegar
- 3 cloves garlic, minced
- 1 tablespoon dried oregano
- 2 teaspoons olive oil
- 1/4 teaspoon salt
- 4 bone-in center-cut pork chops (6 ounces each), trimmed of all visible fat

In a shallow baking dish, combine the broth, vinegar, garlic, oregano, oil, and salt. Add the chops. Turn several times to coat both sides. Cover and marinate in the refrigerator for 30 minutes or up to 4 hours. Turn the chops several times as they marinate.

Coat a grill rack or broiler pan with nonstick spray. Preheat the grill or broiler. Grill or broil the chops, turning once, or until a thermometer inserted in the center of a chop registers 160°F and the juices run clear.

Makes 4 servings

Per serving
Calories 275	*Sodium 230 mg.*
Total fat 12 g.	*Dietary fiber 0 g.*
Saturated fat 4 g.	*Protein 38 g.*
Cholesterol 94 mg.	*Carbohydrates 3 g.*

Good for You

PERFECT PORTIONS

Portion sizes for all foods have become increasingly important for health-conscious folks. Here's a visual cue to help you identify a 3-ounce portion of meat or poultry: If the serving is significantly larger than a deck of cards or the size and thickness of the palm of your hand, cut the portion in half and share it with a friend or save it for another time.

Roasted Leg of Lamb with Mint

Hands-on time: 15 minutes
Total time: 55 minutes

1 boneless butterflied leg of lamb (3 pounds), trimmed of all visible fat

5 cloves garlic

1 tablespoon dried oregano

1/4 teaspoon salt

1/4 teaspoon ground black pepper

1 cup loosely packed fresh mint leaves

1 cup loosely packed fresh parsley

1/4 cup chopped toasted walnuts

1 tablespoon lime juice

2 teaspoons olive oil

1 teaspoon sugar

3/4 teaspoon ground cumin

1 cup fat-free plain yogurt

Preheat the oven to 450°F. Coat a roasting pan with nonstick spray. Place the lamb on a work surface and open like a book.

Mince 3 cloves of the garlic. Place in a small bowl with the oregano, salt, and pepper. Stir to mix. Sprinkle half of the mixture over the lamb. Roll the lamb into its original shape and tie with kitchen string to secure. Cut several ½" slits all over the surface of the lamb. Rub the remaining oregano mixture over the lamb, pressing some into the slits.

Place the lamb in the prepared pan. Roast for 15 minutes. Reduce the oven temperature to 350°F. Roast for 30 to 35 minutes, or until a thermometer inserted in the center registers 160°F for medium doneness. Remove from the oven and allow to rest for 10 minutes.

While the lamb is roasting, in a food processor or blender, combine the mint, parsley, walnuts, lime juice, oil, sugar, cumin, and the remaining 2 cloves garlic. Process until smooth. Add the yogurt. Process until creamy.

Slice the lamb and serve with the mint sauce.

Makes 10 servings

Per serving
Calories 231   *Sodium 147 mg.*
Total fat 10 g.   *Dietary fiber 0 g.*
Saturated fat 5 g. *Protein 31 g.*
Cholesterol 90 mg. *Carbohydrates 4 g.*

Rosemary Roast Chicken

Photograph on page 279
Hands-on time: 20 minutes
Total time: 1 hour and 25 minutes

1 broiler fryer chicken (3 pounds)

3 teaspoons dried rosemary, crushed

1/4 teaspoon salt

1 lemon, sliced

1 small onion, chopped

2 cans (14 1/2 ounces each) fat-free reduced-sodium chicken broth

1 tablespoon cornstarch

1/3 cup Madeira wine or alcohol-free white wine

Preheat the oven to 450°F. Coat a roasting rack and roasting pan with nonstick spray.

Wash the chicken and pat dry with paper towels. (Reserve the giblets for another use.) Season the cavity with 1 teaspoon of the rosemary and the salt. Place the lemon inside the cavity. Place the chicken, breast side up, on the prepared roasting rack. Rub 1 teaspoon of the remaining rosemary over the breast meat under the skin of the chicken. Scatter the onion around the bottom of the pan. Pour in 1 can of the broth.

Roast the chicken for 20 minutes, basting with the pan juices. Lower the heat to 350°F. Roast, basting every 15 minutes, for 45 to 50 minutes, or until a thermometer inserted in a breast registers 180°F and the juices run clear. Transfer the chicken to a cutting board and loosely cover with foil.

In a small bowl, whisk the cornstarch with 1/4 cup of the remaining broth until smooth. Set aside.

Place the roasting pan on the stove top over medium-high heat. Add the wine. Boil for 2 to 3 minutes, scraping the bottom of the pan to remove the browned bits, or until reduced to 1/4 cup. Add the remaining broth. Bring to a boil. Skim off and discard any fat that rises to the top. Pour in the reserved cornstarch mixture and the remaining 1 teaspoon rosemary. Cook, stirring constantly, for 2 to 3 minutes, or until slightly thickened.

Carve the chicken. Remove and discard the skin before eating. Serve with the gravy.

Makes 6 servings

Per serving
Calories 292   *Sodium 332 mg.*
Total fat 5 g.   *Dietary fiber 1 g.*
Saturated fat 1 g.   *Protein 38 g.*
Cholesterol 111 mg.   *Carbohydrates 22 g.*

CHICKEN STOCK

Use the leftover carcass from the roast chicken and reserved giblets (minus the liver) to make homemade chicken stock. In a large pot, combine the chicken carcass, reserved giblets, 1 chopped onion, 2 chopped carrots, 2 chopped ribs celery, 2 bay leaves, 1 teaspoon salt, 1 teaspoon black peppercorns, and 8 sprigs fresh parsley. For a richer stock, you can also add up to 1 pound raw chicken necks or backbones. Add enough cold water to cover by 1". Cover loosely and cook over medium-low heat for 2 hours, occasionally skimming the surface of any foam. Add a little more water, if needed, to keep the ingredients covered. Strain into a large bowl and refrigerate until well-chilled. Remove and discard any fat that hardens on the top. Makes about 8 cups.

California Chicken

Photograph on page 280
Hands-on time: 20 minutes
Total time: 30 minutes

1 tablespoon whole-grain mustard

1 egg white

1 cup fresh bread crumbs

1/3 cup (1 1/2 ounces) grated Parmesan cheese

1 teaspoon grated lemon peel

4 boneless, skinless chicken breast halves (5 ounces each), pounded to 1/2" thickness

1 bunch watercress, trimmed, or 1 small head leaf lettuce

3 large plum tomatoes, chopped

1/4 cup finely chopped red onion

1/4 cup chopped fresh basil

1 tablespoon balsamic vinegar

2 teaspoons extra-virgin olive oil

1/8 teaspoon salt

Coat a broiler pan and rack with nonstick spray. Preheat the broiler.

In a shallow bowl, combine the mustard and egg white. Beat lightly with a fork. In another shallow bowl, combine the bread crumbs, Parmesan, and lemon peel. Dip the chicken into the mustard mixture, turning to coat, and then into the bread-crumb mixture, turning to coat. Place the chicken on the rack in the prepared pan.

Broil 6" from the heat, turning once, for 6 to 10 minutes, or until golden brown, no longer pink, 160°F in the thickest portion when a thermometer is inserted, and with juices that run

clear. If the chicken browns too quickly, turn off the broiler and bake the chicken in a 350°F oven for 15 to 20 minutes, or until no longer pink.

Meanwhile, in a medium bowl, combine the watercress or lettuce, tomatoes, onion, basil, vinegar, oil, and salt. Serve the chicken with the salad.

Makes 4 servings

Per serving
Calories 418	*Sodium 639 mg.*
Total fat 11 g.	*Dietary fiber 2 g.*
Saturated fat 3 g.	*Protein 52 g.*
Cholesterol 125 mg.	*Carbohydrates 24 g.*

Try it — BEYOND THE BASIC

"This zesty chicken dish is quite satisfying. The lemon peel and fresh herbs add an extra bonus to this low-fat updated version of a traditional breaded chicken dish. Try experimenting with different flavored mustards, such as honey mustard or Dijon for a variation," says Jill Goodman, a pediatric social worker.

Oven-Fried Chicken

Hands-on time: 25 minutes
Total time: 1 hour and 40 minutes

1 $1/2$ cups buttermilk

1 egg

$1/3$ cup chopped parsley

1 $1/4$ cups cornflake crumbs

$2/3$ cup unbleached or all-purpose flour

1 teaspoon paprika

$1/4$ teaspoon salt

1 whole chicken, cut into 8 pieces and trimmed of all visible fat

Coat a baking sheet with nonstick spray.

In a medium bowl, combine the buttermilk, egg, and parsley and/or basil.

In a large bowl, combine the cornflake crumbs, flour, paprika, and salt.

One piece at a time, dip the chicken pieces into the buttermilk mixture, then dredge in the cornflake mixture, pressing to adhere. Place on the prepared baking sheet. Refrigerate for 30 minutes or as long as 4 hours.

Preheat the oven to 375°F. Remove the baking sheet from the refrigerator. Coat the chicken with nonstick spray.

Bake for 25 minutes. Remove the baking sheet from the oven. Gently turn the chicken pieces over. Coat with nonstick spray.

Return to the oven. Bake for 20 to 25 minutes, or until a thermometer inserted in the thickest portion registers 170°F and the juices run clear.

Makes 6 servings

Per serving

Calories 347	*Sodium 451 mg.*
Total fat 6 g.	*Dietary fiber 2 g.*
Saturated fat 2 g.	*Protein 36 g.*
Cholesterol 127 mg.	*Carbohydrates 35 g.*

SHARE TO PARE

As you strive to maintain a healthy fat and calorie intake, gargantuan restaurant portions may present a challenge. To tip the scales in your favor when dining out, choose a main dish that appeals to you and your partner and share it. You can add à la carte items such as baked potatoes, salads, and vegetable or clear soups to round out the meal. This technique allows you to indulge in your meal of choice without going overboard on the calories or the fat.

Stuffed Chicken Breasts

Hands-on time: 20 minutes
Total time: 50 minutes

- 1 zucchini, shredded
- 1 small onion, chopped
- 1 1/2 teaspoons dried oregano
- 1/2 teaspoon dried thyme
- 1/2 cup (4 ounces) 1% cottage cheese
- 1/4 cup (1 ounce) grated Parmesan cheese
- 1/2 cup fresh bread crumbs
- 1/4 teaspoon + 1/8 teaspoon salt
- 4 boneless, skinless chicken breast halves (4 ounces each), trimmed of all visible fat

Preheat the oven to 450°F. Coat a baking sheet with nonstick spray.

Coat a large skillet with nonstick spray. Add the zucchini, onion, 1 teaspoon of the oregano, and the thyme. Coat with nonstick spray. Cook, stirring occasionally, over medium heat for 5 to 6 minutes, or until any juices from the zucchini have evaporated. Remove from the heat. Add the cottage cheese, Parmesan, bread crumbs, and 1/4 teaspoon of the salt. Stir to mix.

Place the chicken on a work surface. Butterfly each piece by making a horizontal cut into the thick end of each breast half to create a flap. Do not cut all the way through. Open the cut portion as you would open a book. Lay a piece of plastic wrap over the chicken breast halves. Flatten with the flat side of a meat mallet or heavy skillet to about 1/4" thickness.

Divide one-quarter of the zucchini mixture in the center of each breast half. Roll each breast half into a bundle, tucking in the sides as you roll. Tie each bundle with kitchen string. Place the bundles on the prepared baking sheet. Coat with nonstick spray. Season with the remaining 1/2 teaspoon oregano and 1/8 teaspoon salt.

Bake for 10 minutes. Reduce the oven temperature to 350°F. Bake for 15 minutes, or until a thermometer inserted in the thickest portion registers 160°F and the juices run clear.

Remove from the oven and allow to rest for 5 minutes. Remove the string before serving.

Makes 4 servings

Per serving

Calories 262	*Sodium 638 mg.*
Total fat 5 g.	*Dietary fiber 2 g.*
Saturated fat 2 g.	*Protein 35 g.*
Cholesterol 73 mg.	*Carbohydrates 17 g.*

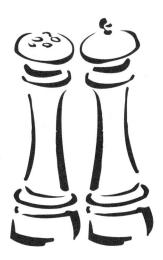

Honey-Roasted Turkey Breast

Photograph on page 285
Hands-on time: 15 minutes
Total time: 1 hour and 15 minutes

1 bone-in turkey breast half
 (2½ pounds)

⅓ cup honey

¾ teaspoon ground cinnamon

⅔-1 cup fat-free reduced-sodium
 chicken broth

Preheat the oven to 350°F. Coat a roasting pan with nonstick spray. Trim all visible fat and excess skin from the turkey breast. Leave just enough skin to cover the top of the breast. Place the turkey, skin side up, in the prepared baking dish. Pour the honey over the turkey. Lift the skin and spread with a spatula to evenly coat the breast. Sprinkle with the cinnamon, rubbing it under the skin. Pour ⅔ cup broth into the baking dish.

Roast for 40 minutes. Remove the skin and discard. Add up to ⅓ cup more broth, if needed, to prevent the glaze in the pan from burning. Roast for 20 minutes longer, or until a thermometer inserted in the thickest portion registers 170°F.

Remove the turkey and let stand for 10 minutes. Pour the pan juices into a serving dish. Skim off and discard any fat. Slice the turkey and serve with the pan juices.

Makes 6 servings

Per serving
Calories 241	*Sodium 89 mg.*
Total fat 1 g.	*Dietary fiber 0 g.*
Saturated fat 0 g.	*Protein 41 g.*
Cholesterol 110 mg.	*Carbohydrates 16 g.*

Cooking Note

The leftover turkey makes terrific sandwiches, so buy a bigger breast, if you like, and increase the pan ingredients accordingly. Add 20 minutes oven time for each additional pound of turkey breast.

TURKEY SANDWICH

Play it Again!

Who can resist a turkey sandwich carved right off the breastbone? In a small bowl, stir together 3 tablespoons whole-berry cranberry sauce and 2 teaspoons low-fat mayonnaise. Stuff a split pita with thinly sliced turkey breast. Spread the cranberry mayonnaise over the turkey. Add shredded lettuce and 2 tablespoons grated apple, if desired.

Caribbean Turkey Kabobs

Hands-on time: 25 minutes
Total time: 55 minutes

4 tablespoons soy sauce

4 tablespoons molasses

2 tablespoons lime juice

1 tablespoon hot-pepper sauce

$1/2$ teaspoon ground cinnamon

$1/4$ teaspoon ground cloves

1 pound boneless skinless turkey tenders, cut into 1" pieces

1 pound sweet potatoes, cut into 1" pieces

1 cup fresh or canned pineapple chunks

1 large red bell pepper, cut into 1" pieces

6 scallions, cut into 1" diagonal pieces

In a medium bowl, combine the soy sauce, molasses, lime juice, hot-pepper sauce, cinnamon, and cloves. Add the turkey. Toss to coat. Cover with plastic wrap and marinate for 30 minutes at room temperature or up to 8 hours in the refrigerator.

Coat a grill rack or broiler pan with nonstick spray. Preheat the grill or broiler.

Set a steamer rack in a medium saucepan filled with 1" of boiling water. Place the sweet potatoes on the rack. Cover and cook over high heat for 15 minutes, or until tender.

Remove the turkey from the marinade. Pour the marinade into a small saucepan. Bring to a boil over high heat. Reduce the heat to medium-low. Cook for 5 to 6 minutes, or until thickened.

Thread the turkey, pineapple, sweet potatoes, bell pepper, and scallions alternately on 8 metal skewers. Place the kabobs on the prepared rack or pan. Grill or broil, basting occasionally with the reduced marinade and turning every 3 minutes, for 12 to 14 minutes, or until and the turkey is cooked through.

Makes 4 servings

Per serving
Calories 372	*Sodium 682 mg.*
Total fat 1 g.	*Dietary fiber 5 g.*
Saturated fat 0 g.	*Protein 38 g.*
Cholesterol 94 mg.	*Carbohydrates 52 g.*

SWEET-AND-SOUR TURKEY

Play it Again!

Leftover turkey kabobs make a wonderful Chinese sweet-and-sour dish. In a medium saucepan, combine 1/4 cup frozen pineapple juice concentrate, 1/3 cup water, 2 tablespoons white vinegar, 1 tablespoon soy sauce, 1 minced clove garlic, and 1 teaspoon cornstarch. Cook, whisking, over medium heat for 2 to 3 minutes, or until thickened. Remove the turkey and vegetables from 4 kabobs. Add to the sauce. Cover and cook over low heat for 5 minutes, or until heated through. Add a little water, if needed, to thin the sauce. Serve over cooked rice. Makes 2 servings.

et's face it. For most of us, dessert is the best part of the meal. Unfortunately, it has gotten a bad rap, and not without good reason. Many desserts are extremely high in fat and calories and shy in nutrients.

Common sense tells us that desserts were created to nourish the spirit, not to sustain the body. They are indulgent treats for special times, and we should wisely choose when to enjoy them.

Enjoy small portions of rich desserts on occasion after a well-balanced meal. During the rest of the time, choose desserts that will provide nutrients. By making fruit the main focus of desserts, vitamins, minerals, and fiber can provide health benefits while satisfying your sweet tooth.

Adjust Desserts

Traditional desserts usually have more fat and sugar than is necessary to make the recipes come out properly. There are many ways to cut the fat and calories while maintaining the satisfying taste. Use the information on page 20 to easily convert your family favorites into healthier versions.

To get you started on preparing healthier desserts, this chapter is full of great-tasting recipes to please your family. Savor every sweet morsel with the assurance that they fit into your healthy eating plan.

Recipes

Chocolate Chippers

Photograph on page 288
Hands-on time: 20 minutes
Total time: 55 minutes

2¼ cups unbleached or all-purpose flour

¼ cup cornstarch

1 teaspoon baking soda

½ teaspoon salt

¼ cup butter or margarine, softened

2 ounces reduced-fat cream cheese, softened

¾ cup granulated sugar

¾ cup packed light brown sugar

1 egg

1 egg white

1 teaspoon vanilla extract

¾ cup chocolate chips

Preheat the oven to 375°F. Lightly coat a baking sheet with nonstick spray.

In a medium bowl, combine the flour, cornstarch, baking soda, and salt.

In a large bowl, combine the butter or margarine and cream cheese. With an electric mixer on medium speed, beat for 1 minute, or until smooth. Add the granulated sugar and brown sugar. Beat until light and creamy. Add the egg, egg white, and vanilla extract. Beat until smooth. Reduce the mixer speed to low. Add the flour mixture in 2 additions, beating just until combined. With a spoon, stir in the chocolate chips. Drop the dough by rounded teaspoonfuls onto the prepared baking sheet.

Bake for 9 to 12 minutes, or until golden. Remove the cookies to a rack to cool. Repeat until all the cookies are baked.

Makes 40

Per cookie
Calories 90
Total fat 3 g.
Saturated fat 1 g.
Cholesterol 6 mg.
Sodium 72 mg.
Dietary fiber 0 g.
Protein 1 g.
Carbohydrates 16 g.

COOKIE TALK

"These chocolate chip cookies tasted great and were quick and easy to make. Knowing they were made with healthy ingredients made them more enjoyable than ordinary cookies," says Sherrie Fleeter, mother of one.

Crisp Sugar Cookies

Hands-on time: 15 minutes
Total time: 25 minutes

2 1/4 cups unbleached or all-purpose flour
1/2 teaspoon baking powder
1/2 teaspoon baking soda
1/2 teaspoon salt
6 tablespoons butter or margarine
1 1/3 cups sugar
1 egg
1/4 cup fat-free milk
1 teaspoon vanilla extract

Preheat the oven to 375°F. Coat a baking sheet with nonstick spray.

In a medium bowl, combine the flour, baking powder, baking soda, and salt.

Place the butter or margarine in a large bowl. With an electric mixer on medium speed, beat until light and creamy. Continue beating, gradually adding 1 cup of the sugar, until blended. Add the egg. Beat until smooth. Add the milk and vanilla extract. Beat until smooth. Reduce the mixer speed to low. Beat, gradually adding half of the flour mixture. Add the remaining flour mixture, beating just until combined.

Place the remaining 1/3 cup sugar on a plate. Shape the dough into 1" balls (about 1 level tablespoon). Roll the balls in the sugar to coat. Place 2" apart on the prepared baking sheet. With the bottom of a juice glass, press the dough into 2 1/2" rounds. If the glass sticks, dip the bottom in some sugar.

Bake for 8 to 10 minutes, or until lightly golden and the edges are tinged with brown. Remove the cookies to a rack to cool. Repeat until all the cookies are baked.

Makes 40

Per cookie
Calories 69   *Sodium 73 mg.*
Total fat 2 g.   *Dietary fiber 0 g.*
Saturated fat 0 g.   *Protein 1 g.*
Cholesterol 5 mg.   *Carbohydrates 12 g.*

FROZEN COOKIE SANDWICHES

Play it Again!

Make your own frozen treat sandwiches with any sugar cookies that may be lingering in your cookie jar. Sandwich 1/4 cup of your favorite fat-free frozen yogurt (slightly softened) between 2 sugar cookies. Refreeze until ready to serve.

Fudgy Chocolate Brownies

Hands-on time: 15 minutes
Total time: 50 minutes

- 1 cup unbleached or all-purpose flour
- 3/4 cup cocoa powder
- 1/2 teaspoon baking powder
- 1/4 teaspoon salt
- 1/4 cup butter or margarine, softened
- 2 ounces reduced-fat cream cheese, softened
- 1 1/2 cups sugar
- 1 egg
- 2 egg whites
- 1 tablespoon vanilla extract
- 1 tablespoon confectioners' sugar

Preheat the oven to 350°F. Coat a 13" × 9" baking pan with nonstick spray.

In a medium bowl, combine the flour, cocoa, baking powder, and salt.

In a large mixing bowl, combine the butter or margarine, cream cheese, and sugar. With an electric mixer on medium speed, beat for 2 to 3 minutes, or until smooth. One at a time, add the egg and egg whites, beating after each addition until smooth. Add the vanilla extract. Beat just to incorporate.

Reduce the mixer speed to low. Gradually add the flour mixture, beating just to combine. Pour the batter into the prepared pan.

Bake for 30 to 35 minutes, or until a wooden pick inserted in the center comes out with just a few moist crumbs. Remove to a rack to cool.

Sift the confectioners' sugar over the brownies.

Makes 24 servings

Per serving

Calories 104	*Sodium 94 mg.*
Total fat 3 g.	*Dietary fiber 1 g.*
Saturated fat 1 g.	*Protein 2 g.*
Cholesterol 10 mg.	*Carbohydrates 19 g.*

Bananas Foster

Hands-on time: 5 minutes
Total time: 10 minutes

1 tablespoon butter or margarine

2 tablespoons dark brown sugar

2 tablespoons apple juice
  concentrate

1/4 teaspoon ground cinnamon

3 bananas, cut in half crosswise and
  halves quartered lengthwise

2 teaspoons vanilla extract

3 cups fat-free frozen vanilla yogurt

Melt the butter or margarine in a medium non-stick skillet set over medium heat. Add the brown sugar, apple juice concentrate, and cinnamon. Cook, stirring, until the sugar melts. Add the bananas. Toss to coat well. Cook for 3 to 5 minutes, or until the bananas are tender. Remove from the heat. Add the vanilla extract. Swirl to combine.

Serve the frozen yogurt topped with the bananas and sauce.

Makes 6 servings

Per serving
Calories 226   *Sodium 68 mg.*
Total fat 2 g.   *Dietary fiber 2 g.*
Saturated fat 1 g.   *Protein 6 g.*
Cholesterol 7 mg.   *Carbohydrates 40 g.*

Good for You

HEALTHFUL TREATS

When trying to balance a healthy style of eating with a sweet tooth, look to nutritious dessert ingredients. Incorporate fruits, low-fat dairy products, and silken tofu for satisfying sweets that will provide your body with valuable vitamins, minerals, and fiber.

Chocolate-Cherry Bread Pudding

Photograph on page 292
Hands-on time: 15 minutes
Total time: 1 hour

- 8 ounces seedless hamburger buns, cut into cubes
- 1/2 cup dried sour cherries
- 1/4 cup cherry liqueur or cherry-flavored juice
- 2/3 cup packed light brown sugar
- 1/3 cup cocoa powder
- 3 1/2 cups 1% milk
- 4 egg whites, lightly beaten
- 3/4 cup prune puree
- 2 teaspoons vanilla extract
- 1 ounce semisweet chocolate, finely chopped
- 1 tablespoon confectioners' sugar

Preheat the oven to 350°F. Coat a medium baking dish with nonstick spray. Place the bread cubes evenly in the prepared baking dish.

In a small microwaveable bowl, combine the cherries and liqueur or juice. Microwave on high power for 1 minute. Let stand for 5 minutes, or until the cherries are plump and most of the liquid is absorbed.

In a large bowl, combine the brown sugar, cocoa, milk, egg whites, prune puree, and vanilla extract. Add the chocolate and the cherries with any remaining liquid. Stir to mix. Pour over the bread cubes. Press down lightly to make sure that all of the bread is moistened. Allow to stand for 15 minutes for the bread to absorb the liquid.

Bake for 35 to 40 minutes, or until slightly puffed and set. Remove from the oven and allow to cool slightly. Sift the confectioners' sugar over the pudding.

Makes 10 servings

Per serving
Calories 242	*Sodium 209 mg.*
Total fat 4 g.	*Dietary fiber 3 g.*
Saturated fat 2 g.	*Protein 8 g.*
Cholesterol 4 mg.	*Carbohydrates 48 g.*

Good for You

PRUNE PUREE

Store-bought prune puree or even baby food prunes make a fine substitute for all or some of the fat in dense baked desserts such as puddings, muffins, and quick breads. You can also make prune puree by combining ¾ cup pitted prunes and ¼ cup water in a food processor. Process, scraping the sides of the bowl, for 1 to 2 minutes, or until smooth. Makes ¾ cup.

Apple-Cheese Strudel

Photograph on page 290
Hands-on time: 30 minutes
Total time: 1 hour and 20 minutes

1¼ cups (10 ounces) 1% cottage cheese

4 ounces reduced-fat cream cheese, softened

½ cup + 6 tablespoons granulated sugar

1½ teaspoons vanilla extract

4 apples, peeled and thinly sliced

2 tablespoons lemon juice

2 tablespoons unbleached or all-purpose flour

2 tablespoons chopped toasted walnuts

1½ teaspoons ground cinnamon

⅓ cup plain dry bread crumbs

12 sheets (17" × 11") frozen phyllo dough, thawed

1 tablespoon confectioners' sugar

Line a sieve with a coffee filter or cheesecloth. Place over a bowl. Fill with the cottage cheese and allow to drain for 15 to 20 minutes.

In a food processor, combine the cottage cheese, cream cheese, ½ cup of the granulated sugar, and vanilla extract. Process for 30 seconds, or until smooth. Set aside.

Meanwhile, in a large bowl, combine the apples, 3 tablespoons of the remaining granulated sugar, lemon juice, flour, walnuts, and cinnamon. Toss to coat.

Preheat the oven to 400°F. Coat a baking sheet with butter-flavored nonstick spray. In a small bowl, combine the bread crumbs and 2 tablespoons of the remaining granulated sugar.

Place 1 sheet of phyllo dough on a work surface with the narrow end toward you. Coat lightly with nonstick spray. Sprinkle lightly with 2 scant teaspoons of the bread-crumb mixture. Repeat layering with 5 of the remaining phyllo sheets, the nonstick spray, and the remaining bread-crumb mixture.

Spread with half of the cheese filling, leaving a 1" border on all sides. Spoon half of the apples evenly on top. Starting at the bottom, roll the dough over the filling twice. Tuck the sides in and continue rolling into a cylinder.

Place, seam-side down, on 1 end of the prepared baking sheet. Repeat with the remaining ingredients to make another strudel. Transfer to the baking sheet. Coat each strudel with nonstick spray and sprinkle with the remaining 1 tablespoon sugar.

Bake for 15 minutes. Reduce the heat to 350°F. Bake for 25 to 30 minutes, or until golden brown and crisp. Remove to a rack to cool for 15 minutes. Serve warm or cool completely.

To serve, sift the confectioners' sugar onto the strudels. Cut each strudel into 6 diagonal pieces.

Makes 12 servings

Per serving

Calories 166	*Sodium 206 mg.*
Total fat 4 g.	*Dietary fiber 1 g.*
Saturated fat 2 g.	*Protein 6 g.*
Cholesterol 8 mg.	*Carbohydrates 28 g.*

Peach Tart

Photograph on page 289
Hands-on time: 25 minutes
Total time: 1 hour and 40 minutes

1 1/2 cups + 2 tablespoons unbleached or all-purpose flour

2 tablespoons + 1/3 cup granulated sugar

1/2 teaspoon salt

1/4 cup cold butter or margarine, cut into small pieces

2 tablespoons reduced-fat cream cheese

3-4 tablespoons ice water

7 ripe peaches, sliced

1 cup coarsely crushed fat-free almond-flavored biscotti

2 tablespoons chopped almonds

2 tablespoons packed light brown sugar

1 tablespoon butter or margarine, softened

In the bowl of a food processor, combine 1½ cups of the flour, 2 tablespoons of the granulated sugar, and the salt. Process until blended. Add the cold butter or margarine and cream cheese. Pulse until the mixture resembles cornmeal. Drizzle 3 tablespoons of the water over the mixture. Pulse until a crumbly dough forms that will hold together when pressed. If needed, add up to 1 tablespoon more water. Pulse to combine.

Turn the dough out onto a work surface. Shape into a disk and wrap in plastic wrap. Refrigerate for 30 minutes.

Preheat the oven to 375°F. Coat a 10" tart pan or pie pan with nonstick spray.

On a lightly floured surface, roll the dough into a 13" circle. Drape it over the prepared pan. Gently press the dough against the sides of the pan, trimming any overhang. Prick the bottom and sides of the crust with a fork. Line with foil. Fill with pie weights or dried beans.

Bake for 15 minutes. Remove the weights and foil. Bake for 10 minutes longer, or until lightly golden. Remove to a rack to cool. Do not turn the oven off.

Meanwhile, in a large bowl, combine the peaches, the remaining 1/3 cup granulated sugar, and the remaining 2 tablespoons flour. Set aside.

In a small bowl, combine the biscotti, almonds, brown sugar, and softened butter or margarine. Using your hands, combine to form coarse crumbs. Spoon the peach mixture into the tart shell. Sprinkle with the crumb topping.

Bake for 35 to 40 minutes, or until the topping is golden and bubbly. Remove to a rack to cool. Serve warm or at room temperature.

Makes 10 servings

Per serving

Calories 265	*Sodium 199 mg.*
Total fat 7 g.	*Dietary fiber 1 g.*
Saturated fat 2 g.	*Protein 5 g.*
Cholesterol 5 mg.	*Carbohydrates 47 g.*

Plum-Blueberry Cobbler

Photograph on page 291
Hands-on time 20 minutes
Total time: 1 hour

8 plums, quartered

1 pint fresh or frozen blueberries

1/2 cup + 4 teaspoons sugar

2 tablespoons + 1 cup unbleached or all-purpose flour

3/4 teaspoon baking powder

1/8 teaspoon salt

1/2 cup buttermilk

1 egg white, lightly beaten

1 1/2 tablespoons vegetable oil

Preheat the oven to 375°F. Coat an 8" × 8" baking dish with nonstick spray.

In a large bowl, combine the plums, blueberries, 1/2 cup of the sugar, and 2 tablespoons of the flour. Pour into the prepared baking dish.

In a medium bowl, combine 3 teaspoons of the remaining sugar, the baking powder, salt, and the remaining 1 cup flour.

In a small bowl, combine the buttermilk, egg white, and oil. Pour into the medium bowl with the flour mixture. Stir until a thick batter forms. Drop the batter in tablespoonfuls on top of the fruit. Sprinkle with the remaining 1 teaspoon sugar.

Bake for 35 to 40 minutes, or until golden and bubbly. Remove to a rack to cool. Serve warm or at room temperature.

Makes 8 servings

Per serving

Calories 238	*Sodium 107 mg.*
Total fat 4 g.	*Dietary fiber 3 g.*
Saturated fat 0 g.	*Protein 4 g.*
Cholesterol 1 mg.	*Carbohydrates 50 g.*

PLUM NUTRITIOUS

Desserts are a wonderful way to end a meal. By starting with fresh fruits, as with this Plum-Blueberry Cobbler, you can easily incorporate more nutrients into a sweet treat. Many desserts have 500 calories or even more per serving, but this cobbler has only 238 calories per serving.

South Pacific Crisp

Hands-on time: 25 minutes
Total time: 1 hour and 10 minutes

1¼ cups coarsely chopped low-fat gingersnaps

1 cup quick-cooking oats

⅓ cup + ½ cup light brown sugar

⅓ cup sweetened shredded coconut

2 tablespoons butter or margarine

½ teaspoon ground cinnamon

1 pineapple, cut into 1" cubes, or 1 can (16 ounces) pineapple tidbits in juice, drained

6 peaches, cut into 1" cubes

¾ cup orange juice

2 tablespoons dark rum or 1 teaspoon rum extract

1 tablespoon cornstarch

1½ pints fat-free frozen vanilla yogurt

Preheat the oven to 375°F. Lightly coat a medium baking dish with nonstick spray.

In a small bowl, combine the gingersnaps, oats, ⅓ cup of the brown sugar, the coconut, butter or margarine, and cinnamon. Using your hands, combine to form coarse crumbs.

In a medium bowl, combine the pineapple, peaches, orange juice, rum or rum extract, cornstarch, and the remaining ½ cup brown sugar. Stir until the brown sugar and cornstarch are dissolved. Pour into the prepared baking dish. Sprinkle with the gingersnap mixture.

Bake for 35 to 40 minutes, or until golden brown and bubbly. Remove to a rack to cool for 15 minutes. To serve, top each portion with ¼ cup of the frozen yogurt.

Makes 12 servings

Per serving

Calories 231	Sodium 81 mg.
Total fat 5 g.	Dietary fiber 3 g.
Saturated fat 2 g.	Protein 3 g.
Cholesterol 0 mg.	Carbohydrates 47 g.

CRISP IN THE MORNING

Not only are fruit crisps the perfect ending to almost any meal but they are also a great way to start the day. Take leftover fruit crisp and create a fabulous breakfast parfait. Spoon ¼ cup fat-free vanilla yogurt into a clear parfait glass or dessert bowl. Sprinkle with 3 tablespoons low-fat granola and top with ¼ cup of the fruit crisp. Repeat the layering once. Top with a dollop of yogurt.

Creamy Chocolate Cheesecake

Hands-on time: 20 minutes
Total time: 5 hours and 35 minutes

18 chocolate graham crackers

2 tablespoons butter or margarine, melted

3 packages (8 ounces each) reduced-fat cream cheese, softened

1 1/2 cups sugar

1 egg

2 egg whites

3/4 cup cocoa powder

1/4 teaspoon salt

1 tablespoon vanilla extract

1/2 teaspoon almond extract

1/2 cup fat-free whipped topping

1/2 cup raspberries

1 cup fat-free caramel sauce, warmed

Preheat the oven to 325°F. Coat a 9" springform pan with nonstick spray.

Place the graham crackers in a plastic food storage bag. Seal the bag and crush the crackers with a rolling pin until they form coarse crumbs. Place in the prepared pan with the butter. Stir to combine and press the crumb mixture onto the bottom and up the sides of the pan. Bake for 10 minutes, or until set. Remove to a rack to cool.

Meanwhile, in a large bowl, with an electric mixer at medium speed, beat the cream cheese and sugar until smooth. Add the egg, egg whites, cocoa, salt, vanilla extract, and almond extract. Beat for 5 minutes, or until smooth and well-combined. Pour into the prepared crust.

Bake for 1 hour and 15 minutes, or until the center is slightly soft. Turn off the oven and leave the cake in the oven for 1 hour. Remove to a rack and cool for 1 hour. Cover and refrigerate for 2 hours or overnight.

Decorate the cake with dollops of the whipped topping and the raspberries. Serve with the warmed caramel sauce.

Makes 16 servings

Per serving
Calories 272
Total fat 11 g.
Saturated fat 6 g.
Cholesterol 41 mg.
Sodium 275 mg.
Dietary fiber 2 g.
Protein 7 g.
Carbohydrates 35 g.

Chocolate Soufflé Cake

Photograph on page 287
Hands-on time: 20 minutes
Total time: 55 minutes

- 1/2 teaspoon + 1 tablespoon unbleached or all-purpose flour
- 2 ounces semisweet chocolate, chopped
- 1 cup granulated sugar
- 2 tablespoons butter or margarine, softened
- 5 tablespoons (2 1/2 ounces) fat-free sour cream
- 1 egg yolk
- 1/4 teaspoon vanilla extract
- 3 tablespoons cocoa powder
- 4 egg whites, at room temperature
- 1/8 teaspoon cream of tartar
- 2 tablespoons confectioners' sugar

Preheat the oven to 350°F. Coat an 8" springform pan with nonstick spray. Dust with ½ teaspoon of the flour.

Place the chocolate in a microwaveable bowl. Microwave on high power for 1 minute. Stir until smooth. Add ¾ cup of the granulated sugar, the butter or margarine, sour cream, egg yolk, and vanilla extract. Stir until well-blended. Add the cocoa and the remaining 1 tablespoon flour. Stir until smooth.

In a large bowl, combine the egg whites and cream of tartar. With an electric mixer on medium speed, beat until soft peaks form. Increase the speed to high. Beat, while gradually adding the remaining ¼ cup granulated sugar, until stiff peaks form. Fold about one-third of the egg-white mixture into the chocolate mixture. Gently fold in the remaining egg-white mixture in 2 additions. Spoon the batter into the prepared pan. Smooth the top.

Bake for 30 to 35 minutes, or until a toothpick inserted in the middle comes out with just a few moist crumbs. Remove to a rack to cool. The cake will fall as it cools, leaving a raised edge. Gently press down on the edges as it cools.

To serve, remove the pan sides. Transfer the cake to a serving plate. Sift the confectioners' sugar over the top of the cake.

Makes 10 servings

Per serving

Calories 160	*Sodium 29 mg.*
Total fat 5 g.	*Dietary fiber 1 g.*
Saturated fat 2 g.	*Protein 3 g.*
Cholesterol 21 mg.	*Carbohydrates 28 g.*

Vanilla Cheesecake with Strawberry Sauce

Hands-on time: 20 minutes
Total time: 8 hours

- 3 egg whites
- 1¹⁄₄ cups vanilla wafer cookie crumbs
- 3 tablespoons + 1¹⁄₄ cups sugar
- 1 tablespoon butter or margarine, melted
- 1¹⁄₂ pounds 1% cottage cheese
- 8 ounces reduced-fat cream cheese, softened
- 8 ounces fat-free cream cheese, softened
- ¹⁄₄ cup unbleached or all-purpose flour
- 1 egg
- 1 tablespoon vanilla extract
  Strawberry Sauce (at right)

Preheat the oven to 325°F. Coat a 9" springform pan with nonstick spray.

Place 1 egg white in a medium bowl. Beat lightly with a fork. Add the cookie crumbs, 3 tablespoons of the sugar, and the butter or margarine. Toss until the crumbs cling together. Press the mixture into the bottom and 2" up the sides of the prepared pan.

In a food processor, combine the cottage cheese, reduced-fat cream cheese, and fat-free cream cheese. Process until smooth. Add the flour and the remaining 1¼ cups sugar. Process until the sugar is dissolved. One at a time, add the egg, vanilla extract, and the remaining 2 egg whites, processing until just blended. Pour over the prepared crust.

Bake for 1 hour and 15 minutes. Turn off the oven but leave the cheesecake in the oven for 30 minutes, or until the edges are a light golden brown and the center still jiggles slightly. Remove to a rack to cool completely. Cover and refrigerate for at least 6 hours.

Serve the cheesecake with the strawberry sauce.

Makes 12 servings

Per serving
Calories 296
Total fat 6 g.
Saturated fat 3 g.
Cholesterol 31 mg.
Sodium 375 mg.
Dietary fiber 1 g.
Protein 13 g.
Carbohydrates 47 g.

A New Twist

STRAWBERRY SAUCE

Hull and quarter 2 pints of strawberries. (Or, use 2 pints frozen unsweetened strawberries, thawed.) Place in a medium bowl with 2 tablespoons sugar and 1 tablespoon lemon juice. Stir until the sugar dissolves. Transfer 1½ cups of berries to a food processor or blender. Process until smooth. Return the puree to the bowl. Stir to mix. Cover and refrigerate for several hours, if desired. Makes 8 servings.

Fresh Berry Shortcakes

Photograph on page 293
Hands-on time: 20 minutes
Total time: 30 minutes

- 2 cups unbleached or all-purpose flour
- 3 tablespoons + 1/3 cup sugar
- 2 teaspoons baking powder
- 1/4 teaspoon baking soda
- 1/4 cup butter or margarine, cut into small pieces
- 2/3 cup + 2 tablespoons buttermilk
- 1 1/2 pints assorted berries
- 2 tablespoons orange juice
- 2 cups fat-free frozen vanilla yogurt

Preheat the oven to 400°F. Coat a baking sheet with nonstick spray.

In a large bowl, combine the flour, 2 tablespoons of the sugar, the baking powder, and baking soda. Cut in the butter or margarine until the mixture resembles cornmeal. Add 2/3 cup of the buttermilk, stirring with a fork until the dough comes together.

Turn the dough out onto a lightly floured surface. Gently pat or roll to 1/2" thickness. Using a 3" round cutter or large glass, cut 8 biscuits. (You may have to pat the dough scraps together to cut out all the biscuits.) Transfer to the prepared baking sheet. Brush with the remaining 2 tablespoons buttermilk. Sprinkle with 1 tablespoon of the remaining sugar.

Bake for 12 to 15 minutes, or until golden. Remove to a rack to cool.

Meanwhile, in a large bowl, combine the berries, orange juice, and the remaining 1/3 cup sugar. Allow to sit for 10 minutes to draw out the berry juices.

Split the biscuits crosswise in half. Place a biscuit bottom on each of 8 dessert plates. Top with the berry filling and a scoop of yogurt. Cover with the biscuit tops.

Makes 8 servings

Per serving
Calories 319	*Sodium 289 mg.*
Total fat 7 g.	*Dietary fiber 5 g.*
Saturated fat 1 g.	*Protein 7 g.*
Cholesterol 2 mg.	*Carbohydrates 59 g.*

Chocolate Cake with Fluffy Chocolate Icing

Hands-on time: 20 minutes
Total time: 45 minutes

CAKE

1 1/2 cups unbleached or all-purpose flour

1/2 cup cocoa powder

1 tablespoon instant espresso powder

1 teaspoon baking soda

1/2 cup butter or margarine, softened

1 cup sugar

1 egg

1 teaspoon vanilla extract

1/2 cup buttermilk

1/2 cup hot water

ICING

1 1/2 cups sugar

3 large egg whites

1/4 cup water

1 teaspoon cream of tartar

1 teaspoon vanilla extract

1/4 cup cocoa powder

To make the cake: Preheat the oven to 350°F. Coat 2 (8") round cake pans with nonstick spray.

In a medium bowl, combine the flour, cocoa, espresso powder, and baking soda.

In a large bowl, with an electric mixer on medium speed, beat the butter or margarine and sugar for 3 to 4 minutes, or until creamy. Add the egg and vanilla extract. Beat on low speed until creamy.

With the mixer on low speed, gradually add the flour mixture, alternating with the buttermilk and water. Pour the batter into the prepared pans. Bake for 25 to 30 minutes, or until a wooden pick inserted in the center comes out clean.

Cool on racks for 5 minutes. Invert the cakes onto the racks. Allow to cool completely.

To make the icing: Meanwhile, in the top of a double boiler, combine the sugar, egg whites, water, and cream of tartar. Place over a saucepan of simmering water. With an electric mixer on high speed, beat for 5 minutes, or until soft peaks form. Add the vanilla extract and beat for 4 to 5 minutes, or until the mixture is thick and glossy and registers 160°F on an instant-read thermometer. Remove from the heat. Sift the cocoa over the frosting and gently fold in. Allow to cool completely, about 20 minutes.

Spread the frosting over the tops and sides of the cooled layers to make a 2-layer cake.

Makes 12 servings

Per serving

Calories 320	Sodium 221 mg.
Total fat 9 g.	Dietary fiber 2 g.
Saturated fat 6 g.	Protein 5 g.
Cholesterol 40 mg.	Carbohydrates 55 g.

Shakes, Smoothies, and Other Drinks

Bottled water is a billion-dollar business in the United States, an affirmation of water's importance to overall health. Health officials recommend from 6 to 10 eight-ounce servings of fluid per day to prevent dehydration and kidney stones and ensure the absorption and utilization of water-soluble vitamins.

To get the fluids that you need each day, you can choose a beverage as simple as water or as elaborate as a smoothie made with several fruits. If you choose tap water on a regular basis, have your water tested to be sure that there aren't large levels of unsafe chemicals. Be sure to monitor your intake of flavored waters and soft drinks with lots of added sugar, which adds a lot of calories without nutrients.

"Blender drinks can be an excellent way to provide our bodies with valuable vitamins, minerals, and fiber. By using different fruits and vegetables and combining them with fat-free milk, silken tofu, or low-fat yogurt, you will have a quick snack that's a wonderful addition to your nutrition for the day," says licensed dietitian Shannon Stovsky, R.D., of the University Hospitals of Cleveland Synergy Program in Ohio.

Coffee as a beverage is more popular than ever, it seems, with the proliferation of coffee bars throughout the country. Because caffeine may interfere with the absorption of calcium, your best bet is to order a decaffeinated beverage with skim milk so that you get the benefits of a low-fat calcium source without the caffeine. In addition, many herbal teas, such as chamomile, lemon zinger, and wild berry, provide delicious liquid refreshment with no fat, calories, or caffeine.

Liquid meals have become a beverage choice for many. Milk- or soy-based beverages are fortified with all of the essential nutrients, vitamins, and minerals and are touted as being not just beverages but all-in-one super meals. But no beverage, however nutritious, can replace the full range of nutrients and fiber found in whole foods.

The recipes in this chapter focus on refreshing and unique ways to incorporate beverages as heart-healthy snacks, as additions to breakfasts, or even as cool desserts. The average person consumes 129 gallons of fluid per year, so make sure that your choices for this large amount of liquid enhance your overall nutritional intake.

Recipes

Mocha Frappé

Hands-on time: 10 minutes
Total time: 2 hours and 10 minutes

1/2 cup boiling water

2 teaspoons instant espresso powder

2 cups fat-free milk

3 tablespoons fat-free chocolate syrup

1 cup crushed ice

In a measuring cup or bowl, combine the water and espresso powder. Stir to dissolve. Pour into an ice-cube tray. Freeze for 2 hours, or until solid.

In a blender, combine the milk, chocolate syrup, and frozen coffee ice cubes. Blend until smooth. Add the ice. Blend until smooth.

Makes 2 servings

Per serving
Calories 147   Sodium 159 mg.
Total fat 1 g.   Dietary fiber 1 g.
Saturated fat 0 g.   Protein 9 g.
Cholesterol 4 mg.   Carbohydrates 28 g.

Try it — MIGHTY MOCHA

"We served this drink to a large crowd, ages 9 to 87, at the lake on a hot summer's day. The grandmothers in the group said, 'It's much more refreshing than iced coffee. It's a great drink for a hot day.' The young adults said, 'It's an excellent way to enjoy coffee on a warm day.' The teens who frequent coffee bars said, "It has a familiar mocha flavor and a refreshing texture.' When you need a drink to satisfy a group of all ages, this is a definite winner," says Mimi Gallo, an art education consultant.

Berry Berry Smoothie

Photograph on page 294
Hands-on time: 5 minutes
Total time: 5 minutes

1/2 cup frozen unsweetened raspberries

1/2 cup frozen unsweetened strawberries

3/4 cup unsweetened pineapple juice

1 cup (8 ounces) fat-free vanilla yogurt

In a blender, combine the raspberries, strawberries, and pineapple juice. Add the yogurt. Blend until smooth.

Makes 2 servings

Per serving
Calories 195   Sodium 79 mg.
Total fat 1 g.   Dietary fiber 3 g.
Saturated fat 0 g.   Protein 7 g.
Cholesterol 2 mg.   Carbohydrates 43 g.

BERRIES

Strawberries and raspberries contain vitamin C, fiber, and the compound ellagic acid, which are all believed to be effective in warding off heart disease and cancer. So the next time you're craving something sweet, a batch of these Berry Berry Smoothies can shore up nutrients and satisfy your sweet tooth at the same time.

Peachy Smoothie

Photograph on page 294
Hands-on time: 5 minutes
Total time: 5 minutes

1 large ripe peach, sliced
1 tablespoon sugar
1 cup fat-free vanilla ice cream
1/2 cup orange juice
   Pinch of ground cinnamon

In a blender, combine the peach and sugar. Add the ice cream, orange juice, and cinnamon. Blend until smooth.

Makes 2 servings

Per serving
Calories 236   Sodium 81 mg.
Total fat 0 g.   Dietary fiber 2 g.
Saturated fat 0 g.   Protein 4 g.
Cholesterol 5 mg.   Carbohydrates 54 g.

Limeade Shiver

Hands-on time: 5 minutes
Total time: 5 minutes

4 tablespoons lime juice
4 tablespoons sugar
1/2 cup fat-free lime sherbet
1 1/2 cups chilled club soda

In a blender, combine the lime juice and sugar. Add the sherbet. Blend until smooth. Add the soda. Blend briefly just to combine.

Makes 2 servings

Per serving
Calories 174   Sodium 61 mg.
Total fat 1 g.   Dietary fiber 0 g.
Saturated fat 1 g.   Protein 1 g.
Cholesterol 2 mg.   Carbohydrates 43 g.

Good for You

DRINK DIFFERENTLY

One sweetened 12-ounce soda contains about 150 calories. This equals approximately 10 teaspoons of sugar. If weight loss is your goal, passing up soda can be a very easy way to cut unnecessary calories. Replace sweetened soda with bottled water, unsweetened iced tea, iced herbal tea, iced decaffeinated coffee, or diet soda. Eliminating just one soda a day for a year adds up to a reduction of more than 54,000 calories!

Tropical Teaser

Hands-on time: 5 minutes
Total time: 5 minutes

2 cups unsweetened pineapple juice

1 banana, cut into chunks

1/4 cup lime juice

1/8 teaspoon coconut extract

2 cups ginger ale

In a blender, combine the pineapple juice, banana, lime juice, and coconut extract. Add the ginger ale. Blend briefly just to combine.

Makes 4 servings

Per serving
Calories 145   Sodium 10 mg.
Total fat 1 g.   Dietary fiber 1 g.
Saturated fat 0 g.   Protein 1 g.
Cholesterol 0 mg.   Carbohydrates 36 g.

Chocolate Malted

Hands-on time: 5 minutes
Total time: 5 minutes

1 1/2 cups fat-free frozen chocolate yogurt

1/2 cup fat-free milk

4 1/2 tablespoons chocolate malted milk powder

In a blender, combine the yogurt, milk, and malted milk powder. Blend until smooth.

Makes 2 servings

Per serving
Calories 340   Sodium 234 mg.
Total fat 3 g.   Dietary fiber 2 g.
Saturated fat 2 g.   Protein 12 g.
Cholesterol 5 mg.   Carbohydrates 74 g.

Good for You

CALCIUM CONTENT

You don't lose any calcium when you switch to reduced-fat dairy products. By replacing full-fat dairy foods with reduced-fat or fat-free versions, you save calories and fat while maintaining your intake of healthful calcium.

A Trip to the Soda Fountain

From classic soda-fountain concoctions to contemporary fruit smoothies, blended beverages are a delightful way to combine liquid refreshment and nutrients into snacks. This list will help you come to terms with these refreshing drinks.

Egg cream/chocolate phosphate. This delicatessen favorite contains no eggs but does whip up into a froth that resembles beaten egg whites. It's made with a combination of milk and chocolate syrup into which seltzer is sprayed. Remember to drink this one fast—it goes flat very quickly.

Float. This is a combination of ice cream and soda often made with vanilla ice cream and root beer. Experiment with your own creative flavor combinations. And, if you remember to drop a small shaving of ice cream in the bottom of the glass before you pour in the soda, it won't fizz up and froth over.

Frappé. Freeze fruit juice or other flavored liquid until it turns to slush, and you'll have a fancy-sounding frappé.

Fruit-juice spritzer. Perfect for the party person who chooses to forgo alcohol, this classy drink is a refreshing combination of fruit juice and sparkling water.

Iced coffee/iced tea. Decaffeinated or regular, these beverages are calorie-free before you add milk and sweetener. So choose low-fat milk and go easy on the sugar. Be adventurous—sample the new flavored varieties, such as apple-cinnamon tea or raspberry-mocha coffee.

Malted milk/malted. This is a milkshake with malt powder added. When made with reduced-fat ice cream and fat-free milk, this wonderful old favorite goes down easily as part of a healthier new lifestyle.

Milkshake. Traditionally a voluptuous combination of whole milk, ice cream, and flavored syrup, milkshakes can now be made virtually fat-free with a host of vibrantly flavored fat-free ice creams, spices, flavored syrups, and fat-free milk.

Smoothie. A legacy of the 1970s, this thick drink is a combination of fruit and frozen yogurt or ice cream pureed in a blender. You can use fresh or frozen fruit and different low-fat flavored yogurt, frozen yogurt, or ice cream to create your own signature smoothie.

Raspberry-Cranberry Mist

Hands-on time: 5 minutes
Total time: 5 minutes

1 cup frozen unsweetened raspberries

1 cup cranberry-raspberry juice

2 tablespoons sugar

1 tablespoon lemon juice

1 cup club soda

In a blender, combine the raspberries, cranberry-raspberry juice, sugar, and lemon juice. Blend until smooth. Add the soda. Blend briefly just to combine.

Makes 2 servings

Per serving
Calories 162	*Sodium 28 mg.*
Total fat 0 g.	*Dietary fiber 4 g.*
Saturated fat 0 g.	*Protein 1 g.*
Cholesterol 0 mg.	*Carbohydrates 41 g.*

DOUBLE RASPBERRY-CRANBERRY MIST

For an intense raspberry flavor, add 1 tablespoon raspberry-flavored liqueur or raspberry syrup before blending.

Banana Split Shake

Hands-on time: 5 minutes
Total time: 5 minutes

2 cups fat-free vanilla ice cream

1/2 cup fat-free milk

1 ripe banana, cut into chunks

3 tablespoons fat-free fudge sauce

2 tablespoons chopped roasted peanuts or toasted walnuts

In a blender, combine the ice cream and milk. Blend until smooth. Add the banana and fudge sauce, in teaspoonfuls, to the blender. Pulse briefly just to mix in without pureeing. Pour into 2 tall glasses. Sprinkle with the peanuts or walnuts.

Makes 2 servings

Per serving
Calories 495	*Sodium 261 mg.*
Total fat 5 g.	*Dietary fiber 5 g.*
Saturated fat 0 g.	*Protein 12 g.*
Cholesterol 11 mg.	*Carbohydrates 98 g.*

NUTS

You'll want to include moderate amounts of nuts in your weekly eating plan. Although high in calories and fat, popular table nuts such as peanuts, walnuts, and almonds contain very little harmful saturated fat. In addition, nuts are high in protein and contain generous amounts of vitamins, minerals, and fiber. They can help lower cholesterol, protect against heart disease, and help prevent cancer.

Frosty Fruity Punch

Hands-on time: 10 minutes
Total time: 1 hour and 10 minutes

- 2 cups apricot nectar
- 2 cups orange juice
- 2 cups unsweetened pineapple juice
- 1 cup apple juice
- $1/2$ cup water
- $1/4$ cup lemon juice
- $1/4$ cup grenadine syrup (optional); see note
- 1 quart carbonated lemon-lime beverage or ginger ale
- 1 pint rainbow sherbet

In a large punch bowl, combine the apricot nectar, orange juice, pineapple juice, apple juice, water, lemon juice, and grenadine syrup, if using. Cover and refrigerate for at least 1 hour to chill.

Just before serving, add the lemon-lime soda or ginger ale. Stir to mix. Add scoops of the sherbet.

Makes 24 servings

Per serving
Calories 76	*Sodium 12 mg.*
Total fat 0 g.	*Dietary fiber 0 g.*
Saturated fat 0 g.	*Protein 1 g.*
Cholesterol 1 mg.	*Carbohydrates 18 g.*

Cooking Note

Grenadine syrup, a red pomegranate-flavored syrup often used to flavor drinks and desserts, is sold in some supermarkets and coffee shops and in liquor stores. Both alcoholic and nonalcoholic varieties are available, so be sure to check labels carefully.

FRUITY PUNCH SORBET — Play it Again!

Any leftover punch can be poured into a plastic container and frozen to make sorbet. To serve, scoop out the number of desired portions into a food processor. Process, scraping down the sides of the bowl as necessary, until smooth.

Citrus Crush

Hands-on time: 5 minutes
Total time: 5 minutes

1 cup unsweetened pineapple juice

1 cup orange juice

3 tablespoons lemon juice

2 tablespoons lime juice

2 tablespoons sugar

2 cups crushed ice

In a blender, combine the pineapple juice, orange juice, lemon juice, lime juice, sugar, and ice. Puree until smooth and frothy.

Makes 2 servings

Per serving
Calories 198	Sodium 11 mg.
Total fat 0 g.	Dietary fiber 1 g.
Saturated fat 0 g.	Protein 2 g.
Cholesterol 0 mg.	Carbohydrates 51 g.

CITRUS SODAS

To make citrus sodas, serve Citrus Crush in frosted tall glasses. Top each serving with 2 scoops fat-free vanilla frozen yogurt and garnish with mint leaves or curls of citrus peel.

Index

Underscored page references indicate boxed text. **Boldface** references indicate photographs.

Enchiladas
   Creamy Black Bean Enchiladas, **224**, 266
   Seaside Enchiladas, 256

F

Fajitas
   Chicken Fajitas, 154
Fats, 10. *See also* Oils
   calories in, 2, 8
   dietary guidelines for, 10, 109
   on food product labels, 232
   omega-3 fatty acids, 4, 10, 143, 271
   reducing, in recipes, 18–19, 20–23
   in restaurant meals, 16–17
Fennel
   Potato-Fennel Gratin, 176
   Risotto with Shrimp, Peas, and Fennel, **222**, 260
Feta cheese
   Greek Pizza, 105
   Greek-Style Appetizer Cheesecake, 50
   Mediterranean Chickpea Salad with Feta, 267
   Mediterranean Flounder, 275
   Spinach Strudel, 105
Fettuccine
   Fettuccine Alfredo Pizza, 104
   Mushroom Fettuccine, 101
Fiber
   daily requirements for, 109, 157, 255
   food sources of, 72, 261
   health benefits from, 261
Fish. *See also* Shellfish
   Asian Fish, 297
   Baked Cod with Mustard Crumbs, **228**, 277
   Big Sur Cioppino, 168
   buying, 3–4, 14, 272
   Cornmeal-Crusted Catfish, **225**, 273
   Creamy Dill Salmon in Phyllo, 295
   Fish Stew with Couscous, 167
   health benefits from, 143, 271
   Italian-Style Baked Fish, 297
   Mediterranean Flounder, 275
   menu ideas, 297

   nutrients in, 12–13
   omega-3 fatty acids in, 4, 10, 143, 271
   Orange Roughy Veracruz, **226**, 298
   Pan-Seared Salmon Salad, 214
   Pasta with Beans and Cajun Salmon, **120**, 143
   Potato Pancakes and Smoked Salmon with Chive
      Cream, **130**, 172
   Red Snapper with Fruit Sauce, 276
   in restaurants, 17
   Salmon Salad Wrap, 214
   Sardine Sandwich, 297
   Seafood Soup, 297
   Smoked Salmon 'n' Bagels, 86
   Sole with Stir-Fried Vegetables, 296
   Steamed Sea Bass in Black Bean Sauce, 274
   storing, 4, 14
   Swordfish Pitas with Herb Chutney, 278
   Teriyaki Tuna Burgers, 94
   Teriyaki Tuna with Pineapple, **227**, 303
   Tuna Burger, 83
   Tuna Pasta, 297
   Tuna Salad Pockets, **66**, 83
Five-a-Day program, 212
Flounder
   Mediterranean Flounder, 275
Flour
   cake, 15, 24
   in pizza dough, 99
   whole wheat, 20, 24
Focaccia
   Onion-Rosemary Focaccia, **67**, 102
Folic acid, 12–13, 117, 270
Food Guide Pyramid, 145, 185, 253
Food safety, 31, 148
Frittatas
   South-of-the-Border Frittata, 32
Frostings, ingredients in, 22
Fruit, 72, 212. *See also specific kinds*
   crisps, for breakfast, 335
   nutrients in, 12–13
   on pizza, 111
   purchasing and storing, 11
   in scones, 42
   serving sizes for, 9
   storing, 142

G

H

V

Conversion Chart

These equivalents have been slightly rounded to make measuring easier.

Volume Measurements

U.S.	Imperial	Metric
¼ tsp.	–	1.25 ml.
½ tsp.	–	2.5 ml.
1 tsp.	–	5 ml.
1 Tbsp.	–	15 ml.
2 Tbsp. (1 oz.)	1 fl. oz.	30 ml.
¼ cup (2 oz.)	2 fl. oz.	60 ml.
⅓ cup (3 oz.)	3 fl. oz.	80 ml.
½ cup (4 oz.)	4 fl. oz.	120 ml.
⅔ cup (5 oz.)	5 fl. oz.	160 ml.
¾ cup (6 oz.)	6 fl. oz.	180 ml.
1 cup (8 oz.)	8 fl. oz.	240 ml.

Weight Measurements

U.S.	Metric
1 oz.	30 g.
2 oz.	60 g.
4 oz. (¼ lb.)	115 g
5 oz. (⅓ lb.)	145 g.
6 oz.	170 g.
7 oz.	200 g.
8 oz. (½ lb.)	230 g.
10 oz.	285 g.
12 oz. (¾ lb.)	340 g.
14 oz.	400 g.
16 oz. (1 lb.)	455 g.
2.2 lb.	1 kg.

Length Measurements

U.S.	Metric
¼"	0.6 cm.
½"	1.25 cm.
1"	2.5 cm.
2"	5 cm.
4"	11 cm.
6"	15 cm.
8"	20 cm.
10"	25 cm.
12" (1')	30 cm.

Pan Sizes

U.S.	Metric
8" cake pan	20 × 4-cm. sandwich or cake tin
9" cake pan	23 × 3.5-cm. sandwich or cake tin
11" × 7" baking pan	28 × 18-cm. baking pan
13" × 9" baking pan	32.5 × 23-cm. baking pan
2-qt. rectangular baking dish	30 × 19-cm. baking pan
15" × 10" baking pan	38 × 25.5-cm. baking pan (Swiss roll tin)
9" pie plate	22 × 4 or 23 × 4-cm. pie plate
7" or 8" springform pan	18 or 20-cm. springform or loose-bottom cake tin
9" × 5" loaf pan	23 × 13-cm. or 2-lb. narrow loaf pan or pâté tin
1½-qt. casserole	1.5-liter casserole
2-qt. casserole	2-liter casserole

Temperatures

Fahrenheit	Centigrade	Gas
140°	60°	–
160°	70°	–
180°	80°	–
225°	110°	–
250°	120°	½
300°	150°	2
325°	160°	3
350°	180°	4
375°	190°	5
400°	200°	6
450°	230°	8
500°	260°	–